Sightings

SIGHTINGS

Reflections on Religion in Public Life

Edited by Brett Colasacco

Foreword by Willemien Otten
Introduction by W. Clark Gilpin

WM. B. EERDMANS PUBLISHING COMPANY
GRAND RAPIDS, MICHIGAN

Wm. B. Eerdmans Publishing Co.
4035 Park East Court SE, Grand Rapids, Michigan 49546
www.eerdmans.com

Published 2019
Printed in the United States of America

28 27 26 25 24 23 22 21 20 19   1 2 3 4 5 6 7 8 9 10

ISBN 978-0-8028-7665-2

Library of Congress Cataloging-in-Publication Data

A catalog record for this book is available from the Library of Congress

The one hundred essays in this volume were previously published in *Sightings*, a digital journal. Permission to print this content has been provided by the editorial board of *Sightings*.

Contents

CONTENTS

Editor's Note

BY BRETT COLASACCO

This book contains just a sample of the roughly two thousand columns *Sightings* has published over the past two decades—both as a semiweekly email newsletter and on the website of the Martin Marty Center at the University of Chicago Divinity School. The selection process was an arduous one, and we make no pretense that these are the hundred "best" columns we have ever published (though many of them probably are); rather, these are the hundred columns which, in our judgment, best tell the story of *Sightings* and the Marty Center.

Sightings could not have come this far without the inspiration and guiding light provided by its founder, the indefatigable Martin Marty, who has authored every other *Sightings* column for the publication's first twenty years. Indeed, it would have been easy to fill an anthology of this kind using only Marty's columns. But we decided that it would be a more fitting tribute to Marty's legacy to highlight the ways in which others have taken up the model that he established and made it their own. This volume therefore contains thirty-one columns by Marty and sixty-nine by a diverse array of other contributors. The short biographical statement following each non-Marty column reflects who authors were, where they were, and what they were doing at the time of composition. Many of them, of course, have since gone on to different roles in institutions of higher education, religious organizations, and other sectors of civil society.

I personally owe a tremendous debt of gratitude to the previous editors of *Sightings*: R. Jonathan Moore, Jonathan Ebel, Elizabeth Hayes Alvarez, Jeremy Biles, Kristen Tobey, Shatha Almutawa, and Myriam Renaud. This book builds upon an earlier compilation of thirty-four columns assembled in celebration of the tenth anniversary of the Marty Center and published as a special issue of the Divinity School's magazine *Criterion* in 2008. I want to acknowledge Richard Rosengarten, former dean of the Divinity School, for selecting the columns that comprised that collection—selections from which I have found very few reasons to depart.

I would also like to thank Willemien Otten, Clark Gilpin, Wendy Doniger, Laurie Zoloth, David Nirenberg, Trevor Thompson, Linda Bieze, Terren

Wein, and Joel Brown, without whom this project would never have come to fruition. Still, I must reserve my deepest gratitude for Marty himself. To Marty: it has been an honor to serve as your editor; may this book honor you on the occasion of your ninetieth birthday and on the twentieth anniversary of the Center that will continue to honor your legacy for years and decades to come.

Foreword

By Willemien Otten
Director, The Martin Marty Center

Before you lies a volume that contains what can best be seen as scrapbook pages from the Martin Marty Center as it has developed over the past two decades. Like most scrapbooks these pages show snapshots—these are the *Sightings* columns gathered by the publication's insightful editor Brett Colasacco. As I contemplate the profiles of the authors who wrote these columns, I count a number of significant people: our faculty members, yes, but also students, alumni, and other scholars or important practitioners in the field of religion. First among them, of course, ranks Martin Marty himself, prolific author and proficient historian of American religion. It is after him that the University of Chicago Divinity School's Martin Marty Center has been named, and it has carried this name as a badge of honor for twenty proud years now.

Like any scrapbook, however, this book of columns should also belong to someone, someone whose ambiance, cultural values, and mindset it reflects. But to whom do these columns belong? Here my question, innocent and off the cuff as it may seem, does not have an obvious or immediate answer. And so the plot thickens. Indeed, the columns all have authors, and these hold a kind of intellectual ownership over what they wrote, even if among them Marty excels as the most constant and regular voice. Still, the columns were also all written at the invitation of, or in some cases volunteered to, *Sightings*, which is the official public digital forum of the Marty Center. The scrapbook thus seems to belong jointly to Martin Marty and to the Center. As far as I can see, that conclusion is no indication of ambiguity or attempt at obfuscation but instead indicative of a good thing. This good thing, however, is not a simple thing, so let me explain further.

The Marty Center would not exist as such without the one who lent it his name, Martin Marty. So much seems obvious. But it is important to note that the Center already existed before Marty's name was attached to it, known then as the Institute for the Advanced Study of Religion. In fact, I myself was once a senior fellow there in the early 1990s, on leave from what was then my home institution, Loyola University of Chicago; Frank Reynolds was director at the time. Upon Marty's retirement in 1998, his name became attached to the Institute and, looking back, we can now only conclude that Marty came, saw, and conquered! For the name and the role of the Center have recently been recalibrated and clarified as the Martin Marty Center for the Public Understanding of Religion, thereby appropriately mirroring what has really been his own life's mission and the essence of his scholarship. In sum, then, *Sightings* is jointly owned, I would say, by both Martin Marty and the Martin Marty Center. Where they intersect, and hence where *Sightings* has found and continues to find its pivotal place, is in their deep appreciation for and enduring valuation of efforts to increase the public understanding of religion.

To have a shared and agreed-upon mission does not by definition make that mission a smooth one. Religion is a dangerous thing or, as former dean of the Divinity School Margaret M. Mitchell liked to say, studying religion is "playing with fire." Many explosions—not only figurative ones, as she meant her expression to convey, but also literal ones—have been set off for religious reasons, not least in the two decades of the Martin Marty Center's existence. By contrast, religion can sometimes also seem like the weather: everybody has an opinion, and claims to be some kind of expert, and none of it sticks. Not all of those opinions are therefore wrong, by the way, as life experience can count as a form of intuitive religious knowledge; but there are always more things to know and deeper things to reflect upon and, especially, ponder more systemically. A third problem of religion, besides its explosive character and its status as the subject matter of fickle opinion, is that in our Enlightenment culture (for which modern universities still seem to serve as a near-invincible bulwark) religion tends to be banished to the private sphere, and hence has all but disappeared. "Oh, that's your religion" is usually meant to end a conversation, if not quash discussion altogether, rather than opening up a serious debate. What then are the reasons behind the Center's firm conviction to want to think about enhancing the public understanding of religion? Would it not be far preferable just to stop "playing with fire" and adopt the safe, if somewhat clinical, Enlightenment rules of not invoking or involving it concretely, simultaneously dismissing any untried and untested religious opinions as we do the weather wisdom of old almanacs: *there once was a time when people thought . . . ?*

Yet if there is anything that scholars of religion have learned from the demise of the once-powerful secularization thesis, it is that religion does not go away easily. In fact, it does not go away at all, and neither does it let itself be domesticated or compartmentalized in convenient or easily digestible ways. Modern developments do not at all show that it is on the wane. True, mainstream Christian confessions in the United States and continental Europe are struggling, and the number of "nones"—that is, people who do not define themselves in relation to a known church or established religion—has sharply increased, especially among millennials. Yet with his Fundamentalism Project, Martin Marty long foreshadowed not only how religious affiliations could go underground and rise up again but also how they can morph into new movements that are less institutionally rooted and more reliant on a powerful charismatic or evangelical leader whose force and magnetic attraction should never be underestimated. The religious landscape, in other words, is continuously in flux, and it is an understatement to say that the last decades have seen a little more flux than usual. To pursue my earlier analogy with the weather, one could perhaps speak of a religious "climate change" problem.

For a Divinity School that is itself, in the words of President Robert J. Zimmer, the "Institute for the Advanced Study of Religion" at the University of Chicago, it seems critically important to establish the Martin Marty Center as the place where its faculty can weigh in on current problems and events and can take stock of what the most important recent religious developments are, in order to try to see where they will lead. The Marty Center is hence the place where faculty can develop positions—even if initially perhaps through provisional position papers—by inviting both religious specialists and nonreligious experts to help us map out the field of religion for the next few decades, inside but also outside the United States. An academic institution such as the Divinity School (though one significantly enriched by a respected and highly prized Master of Divinity program) always has to be on guard against the esoteric fallacy, the idea that knowledge in and by itself is the answer and remedy to every problem. It is here that the Marty Center is a healthy *complement* to the Divinity School, as it were, in that it sets out to disseminate that knowledge, following it through so to speak, as the Center carries out its mission of furthering the public understanding of religion. In doing so, the Marty Center is also a *compliment* to the Divinity School whose richness of specialties, dynamic faculty, rigorous programs of study, and relentless pursuit of knowledge unearth problems that put us above the occasion and ahead of the curve. While Martin Marty is no doubt unique, over the years there have been other faculty members who embody that same rare combination of deep knowledge and ebullient social communication: Paul Mendes-Flohr in Judaism, Bernard McGinn in Catholicism, Wendy Doniger in Hinduism, William Schweiker in theological ethics. It takes a village to raise a child, as the saying goes, but it takes a culture to form a scholar. It is within the culture of the Divinity School that the Martin Marty Center has its place, and it is by that culture, recently reinvigorated by Deans Laurie Zoloth and David Nirenberg, that it continues to be nourished.

Reflecting upon the above interface of the Divinity School with the Martin Marty Center leads me to switch back to Martin Marty and these *Sightings* columns a final time. Our culture has a tendency to divide knowledge into specialized theory and applied science, and its respective experts into "theorists" and "practitioners." Not only does it seem a foregone conclusion that one cannot do or be both, but it seems *hubris* even to try. In a recent talk that Marty gave at Augustana Lutheran Church of Hyde Park on the occasion of the five-hundredth anniversary of the Reformation, I saw on display once again how Marty straddles that divide effortlessly, not only graciously but, above all, effectively. It is not that he transcends the divide; it just does not seem to affect him. I am not sure that can be said of all of us scholars in the Divinity School, however hard we try. But I am confident that there are enough scholars to go around who have caught the infectious bug of wanting to make clear to a wider audience that religion is not just a factor but an actor; that it matters—to the academy, to our private lives, to politics and the economy, to society at large. Rather than invoking *hubris*, the Martin Marty Center makes the wager that there is not only a place for the public discussion and understanding of religion but a need for it. I therefore hope you will go through these *Sightings* columns as you would through the scrapbook pages of a beloved friend, breathing in the profile not just of the individual authors, or of Martin Marty himself, but also of our Martin Marty Center. I especially hope you will come away more appreciative and supportive of all that it stands for, aspires to be, and reaches out to achieve.

Introduction: Reflections on *Sightings*

By W. Clark Gilpin
Former Director, The Martin Marty Center

The term "sightings" reflects a central characteristic of the University of Chicago Divinity School's Martin Marty Center—and of Martin Marty. Before you turn to enjoy selected *Sightings* columns by Martin Marty and his colleagues, I invite you to spend a moment with the word itself: "sightings." The word connotes not only noticing but also recognizing or interpreting what it is that we have noticed. In this case, the aim is to interpret the many roles that religion plays in public life and culture, some roles that are highly visible and others that are powerfully invisible. In the religiously pluralistic culture of the United States, catching sight of the various visible and seemingly invisible influences of religion in civil society requires both curiosity and a willingness to collaborate with other interpreters whose angle of vision enables them to glimpse religious influences that we might not otherwise notice. Such interpretation through collaborative curiosity is a distinguishing feature of Martin Marty's scholarly career, a central aspiration of the Marty Center, and a deeply embedded tradition in the intellectual culture of the Divinity School itself.

The idea of publishing a weekly series of short commentaries on the varied cultural influences of religion arose in 1996. Martin Marty, the Fairfax M. Cone Distinguished Service Professor of the History of Modern Christianity, had received a planning grant from the Pew Charitable Trusts in order to launch the Public Religion Project. As that project developed over the next several years, Marty and the project's codirector, Edith Blumhofer, professor of history at Wheaton College and director of Wheaton's Institute for the Study of American Evangelicals, pursued the implications of a concise, yet suggestive, mission statement:

> *The Public Religion Project exists to promote efforts to bring to light and interpret the forces of faith within a pluralistic society.*

Two features of this mission statement have proven especially consequential for the twice-weekly publication of *Sightings* over the ensuing twenty years. First, by promoting "efforts to bring to light" the forces of faith, both the Public Religion Project and *Sightings* aimed to create a space where criticism could occur and mutuality could prosper. Second, the mission statement emphasized the multiple forms that religion takes in public life. Modern society is "pluralistic," and the "forces" of faith exert themselves in many, sometimes conflicting ways. Indeed, project directors Marty and Blumhofer forthrightly noted that leaders at the Pew Charitable Trusts and the University of Chicago, along with many other responsible observers, "were disturbed that it was difficult to get anywhere in addressing the profound issues of society without finding arguments go uncivil when religious voices were present" (*Public Religion in America Today*, 1997). A central tension has thus propelled the writing and editing of *Sightings*. How do we cultivate the collaborative curiosity that takes notice of the innumerable public faces of religion and engagingly interprets their significance for civil society, without descending into factional editorializing? How do we "promote efforts to bring to light and interpret" *public* religion when many skeptical voices would suggest that "a pluralistic society" is better served by *private* religion?

In the years since the Public Religion Project, a series of directors of the Marty Center and graduate-student and alumni editors of *Sightings* have negotiated these questions on a weekly basis. To the extent that directors and editors have succeeded in this negotiation, it has been, in no small measure, because they accepted and capitalized on the limits and strengths of who we are. That is, we are scholars who study religion in its myriad historical and contemporary manifestations. Our contribution to the much larger conversation about the place of religion in public life is the limited but, I would suggest, indispensable public responsibility of scholarship to set current issues in longer histories and wider societal contexts.

On the one hand, *Sightings* has operated on the premise that scholarly interpreters can observe and call attention to the presence and influence of religious ideas and practices in arenas of public life—politics, economics, or the arts—where this influence might otherwise go unobserved. When bringing into plain sight the influential presence of religious assumptions and practices that might otherwise escape the notice of a modern audience, *Sightings* columns tend to be descriptively analytic, calling attention to religious themes embedded in the narrative of a current film or tacitly invoked in political appeals to national identity.

On the other hand, throughout world societies today, the roles of religion in public life are quite visible, and it might seem that scholarship is entirely unnecessary to "bring to light" the forces of faith. Religions are functioning in ways that have become all too evident—even disturbing—to citizens and members of the academy. This public presence of religion frequently excites strong opinions, which tend to trade either on misleading generalizations or on sharply drawn dichotomies. In response, *Sightings* has had the somewhat different scholarly obligation to step back from the immediate controversy and offer interpretive judgments about the social, historical, and theological reasons that religion is evoking a given public debate in politics, the arts, or public culture. To return to the original mandate of the Public Religion Project, the task is not only to "bring to light" the forces of faith but also to "interpret" the forces of faith.

In both bringing to light and interpreting, *Sightings* needs to encourage and foster response and dialogue between writers and readers. In designing the Public Religion Project, Marty saw that mass communication has decisively shaped the arena within which such dialogue could occur. How, he asked, "do things become 'public' except through mass media?" At the same time, Marty observed that the scope and depth of religion's influence in modernity requires for its clarification "the conversation between scholars and practitioners, interpreters of communities and participants of communities" (Marty and Blumhofer, *Public Religion*). At its current state of development, *Sightings* is uneasily balanced—as is our society as a whole—on this pivot between mass communication and sustained conversation to which Marty has called our attention. As you read *Sightings* columns from the past twenty years, I hope you will discover that, beyond merely catching sight of religion, a conversation has begun. Begun—but more remains ahead of us. The collaborative curiosity that propels a civil conversation on public religion is Martin Marty's distinctive gift and his lasting contribution to the University of Chicago Divinity School and its Martin Marty Center.

1. Counting

SEPTEMBER 22, 1999
BY MARTIN E. MARTY

Counting may not be the most exciting thing we do, and reading about counting may not give receivers of *Sightings* much to develop into editorials, talk-show topics, or lecture and sermon illustrations. But keeping track of news everywhere goes with the job, and it informs our venture if now and then we report on statistical reckonings. To the point:

For exactly one month after the Fourth of July, we monitored and clipped—made confetti of, really—all stories dealing explicitly with religion and religiously named groups and incidents in the very secular *New York Times*. This was done as background to a report for an executives' meeting in Toronto; they wanted a sense of happenings on the global scene. We don't usually do globes, either. But, here goes: Kashmir, with Hindu-Muslim war, rated twelve stories, and China's pursuit of the Falun Gong spiritual movement garnered eleven full-length mentions. Tied with eight each were stories about the Serbian Orthodox Church wrestling with the current government, Iranian protests testing the Islamic fundamentalist government, and the Northern Ireland Protestant-Catholic crisis. Seven stories reported Israel's new leadership adjusting to life with ultra-Orthodox Jewish parties. There were three news stories about Algerian Muslims, two British and two South African news accounts, and one each from twenty-one other nations.

Clearly, religion is surging around our post-secular globe, and much of it is violent. Of course, it is conflict and not stability or serenity that makes news, so the reporting is by definition a distortion, and when we get close to home, more sides of religion come out. *The New York Times* had fifty stories outside its Arts sections on religion in the United States. While numbers of these had to do with the World Church of the Creator and killings by a member, there were numerous stories with tender references to Catholic rites after the death of John F. Kennedy, Jr.

Let us just jumble together proper nouns from other stories to indicate scope: Woodlands United Methodist Church; the United Church of Christ; theologians comment on embryo research; the Rev. Jesse Jackson as spiritual adviser; Representative Gephardt bows to pressure and replaces a Muslim appointee with a Christian one; religion and millennial fears; House vote on religious freedom "trivializes religion" editorial; candidates Gore and Bush say more on "faith-based" welfare and historian Gertrude Himmelfarb editorializes in favor of it; witches; angels; alternative spirituality; prayer by victims of insurance fraud; and dozens more. There were also twenty-one "spirituality" and "religious" art stories. Yes, we are secular. And we are religious, too.

2. America's Mythical Religious Past

October 12, 2000
By Catherine A. Brekus

On the first day of the course I teach on Religion in Colonial America at the University of Chicago Divinity School, I often ask students to tell me what they already know about early American religious history. Since many of them are new to the field, they know relatively little about religious leaders or worship practices, but almost all of them have strong assumptions about the past.

Influenced by the rhetoric of conservative religious activists and politicians, some describe America as a "Christian nation" where everyone shared a common set of values. Others claim that the colonies were a haven for religious liberty. Pointing to the stories of the Pilgrims and Puritans who fled to New England to escape religious persecution, they imagine a world where people of all faiths were allowed to worship freely.

Yet as students begin reading documents (whether church records, legal statutes, or personal religious narratives), they are surprised to discover that these two images of early America reflect popular national myth, not historical reality. These images say far more about our modern concerns than they do about the real people who lived and worshipped in the past.

First, although it is certainly true that most early Americans were Christian (with the notable exception of large numbers of Indians and African-born slaves), they disagreed about what constituted "true" Christianity. In the South, for example, Anglicans and Baptists clashed over infant baptism, and in New England, Puritans accused Quakers of being heretics because of their belief in immediate inspiration. (While the Puritans insisted that the Bible was God's final revelation, the Quakers claimed that God continued to speak to humans through the "inner light.") In Maryland, originally founded by Roman Catholics, Protestants eventually seized power and forbade Catholics to vote, hold public office, or worship outside of private homes. Rather than describing themselves as part of a unified, Christian culture, early Americans emphasized the theological divisions that splintered them into competing denominations.

Second, despite the popular image of America's deep commitment to religious liberty, few of the original thirteen colonies allowed people to worship freely. With the exception of Pennsylvania, New Jersey, Delaware, and Rhode Island, every colony had an "established" church that was closely linked to the government. For example, everyone who lived in seventeenth-century Virginia, no matter what their personal beliefs, was legally required to attend the Anglican Church and pay assessments for ministers' salaries. If people refused to pay their taxes, they were publicly whipped or imprisoned. As the colonies became more religiously plural in the eighteenth century, these harsh laws began to disappear, but it was not until 1791, with the passage of the Bill of Rights, that all Americans were guaranteed the right to worship (or not to worship) as they wished.

If my conversations with students are an accurate index of what the public knows about the past, then most people have forgotten the religious battles in early America. Yet at a time when politicians and activists search for a "usable past" that will justify their vision for the present and future, we must move beyond the myths that have framed so many of our national conversations about religion in public life. On one hand, conservatives who want America to return to its identity as a "Christian country" rarely acknowledge that religious diversity has been an enduring feature of American life. On the other hand, liberals who want politicians and activists to keep their religious beliefs "private" rarely mention the Baptists, Quakers, and other religious dissenters who once fought for the right to express their beliefs in public.

To be sure, history doesn't offer any easy answers to our national debates about religion. But unless we wrestle with the legacy of our past, it will be harder to chart a path toward the future.

Catherine A. Brekus is assistant professor of the history of Christianity at the University of Chicago Divinity School.

3. Mourning a Monsignor

MAY 29, 2001
BY MARTIN E. MARTY

Sighting religion in the public realm does not take one away from the organized church if one finds clerical leaders "out there" like the most public priest we have known, Chicago's Monsignor John "Jack" Egan.

The best-known and most loved (and sometimes, by exactly the right people, the most hated) priest hereabouts, he was nationally known for his passion for justice, his compassion, and his friendliness. Years ago, those of us who straggled or cowered at the rear of the civil rights events knew he was always up front. Egan was booted out of town by then-Cardinal John Cody and brought back as a first move by his successor, Joseph Cardinal Bernardin. The moves in both directions, and his summons to Notre Dame by Father Theodore Hesburgh, are all tributes to the monsignor.

Passingly, he was for the ordination of women and the priesthood for married men, but he was also fiercely loyal to the church he considered both holy and broken: "I label myself a dissenter. Yet prayerful, responsible dissent has always played a role in the church." In his pattern of loyalty, as in so many other expressions, he reminded one of Dorothy Day of blessed memory.

This is not a merely local story, since Egan had national influence. A related story also has a Chicago tagline and national implications. On May 19, the very day friend Egan died, Francis Cardinal George ordained only ten men to the priesthood. Remember, the Archdiocese of Chicago is as populated as all but five or six entire Protestant denominations in America. We noted that the majority of the new priests are from foreign lands, including one from a place called "Lutheranism." As for these new "poor world" priests, more power to them and may their numbers increase, bringing new perspectives and gifts—we've seen some in action.

Where, however, are the people with names like "Egan"? Or the Poles or Italians or Czechs who vastly, vastly outnumber Indonesians, Filipinos, and others from nations now supplying Chicago with priests? This is not the place for a Protestant to lobby or advise. ("If they have not heard the voices of the Jack Egans, surely they will not hear the voices of outsiders.") Such advice in this context would be in bad taste and come with ill grace, since most non-Catholic denominations are having similar problems of undersupply in pastoral vocations.

One can celebrate the remarkable burst of activity by lay men and lay women in today's not-yet-priestless Catholicism. But something will be missing from public life when no one is wearing the clerical collar as a special identification, a scandal, a sign, as Egan did. So our tears at the memorial were because we have lost Egan—but also, much more than that.

4. Pearl Harbor, Sarajevo, and the Events of September Eleventh

SEPTEMBER 26, 2001
BY EDWARD McGLYNN GAFFNEY, JR.

As we grapple with the terrifying events of September 11, 2001, we are haunted by analogies from our past. But historical analogies require careful examination, for choosing among them influences the way we will think, speak, and act.

Commentators have compared the attacks on the World Trade Center and the Pentagon to Pearl Harbor because both attacks came without warning. With Pearl Harbor as the primary analog, the attacks on New York and Washington were quickly termed "acts of war." That is understandable but dangerously imprecise. It cloaks massive illegality under the guise of rules of engagement—the very thing that terrorists deny by their outrageous transformation of civil aircraft into weapons of destruction.

The attacks on New York and Washington were also unlike Pearl Harbor in that the destruction wrought by Japanese forces had an obvious and official governmental return address. As President Bush acknowledged in his address to Congress last week, the perpetrators of the recent attacks are a "collection of loosely affiliated terrorist organizations," and "there are thousands of these terrorists in more than sixty countries." This is not the language of war but of crime.

The analogy with Pearl Harbor limps badly and leads to policy judgments of dubious value. The recent atrocities have a much closer precedent in the events leading up to World War I. On June 28, 1914, Francis Ferdinand, heir to the throne of the Austro-Hungarian Empire, was assassinated in Sarajevo. The Austrian investigation into the terrorist attack could not establish a firm connection with Serbia, the likeliest suspect in harboring, if not organizing the assassination. In the meantime, revulsion against the deed abated. When the Austrians decided to act against Serbia (without clear evidence or clear aims—just to "punish" Serbia), they did not have the kind of support that would have prevented the grievance from erupting into global conflict with devastating consequences for decades.

This is not the time to launch smart or dumb bombs in a war that cannot be won from the skies. The objective of locating a suspect is a just one. The killing of innocent men, women, and children who live in their neighborhoods is not. It will not avenge our painful loss. It will recruit new members for the terrorists. This is not even the time to launch an invasion of infantry divisions in a war that the Russians can assure us will not go well for us, and will only rally impoverished Afghanis around leaders under whom they chafe.

It is time to call off the war metaphor. We are dealing not with acts of war committed by a nation-state but with massive criminality that calls for an extraordinary effort to identify and locate the perpetrators, and to bring them to justice. Not infinite justice, but human justice—the only kind we are capable of: condign, focused, measured, and appropriate.

This is the time—as with any organized criminal activity—to follow the money and freeze the assets of known criminals. This is the time for making it much more difficult for thugs to hijack civil aircraft. This is the time to forge a new level of international cooperation in the investigation of this crime, including the expansion of our links to countries toward whom we have not "tilted" in the past, Pakistan and India among them.

All of these things can be done without the rhetoric or actions of war. To follow the rule of law under these most painful circumstances is to deny the lawless the power of their claim that might is right. Human Rights Watch put this point well: "There are people and governments in the world who believe that in the struggle against terrorism, ends always justify means. But that is also the logic of terrorism. Whatever the response to this outrage, it must not validate that logic. Rather, it must uphold the principles that came under attack [on September 11], respecting innocent life and international law. That is the way to deny the perpetrators of this crime their ultimate victory."

The attacks on New York and Washington were on twin symbols of American economy, culture, and democratic governance. Americans correctly understand that this assault was aimed squarely at our institutions and at our national identity. But this assault was also on principles of respect for civilian life cherished for centuries by all civilized people. Remembering that will help keep our reply focused and proportionate to the evil at hand. It is profoundly American to make critical distinctions between the guilty and the innocent; between perpetrators and innocent civilians in their neighborhoods; and between those who commit atrocities and those who may simply share their religious beliefs, ethnicity, or national origin.

These distinctions were hard won in American history. When we beg God to bless America, our prayer should be for greater awareness of these distinctions, which are divine blessings on all humankind.

Ed Gaffney teaches international law and the use of force at Valparaiso University School of Law.

5. An Extraordinary Discussion

OCTOBER 3, 2001
BY JEAN BETHKE ELSHTAIN

On Thursday, September 20, only hours before his speech before Congress, President George W. Bush spent over an hour talking and praying with a group of twenty-some leaders of America's diverse religious communities. I was surprised and honored to be included in the meeting—this despite the fact that I can by no means be described as a leader of a particular religious community. I would like to give readers of *Sightings* a sense of how the event unfolded.

My hunch is that someone on the White House staff decided that they needed a representative from one of America's leading divinity schools and chose me because I have in the past addressed the ethics of war and war-making. I did not know most of those included. I recognized Franklin Graham, son of Billy Graham, from media sightings. I greeted Cardinal Bernard Law of Boston by name because he was, in fact, the one person I had met in the past.

We gathered, as requested, at 12:15 p.m. at the northwest appointments gate of the White House. We cleared security and were then ushered into the Eisenhower Executive Office Building across from the White House. There we gathered together, greeted one another, and shared expressions of peace and concern. I found it rather extraordinary that the single most ecumenical event I have ever attended had been put together by the White House. All Christian orientations were represented, as were members from the Orthodox, Jewish, Sikh, Hindu, Buddhist, and Muslim communities.

We discussed a proposed statement—put together by a member of our group, not by the White House—for around forty minutes. A few of us made proposals for additions and corrections. These were accepted and the statement was signed by all of us. We offered up our prayers for the bereaved. We lifted up those who "selflessly gave their lives in an attempt to rescue others." We expressed our gratitude that "the president has spoken out early and clearly to denounce acts of bigotry and racism directed against Arabs, Muslims, and others in our midst. To yield to hate is to give victory to the terrorists." We called the attacks of September 11 acts against all of humanity—over sixty other countries lost citizens in the attacks—and we argued that there was a "grave obligation to do all we can to protect innocent human life" because "the common good has been threatened by these attacks." We called for a response that was just and peaceful—understanding, as many of us do, that the claims of justice and of peace must guide any reaction.

After our deliberations concluded, we were ushered to the Roosevelt Room of the White House. Chairs were arranged in a circle. There was no table. When the president entered the room, he greeted people he knew by name and asked us to be seated. When he noticed that the chairs on either side of him were empty—people giving the president some room—he gestured and said, "Come on in here. I feel lonely down here." People scooted in. The president then offered twenty to twenty-five minutes of reflection on the situation, indicating the need to steer a careful course between calling for Americans to be attentive and doing so in a way that doesn't instill fear in hearts already bestirred and stunned by what had happened. He indicated that he would oppose anyone who singled out those of the Muslim faith or Arab background for acts of vigilantism and bigotry as Islam, he stated, is a "religion that preaches peace" and those who had hijacked Islam to murder nearly seven thousand people did not represent Islam.

The president discussed the terrible day, going over some of the events as he experienced them, doing what so many Americans are doing in trying to come to grips with what happened. He told us that it is clear the White House was a target; that it was an "old building made of plaster and brick" and that had it been struck it would have been demolished and many people killed, "including my wife." (He paused and choked up at that thought.) The overall sense the president conveyed was that of a man who is horrified, saddened, clear about his constitutional responsibility to protect the country and her citizens, determined to build an international coalition and not to go it alone, equally determined to respond in a way that is measured and not unlimited.

Following this gripping presentation, the president asked us to share concerns and thoughts. Some among the group lifted up particular scriptural passages they found apt for our tragic circumstance. Others—the representatives of the Sikh, Hindu, Buddhist, and Muslim communities—brought their support and thanked the president for his words against bigotry.

Deciding this might be my only opportunity to offer advice to a president of the United States face-to-face, I indicated that I taught "political ethics," to which the president responded jocularly (as do most people when I tell them this), "Is there such a thing?" I replied, "I like to think so, and I believe you are attempting to exemplify such in operation through this crisis." I then said that a president's role as "civic educator" has never been more important.

That he must explain things to the American people and teach patience to an impatient people—the need to sacrifice to a people unused to sacrifice. The president indicated he was aware of this important responsibility and it was clear that he had already given the civic education role some thought.

The entire meeting was unhurried, casual, thoughtful. As the president's aides began to gather in the room, it was clear the meeting—now well into its second hour—was about to end. One of our group asked, "Mr. President, what can we do for you?" He indicated that we could "Pray for me, for our country, for my family." He believes in the efficacy of prayer and needs wisdom and guidance and grace, he said. A Greek Orthodox archbishop was invited to lead us in prayer. We all joined hands in a prayer circle, including the president. It was a powerful and moving moment. As the prayer ended and we began to rise, one among us began, haltingly, to sing "God Bless America," a distinctly unchauvinistic song that Americans have turned to over the past few weeks. We all began to join in, including the president. He then mingled, shook hands, and thanked us as we left.

All of us were aware we had participated in an extraordinary event. People shared addresses and business cards. We departed the White House to face a bank of cameras—always set up on the lawn. It began to rain softly. I stood next to my Sikh colleague and found myself gently patting him on the shoulder. I said, "I hope you don't mind my doing that." He said, "No, of course not. Please. I find it reassuring, very reassuring."

As I got into a taxi for the long ride to Baltimore-Washington International Airport, I realized that I had no desire to "spin" the event, to analyze it to bits, or to engage in some sort of tight exegesis. Sometimes events just stand. They are what they are. If the president had simply wanted a public relations event, he would have done a quick photo-op (preferably the prayer circle scene, no doubt); cameras would have been whirring; we would have had a few well-timed and choreographed minutes. None of that happened. It was clear that the president wanted counsel; that he sought prayer; that he also hoped to reassure us that he understood the issues involved.

It was an afternoon I will not soon forget. I am grateful that I was able to join a group of my fellow citizens and members of our diverse religious communities for an extraordinary discussion with the president of the United States.

Jean Bethke Elshtain is the Laura Spelman Rockefeller Professor of Social and Political Ethics at the University of Chicago Divinity School. [Ed. Note: Professor Elshtain passed away on August 11, 2013.]

6. Of Patriots and Saints

FEBRUARY 7, 2002
BY JONATHAN EBEL

Those who watched Sunday's Super Bowl were treated to a seemingly miraculous game. After appearing to fall apart in the game's final two minutes, the New England Patriots, fourteen-point underdogs, defeated the St. Louis Rams on a last-second field goal. For once in a great many years the game helped viewers forget the halftime kitsch and the much-anticipated, strangely uncreative array of commercials.

Woven into this year's tapestry of sport, show, and commercialism was an unusual attention to religion. Not since Sandy Koufax refused to pitch a World Series game on Yom Kippur or Cassius Clay accepted Islam has the faith of athletes received as much coverage in the sports media. The reasons for the attention are many, but prominent among them are the role that Christianity plays in the lives of so many of the St. Louis Rams, and their readiness to talk so openly about their faith.

In the week before the Super Bowl the *Chicago Tribune* ran two stories, Melissa Isaacson's "Keeping the Faith" and Rick Morrissey's "Preaching Has Its Place, but It's Not Here," sparked by the public Christianity of the St. Louis Rams. ESPN Radio host Dan Patrick, usually given to standard sports talk-radio material, put his spin on the topic when he invited an agnostic player to talk about the dynamics of a religious locker room from a non-religious perspective. To their credit, these journalists and many more across the country waded into unfamiliar waters. They treated what they found there with varying degrees of success.

Rick Morrissey, lead writer of the *Chicago Tribune*'s venerable "In the Wake of the News" column, handled the topic most clumsily, complaining in column length that St. Louis Rams quarterback Kurt Warner, the National Football League's Most Valuable Player, talks about God too much and is unjustifiably disappointed when his message doesn't make its way into the sports page. "Many devout Christian athletes complain that whenever they refer to their religious beliefs during media interviews, their testimony often is edited out by heathen sportswriters wearing stained golf shirts." Morrissey continues, "There is a reason for this separation of church and sport: When people open up their sports section in the morning, they don't do it to read Warner's views on being born again." If Morrissey has in mind the notoriously hard to "church" 18-24 demographic, then he is probably right. But if, as he should hope, his readership extends beyond the sports-bar set, Morrissey might find quite a few more readers who, for many reasons—some surely not to Kurt Warner's liking—take an interest in the role religion plays in the life of a successful team.

According to fellow *Tribune* columnist Melissa Isaacson, one such interested party, the New Orleans Saints football team, hired a "voodoo priestess to cast a spell on the Rams" before a playoff game last year. The Saints won the game, and Warner arrived in New Orleans this year with passages of scripture to "counteract any sorcery." St. Louis lost again.

ESPN Radio personality Dan Patrick devoted a segment of his program to discussing religion and professional football with New York Giants offensive lineman Glenn Parker, an agnostic. His experiences were, generally, that prayer and openly religious acts including the attribution of victory to God did as much harm to the team as they did good. When a quarterback says that we won and he played well because God wanted him to, the lineman said, it makes all of us wonder what, exactly, we contributed to the effort.

What lessons on religion can we learn from the words and experiences of the spectacularly wealthy, super-athletic who dominate our television screens every weekend? Do we need Eugene Robinson, formerly of the Atlanta Falcons, to show us that the Christian citizen by day might solicit a prostitute by night? Do we need defensive great and ordained minister Reggie White to show us that religious authority doesn't always come with clarity of thought on matters of race? Do we need players uncomfortable with public expressions of faith to demonstrate to us that religion can be an alienating influence? For that matter, ought we to ask Kurt Warner (who said, according to Isaacson, "I'm not saying He's picking sides . . . but I think He wants me to be successful because I'm going to glorify His name") and his Christian teammates where God was as Adam Vinatieri's field goal sailed through the up-rights Sunday night?

The answer to each of these questions is "No." We shouldn't turn to Warner for theology any more than we turn to Augustine or Tillich for play-by-play. But given the extent to which athletes have come to dominate public consciousness, we do well to look closely at how religion functions among them. Their problems and triumphs, and religious sensitivities, may be more publicized than ours, but they are certainly in the same ballpark.

Resources

Isaacson, Melissa. "Keeping the Faith." *Chicago Tribune.* January 31, 2002. http://articles.chicagotribune.com/2002-01-31/sports/0201310342_1_rams-practice-field-grant-wistrom-mike-martz.

Morrissey, Rick. "Preaching Has Its Place, but It's Not Here." *Chicago Tribune.* February 2, 2002. http://articles.chicagotribune.com/2002-02-02/sports/0202020193_1_god-lighting-christianity.

Jonathan Ebel is the managing editor of Sightings, *and a doctoral candidate in the history of Christianity at the University of Chicago Divinity School.*

7. "The Women" Are Everywhere

MARCH 14, 2002
BY AMY HOLLYWOOD

In "Where Are the Women?" (*The Nation*, October 4, 2001), Katha Pollitt called attention to the plight of Afghan women under the then-ruling Taliban. After describing the harshest of the measures against women under the Taliban (legally women could not work, go to school, or leave their houses without a male escort, and they were denied almost any form of health care), Pollitt compares "the Taliban's crazier requirements" for women to "the obsessive particularity of the Nazis' statutes against Jews" in the years preceding and during World War II. Pollitt goes on to decry the widespread "notion that the plight of Afghan women is a matter of culture and tradition, and not for Westerners to judge."

While the appeal-to-the-Nazis is a much overused and sensationalistic rhetorical strategy, I can understand the sense of urgency that leads Pollitt to deploy it in this case. I share her concern for the plight of Afghan women and her continued worry about the fate of women in Afghanistan after the Taliban's fall (see "After the Taliban," *The Nation*, November 29, 2001). (For a more historically informed and nuanced view of the situation in Afghanistan, however, see Charles Hirschkind and Saba Mahmood's "Feminism, the Taliban, and the Politics of Counter-Insurgency," forthcoming in *Anthropological Quarterly*.) What concerns me here—and led to my first ever, albeit unpublished, letter to the editor—is the way in which Pollitt goes on to conflate the Taliban with "religious fanaticism" and religious fanaticism with the teachings of every "major religion." According to Pollitt, "the connections between religious fanaticism and the suppression of women are plain to see (and not just applicable to Islam)." "Show me," she challenges, "a major religion in which the inferiority of women, and God's wish to place them and their dangerous polluting sexuality under male control, is not a central original theme."

For Pollitt, religion is a static site of beliefs and practices oppressive to women. She shows no recognition of or concern for the fact that religion might do other things crucial for some people's—among them women's—flourishing, nor does she acknowledge that religious traditions are complex, changing, and contested (both from within and from without). Most crucially, Pollitt's ignorance of the complexity of religious traditions leads her to play directly into the hands of the Taliban and other modern religious movements that make misogyny central to their belief and practice. Feminist scholars of Judaism, Christianity, Islam, and Hinduism, to name only the religions about which I have some knowledge, demonstrate the complexity of women's positions within these traditions. There is no single view about women or women's sexuality within the Hebrew Bible, the New Testament, the Koran, or the sacred scriptures of India (and the Koran may well come off the best here, as Azizah al-Hibri argues in a recent exchange with Susan Moller Okin). To suggest that there are monolithic conceptions of women or women's sexuality at the core of these traditions implicitly legitimates narrow and distorting misogynist readings and misreadings of their central texts and practices.

Of course I don't deny the extraordinarily patriarchal cast of much religious history; yet the subordination of women occurs in different ways and to different degrees within these complex traditions and is often accompanied by substantial goods. We can only begin to contend with and critique the religious subordination of women when we understand the complexity of religious traditions, recognize the emancipatory and egalitarian countercurrents that often exist within them, and, finally, accept that religions may satisfy desires and aspirations unmet by Western secular political ideologies.

Pollitt consistently provides sophisticated and informed feminist analyses of contemporary politics. The same attention and care must be given to religion if Western feminists hope to meaningfully ally themselves with women internationally, for many women throughout the world (as in the West) are struggling to achieve equality and fulfillment within existing religious traditions. When Pollitt claims that these traditions are necessarily and irrevocably harmful to women, she renders her conception of feminism immediately unpalatable to a substantial number of women who otherwise share her concern for women's physical, psychological, and spiritual well-being. Religious women's values may not be—in fact, at times probably won't be—couched in the same terms or even be the same as Pollitt's or, for that matter, my own, shaped as Pollitt and I both are by modern Western liberalism and socialism (themselves deeply indebted to the Christian tradition).

Yet it's a mistake for Western women to assume from the outset the superiority of purportedly secular Western values. Rather we have to search for points of agreement between ourselves and women from different traditions, argue for the validity of our particular views, and—perhaps most importantly—allow these views to be questioned and challenged by the deeply cherished values of women different from ourselves. Only then can a truly international women's movement flourish.

Resources

Pollitt, Katha. "After the Taliban." *The Nation.* November 29, 2001. https://www .thenation.com/article/after-taliban.

———. "Where Are the Women?" *The Nation.* October 4, 2001. https://www .thenation.com/article/where-are-women.

Amy Hollywood (PhD, University of Chicago Divinity School) teaches in the Religion Department at Dartmouth College and is currently a Martin Marty Center fellow and visiting associate professor of theology and history of Christianity at the University of Chicago Divinity School.

8. Of Troubled Hearts

MAY 30, 2002
BY CHRISTOPHER BEEM

"Do not let your hearts be troubled." I recently heard my parish priest read Jesus's words from the Gospel, and apply them to the ongoing crisis in the Catholic Church. I found that I was not persuaded. Of course, I accept the idea that ultimately and fundamentally, Christ is in charge of his church. But I worried that an overeager search for quietude is a recipe for quietism—that is, inaction in the face of grave problems.

I felt the same uneasiness as I listened to the American Cardinals report on their meeting at the Vatican. Church leaders were so eager to move beyond this scandal, so eager to restore untroubled hearts to the American laity, that they passed over the really hard questions.

The crisis in the church is not and never was about pedophilia. Any profession that deals with children will attract some few who would prey upon them. The crisis rather is about a leadership that routinely placed the welfare of the institution—the preservation of appearances, finances, and the status quo—ahead of the welfare of children.

Commentators repeatedly noted the extraordinary nature of the Vatican meeting. And indeed, the meeting was an extraordinary opportunity to address this far more scandalous sin. And yet at the end of it, we were told that we should find it extraordinary that the pope declared pedophilia a sin and a crime. I already knew that. Indeed, I know that aiding and abetting a crime is also a crime. In an extraordinary meeting, church leaders would have asked why they acted like criminals.

I believe these men when they say that they love our children. But the fact remains that our children are not their children. The responsibilities, burdens, joys, and sorrows of parenthood are not theirs. The more I think about it, the more I believe this to be the heart of the matter. Bernard Cardinal Law is not a parent. If it were otherwise—if he were a father—I cannot believe he would have treated children with such chronic and wanton callousness.

Those who are parents—lay men and women—bring an insight to the Christian pilgrimage that the church leadership does not have. And the current crisis demonstrates with appalling clarity that they desperately need that insight. I am not an authority on canon law, so I will simply ask the question: Can the Pope appoint someone who is not a priest, or who is not a man, to the position of cardinal or bishop? That is, can he appoint a mother or father to genuine church leadership? Perhaps he cannot. But the more operative issue, of course, is that he will not. The extraordinary opportunity came and went. And it is all too likely that neither he, nor his successor, nor the American church leadership, will ever summon the courage to ask this question. But until they do, the current crisis may be weathered, but it will not have passed. Indeed, until they do, I am unable to avoid the sad conclusion that the leadership of the Catholic Church is incorrigible and that my heart will and should remain deeply troubled.

Christopher Beem received his PhD from the University of Chicago Divinity School in 1994. He is a member of Holy Family Parish in Whitefish Bay, Wisconsin.

9. A Letter from Jerusalem: Christmas 2002

DECEMBER 19, 2002
BY ITHAMAR GRUENWALD

Christmas this year cannot be like any Christmas in previous years. In the year that has passed, the Church of the Nativity was turned—for a while—into a beleaguered fortress. Arab Palestinians forced their way into the church, and Israeli troops and armor forced them out. War makes horrible things happen. Whether it is the Palestinian police or the Israeli army, midnight mass is conducted with guns protecting the Holy Host.

The war that now plagues the Holy Land leaves no one indifferent. Christmas this year is therefore a moment that generates serious meditation. International terrorism has forced the world into a new situation, one in which thoughts lose their needed consistency. May God help and direct those who, under the circumstances, have to think twice or thrice before taking action.

Christmas 2002 is a time to look beyond the Christmas tree, the lights, and the other decorations and festivities. It is a time for a new resolve and a clear determination to celebrate birth and condemn everything that marks the reverse of a birth event.

In a wider historical context, Christmas brings up reflections on the role the Jewish setting had in shaping the events connected with the rise of Christianity. Jesus was born a Jew. The manger was a Jewish manger. Christians believe that a light was shining in Bethlehem, a divine light, which had yet made no theological divisions. A light utterly removed from the dark night of human compassion as experienced in the events of 2001 and 2002.

When, however, a parting of the ways came into effect, we, the Jews, were pushed aside, condemned, and damned. Can we, then, rejoice with our Christian friends at Christmas time? In his memoir, *From Berlin to Jerusalem*, Gershom Scholem tells that in his family they used to celebrate Christmas, with a Christmas tree and everything. I heard the same story from my father who emigrated in 1933 from Berlin to, then, Palestine. This is how Jewish people in Germany understood and enacted their emancipation from a status of ethnic minority. In their eyes, this opened the door to a positive assimilation, or, in more modern terms, to civil acculturation. Scholem even tells that at one point his mother put the picture of Theodor Herzl, the founder of Zionism, under the Christmas tree—a remarkable mode of messianic transposition. Scholem remarks, though, that since then he always left home at Christmas time.

What are we to do, here in Jerusalem, on this day? I can speak for myself. This is a moment for me to share a few thoughts with friends, known and unknown. From a global village, we have moved into a new kind of global war. To protect our own house, we have to protect the house of a close-by or distant neighbor. I find myself meditating on what differences and alienation can cause. Thus, differences that have separated us, Jews and Christians, in the past should be allowed to dissolve; at least, let's give joint efforts their chance. Whether this concerns our environment, our social structure, or the acuteness of our sense of justice, we have a lot to do together. Perhaps it will simply be our ability to notice the hand that is stretched out to us and respond, with consideration, to the needs that the gesture expresses. It will certainly be reflected in our sincerity and prayers for peace. We have a lot to do together.

It is a Jewish custom to greet friends on the days that mark Jewish holidays and festivals with the words "Chag Same'ach," a happy holiday. In Christian terms, this will equal "Merry Christmas."

Ithamar Gruenwald lives in Jerusalem. He teaches at Tel Aviv University, Israel, in the Department of Jewish Philosophy and the Program in Religious Studies.

10. Ryan's Commute

JANUARY 20, 2003
BY MARTIN E. MARTY

When former Illinois governor George Ryan commuted the death sentences of 167 inmates on Illinois's Death Row earlier this month, he prompted a new round of intense theological and moral debate. *National Review* editor-at-large John O'Sullivan weighed in from the furiously-opposed-to-commutation side (January 14), ignoring religious voices and shooting down the arguments of the "academic, media and political elites." O'Sullivan makes clear that the "elites" have to be wrong because "70 percent of [the American people] endorse capital punishment."

As O'Sullivan paints it, this is "the latest skirmish in the ongoing culture war" between "the people" and those "elites," including Ryan's approving Northwestern University audience with their "obscene" applause. By overlooking the religious perspective, O'Sullivan missed hearing the emphatic anti-death-penalty voices of Pope John Paul II, the Catholic bishops, and leaders of many other-than-Roman Catholic church bodies who, thus, also had to be wrong, if not evil.

Had he monitored the whole religious front, O'Sullivan could also have found some pro-capital-punishment elites, especially among "evangelicals" or the "Christian right"—often the politically best-connected of American religious leaders. From many of them, he would have heard enthusiastic support for capital punishment. Why? They usually quote some biblical passage or invoke ancient precedents, in or out of context, to justify the killing. In doing so, they counteract their own views of conversion, repentance, and eternal destiny.

Ryan pointed out this apparent contradiction in his side comments. Aware that many of the executed were born again or otherwise converted, he wondered why any believers in heaven and the death penalty would see execution as preferable to life in prison. He'd been to many funerals where the preacher professed that the dead were now in a better place, in bliss. Why, he asked, send these killers prematurely to a better place? Prison has to be less blissful.

And there's a flip side to Ryan's observation that's equally hard to resolve from an evangelical perspective: execution of the not-yet-born-again prisoners. By choosing to execute them, the time needed to come to repentance is prematurely cut off; the opportunities for the evil ones to repent are taken away.

I remain puzzled even after the back-and-forth I had with prison minister Charles Colson after he announced his conversion to the pro-capital-punishment camp some seasons ago. When such an aborting of conversion possibilities is pointed out to these evangelizers, they either ignore the issue or respond in predestinarian terms: if God had it in mind and plan for sinners to be saved, they say, God would have acted to save before the executioner killed.

Those who are so sure of what God had in mind might, one would think, be cautious about being the agents of such cutting short and thus such sending of sinners to eternal punishment. We'll monitor future responses.

Resource

O'Sullivan, John. "Obscene." *National Review.* January 14, 2003. http://www .nationalreview.com/article/205518/obscene-john-osullivan.

11. Milton, Mass., Mary

SEPTEMBER 7, 2003
BY ELIZABETH HAYES ALVAREZ

Recently, an image of the Virgin Mary appeared in the window of a Massachusetts hospital prompting 25,000 visitors. The hospital took no official position as to the authenticity of the apparition but tried its best to accommodate the pilgrims who were regularly gathering in its parking lot. The Boston archdiocese was contacted for help. Cameramen and news reporters soon followed. Eventually, the majority of the media-consuming public glimpsed the sight of what appeared to be the Madonna, head bowed and set in frosted glass. But other than etchings in glass, what do we see in scenes such as these? In our rational and cynical culture, how do we explain the attraction, as observers and participants, to miracles and the supernatural?

The church and the media are in similar binds when they seek to address these happenings. The church has historically taken a wait-and-see approach, loath to dismiss the possibility of the supernatural or quash the faith of the people, yet prudent in wanting to protect (or control depending on your viewpoint) theology and worship. The media also strive to respect rather than dismiss "folk" religious expression but, as serious news, generally feel compelled to add an alternate explanation. This can border on the ridiculous as when a recent Associated Press account included commentary by Joe Nickell, a senior research fellow at the Committee for the Scientific Investigation of Claims of the Paranormal, providing a parenthetical non-miraculous explanation (mineral deposits) in their coverage of the hospital appearance. What's needed, instead of squeamishness over the existence of faith, is thoughtful reporting on religion.

The interesting questions that arise from these events are not "Why is there still faith?" but "What is going on in religion? Why Mary?" Since the Second Vatican Ecumenical Council, which downplayed and clarified the role of the saints while formally incorporating a detailed Mariology into the Dogmatic Constitution of the Church, at least thirty Marian apparition claims have made news in the US.

Within the Roman Catholic Church, teaching on Mary continues to be expanded and veneration encouraged. The current pope's devotion is well known. During his pontificate, Pope John Paul II has declared the "Marian Year" (1987); issued the encyclical, *Redemptoris Mater*; delivered, from 1995 through 1997, seventy Wednesday catecheses on Mary; and declared the "Year of the Rosary," from October 2002 to October 2003. Pope John Paul II has recently instituted a new set of mysteries, the Luminous Mysteries, to contemplate in the rosary prayer through which, he explains, the face of Christ is contemplated in the "school of Mary."

On a "folk" level, interest in the Holy Mother abounds. The internet overflows with sites and webrings devoted to her. Conservatives and liberals alike claim her as their own, putting forth wildly differing accounts of her role in faith and her intentions for mankind. She has been reclaimed as a traditionally Christian, but newly understood, female locus of devotion by the "not religious, but spiritual" folk, while at the same time serving as the standard-bearer for conservatives in the pro-life movement (complete with a pro-life rosary).

Apparition sites like the one in Milton, Massachusetts, abound throughout the world, drawing thousands of pilgrims each year. And new ones crop up all the time. There was even a follow-up story that said people were now claiming to see the image of the cross on the hospital's chimney stacks. Somehow that story never grabbed hold (or we had already moved on). But despite our ability to see what is or isn't there, we recognize that faith in America continues to flourish in parking lots as well as parishes—with or without a permit.

Elizabeth Hayes Alvarez is the managing editor of Sightings. *She is a PhD candidate in the history of Christianity at the University of Chicago Divinity School.*

12. Cracking *The Da Vinci Code*

SEPTEMBER 24, 2003
BY MARGARET M. MITCHELL

Besieged by requests for my reaction to *The Da Vinci Code*, I finally decided to sit down and read it over the weekend. It was a quick romp, largely fun to read, if rather predictable and preachy. This is a good airplane book, a novelistic thriller that presents a rummage sale of accurate historical nuggets alongside falsehoods and misleading statements. The bottom line: the book should come coded for "black light," like the pen used by the character Saunière to record his dying words, so that readers could scan pages to see which "facts" are trustworthy and which patently not, and (if a black light could do this!) highlight the gray areas where complex issues are misrepresented and distorted.

Patently inaccurate:

In his own lifetime Jesus "inspired millions" to better lives (p. 231); there were "More than *eighty* gospels" (p. 231; the number eighty is factual-sounding but has no basis); "The earliest Christian records" were found among the Dead Sea Scrolls (including gospels) and Nag Hammadi texts (pp. 234, 245); the Nag Hammadi texts "speak of Christ's ministry in very human terms" (p. 234); the marriage of Mary Magdalene and Jesus is "a matter of historical record" (p. 244); Constantine invented the divinity of Jesus and excluded all gospels but the four canonical ones; Constantine made Christianity "the official religion" of the Roman Empire (p. 232); Constantine coined the term "heretic" (p. 234); "Rome's official religion was sun worship" (p. 232). There are more.

Gray areas:

"The vestiges of pagan religion in Christian symbology are undeniable," but that does not mean "Nothing in Christianity is original" (p. 232). The relationship between early Christianity and the world around it, the ways in which it was culturally embedded in that world, sometimes unreflectively, sometimes reflexively, sometimes in deliberate accommodation, sometimes in deliberate co-optation, are far more complicated than the simplistic myth of Constantine's Stalinesque program of cultural totalitarianism. Further, Constantine's religious life—whether, when, how, and by what definition he was Christian and/or "pagan"—is a much-debated issue because the literary and non-literary sources (such as coins) are not consistent. That Constantine the emperor had "political" motives (p. 234) is hardly news to anyone! The question is how religion and politics (which cannot be separated in the ancient world) were interrelated in him. He is as hard to figure out on this score as Henry VIII, Osama bin Laden, Tammy Faye Bakker, and George W. Bush. Dan Brown has turned one of history's most fascinating figures into a cartoonish villain.

"Paganism" is treated throughout *The Da Vinci Code* as though it were a unified phenomenon, which it was not ("pagan" just being the Christian term for "non-Christian"). The religions of the Mediterranean world were multiple and diverse and cannot all be boiled down to "sun-worshippers" (p. 232). Nor did all "pagans" frequently, eagerly, and with mystical intent participate in the *hieros gamos* (ritual sex acts). "The Church" is also used throughout the book as though it had a clear, uniform, and unitary referent. For early Christian history this is precisely what we do not have; rather, we have a much more complex, varied, and localized phenomenon. Brown presumes "the Church" is "the Holy Roman Catholic Church," which he thinks had tremendous power always and everywhere, but ecclesiastical history is a lot messier.

Brown propagates the full-dress conspiracy theory for Vatican suppression of women. Feminist scholars and others have been debating different models of the "patriarchalization" of Christianity for decades. Elisabeth Schüssler Fiorenza's landmark work, *In Memory of Her* (1983), argued that while Jesus and Paul (on his better days) were actually pretty much pro-women, it was the next generations (the authors of letters in Paul's name like 1 and 2 Timothy and others) who betrayed their feminist agenda and sold out to the Aristotelian, patriarchal vision of Greco-Roman society. Others (unfortunately) sought to blame the misogyny on the Jewish roots of Christianity. More recently it has been argued that the picture is more mixed, even for Jesus and Paul. That is, they may have been more liberal than many of their contemporaries about women, but they were not all-out radicals, though they had ideas (such as Galatians 3:28) that were even more revolutionary than they realized (in both senses of the term). Alas, no simple story here. And while obsessing over Mary Magdalene, *The Da Vinci Code* ignores completely the rise and incredible durability and power of the other Mary, the mother of Jesus, and devotion to her that follows many patterns of "goddess" veneration (she even gets the Athena's Parthenon dedicated to her in the sixth century).

This list is just a sample. A "black light" edition of *The Da Vinci Code* would, however, be unnecessary if readers would simply take the book as fiction. But there is an obstacle: the first page of the book reads, under the bold print headline "Fact": "All descriptions of . . . documents, and secret rituals in this novel are accurate."

Resource
Brown, Dan. *The Da Vinci Code*. New York: Doubleday, 2003.

Margaret M. Mitchell (PhD, University of Chicago Divinity School) is associate professor of New Testament at the University of Chicago Divinity School and the chair of the Department of New Testament and Early Christian Literature at the University of Chicago.

13. Remembering Martin Luther King

JANUARY 19, 2004
BY MARTIN E. MARTY

Our house has always remembered Martin Luther and Martin Luther King. Our children sometimes confused the two. Son John's teacher once advised me to confront our six-year-old about his fibbing. "He claimed to have spent a week in a dormitory with Martin Luther"—whose name had come up in a Lutheran Sunday School class. I confronted John who, in all innocence, insisted he told the truth: we had spent a week with him (when I duoed with King at Hampton Institute) in the summer of 1962. Between sessions, the civil rights leader played with our five boys, hoisting them to a low-lying tree branch and catching them as they jumped.

Needless to say, we spent time telling our little Lutherans about the other Martin Luther. But King always remained vivid to them, as he does to millions of Americans and world citizens who have at best a vague knowledge of who Martin Luther was.

I begin so informally because King often gets elevated to iconic status, fit into remote niches, described as so full of gravitas that he could not unbend. He could unbend. But I must move on from the fond recall to the less familial, less personalized, and weightier theme for this week.

We argue much these days about how the religious and the civil orders do or should interact. Some think God and the public are served by sculptures and plaques and imposed prayer in public places. Here is my take on how King instead related the two orders. Sociologist Michael Hill, citing Max Weber, showed the difference between the charismatic religious leader, who typically says of a text, "It is written, but I say unto you," and the religious virtuoso, who says, "It is written, and I insist." "The religious virtuoso follows what he takes to be a pure and rigorous interpretation of normative obligations which already exist in a religious tradition." In American culture, biblical texts were in that tradition.

King, in this sense, was a virtuoso with two sets of texts, neither of which he imposed and both of which he used to persuade. In one pocket were civil texts, especially the Declaration of Independence and the Constitution. King would figuratively wave them and say that since 100 percent of the population was committed to these, he "insisted" that they be responded to by and realized among all citizens. In the other were biblical texts, as befit the pocket of an African American preacher. He would cite Isaiah or Micah or John the Baptist or Jesus and say, in effect, since 80 percent of you profess to be responsive to these texts, I insist that you try to help realize the justice of which they speak.

For at least a moment in 1965, enough people in the White House, the Congress, the Court, the legislatures, and the general public responded and more civil rights were realized. King was religious and he put religion to work when he wanted to reach the conscience of the public. Civil law came into the picture not for the imposition of religion but the assurance of rights.

At our house each year we remember King's use of texts and his persuasive and courageous achievements. We also fondly recall and celebrate the important then-young man who, in 1962, had time for the five little boys on the tree branch.

Resource

Hill, Michael. *The Religious Order*. London: Heinemann, 1973.

14. Tru-Envy?

April 15, 2004
By Jon Pahl

I saw the first dandelion in my lawn yesterday, and today two advertisements for lawn care companies arrived in my mailbox. Call it a coincidence, but for many in America, such a conjunction of signs would be the trigger of a largely unconscious religious crisis.

Lawn care is big business in America. Estimates of the amount spent on professional lawn care services vary, but a recent Harris survey put the total at $28.9 billion in 2002, which calculates to roughly $1,200 per household, spread over the 24.7 million households who use such services.

And that doesn't take into account the products consumers purchase for do-it-yourself devotion to the righteous icon of the American lawn. According to a 2002 article by Craig Wilson in *USA Today*, there are roughly 30 million acres of these little shrines to uniformity across the US. Their care demands 300 million gallons of gas per year, 70 million pounds of pesticides, and roughly one billion hours in labor.

All in all, something must be motivating so many in America to devote themselves to a blessed rage for order that may have bad implications for our public life together.

Most notably—pesticides and herbicides kill things. Take dandelions, for example. The impact of lawn care chemicals on humans and domestic animals is open to debate, but most children find dandelions pretty, and they are (in fact) a food source. What happens to make adults want to kill them?

Virginia Scott Jenkins, in her wonderfully researched *The Lawn: A History of an American Obsession*, traces the desire to kill weeds historically. She notes that the current rage for a chemically dependent lawn emerged after World War II, and she argues that "American front lawns are a symbol of man's control of, or superiority over, his environment."

Such a symbol is, by the definition of a lawn, a public one. Is it also religious? One of the ads I received was on four-by-ten-inch card stock. It featured a long picture of a green hedge with a man staring over it with the words "TRU envy" next to him. On the flip side of the card, it encouraged me to call the company "now for a greener lawn. Your neighbors will notice." Then, in smaller print, it continued: "You can enjoy a lawn your neighbors will envy."

Now, call me old-fashioned, but I thought envy was a sin? And I'm supposed to inspire it in my neighbors? I suppose a way to put the best construction on this ad would be to say that it appeals to my pride: that in the eyes of my neighbors I will appear noble, good, and pure for the greenness and uniformity of my lawn.

Or maybe the ad appeals to my fear and shame: that my neighbors won't love me if I grow a motley lawn. And isn't that a dangerous facet of many religions? Believers have their identity defined for them over and against some other who is defined as a threat and to whom they must demonstrate their superiority—even to the point of sacrifice and killing—to display that their faith is real and true.

Even more pointedly, isn't that the way much of public religion works in America? We seem somehow uncertain of our salvation, so we seek enemies to conquer and control, and we seem driven constantly to display our power for others to see. Can there be a connection between the way we treat dandelions and the way we treat our neighbors? The way we treat the poor and sick and suffering of the world?

Honestly, I hope not. And the structures are in place for people to make wiser spiritual choices: to devote ourselves to places of grace that are not constructed for us by corporate products. That is the beauty of the lively experiment that is protected by the First Amendment.

But, at present, that $28.9 billion we're spending seems to be leading us directly into the temptation to kill things with poison, to try to control the uncontrollable, and to desire to be the envy of our neighbors. Not much seems "tru" about that.

Resource

Jenkins, Virginia Scott. *The Lawn: A History of an American Obsession*. Washington, DC: Smithsonian Books, 1994.

Jon Pahl (PhD, University of Chicago Divinity School) teaches American religious history at the Lutheran Theological Seminary at Philadelphia.

15. Supreme Court Theology

SEPTEMBER 9, 2004
BY BRIAN BRITT

College religion courses come in many varieties, with no consistency in labeling. "Theology" at one school may be called "religious studies" at another, and at still others missionaries are trained under the rubric of "intercultural studies." While many church-affiliated colleges minimize their denominational identity, the study of theology flourishes at some state universities, and non-denominational Christian colleges, according to a recent *New York Times Magazine* article, have grown 67 percent in the last ten years.

These conflicting trends reveal unresolved tensions about religion and higher education in American life. Is the study of religion a kind of religious practice? Is a major in religion, or any other subject, really just a form of job training? With its 7–2 decision in February to uphold a Washington state law denying scholarships to theology and ministry students (*Locke v. Davey*), the Supreme Court has calmed the nerves of People for the American Way and others worried about government support for "faith-based" institutions, but it has also codified two major confusions in the law of church and state.

In the case, Joshua Davey was denied a state scholarship available to all undergraduate majors *except* "theology" majors. While Davey's major in pastoral ministries was undoubtedly designed to prepare for a career in the church, the statute in question applies to "theology" without defining the term, a problem overlooked even by the dissenting opinion of Justices Scalia and Thomas. In fact, Davey's college study led him to Harvard Law School, where he is currently enrolled.

The first confusion here is the idea that the boundaries of church and state are crossed only by "theology" majors. Davey attended Northwest College, a fully accredited evangelical institution affiliated with the Assemblies of God. Northwest offers many religiously based undergraduate majors. Students who major in intercultural studies at Northwest, for example, take courses on "Intercultural Ministries" and "Multicultural Evangelism." The entire curriculum is permeated by the religious identity of the college. As Chief Justice Rehnquist admits, the vague state law must be read along with the state constitution, which prohibits state funding of degrees that are "devotional in nature or designed to induce religious faith," a standard that could apply to all degrees at Northwest.

The second, related confusion is the implication that all theology majors are studying to prepare for the ministry. Even the two dissenting opinions blur theology and ministry, claiming that "Today's holding is limited to training the clergy." Most departments of theology and religious studies belong to the humanities and liberal arts, beside English, history, and philosophy. Religion students are famously impractical people, but at schools like Williams College or Virginia Tech (where I teach) those who go on to the ministry are a minority. Most theology and religion faculty belong to the American Academy of Religion, an organization of over nine thousand members whose primary mission is to promote "reflection upon and understanding of religious traditions, issues, questions, and values," not the training of church leaders.

With provisions in thirty-seven states strictly preventing the use of state funding for religious purposes, legal scholars attribute laws like Washington's to the legacy of the anti-Catholic Blaine Amendments of the nineteenth century. And at least fourteen states specifically bar theology students from receiving state aid. The Washington law ("No aid shall be awarded to any student who is pursuing a degree in theology") does not dispute the educational validity of theology majors, which are offered at accredited and mostly tax-exempt institutions, but it takes exception to what these majors might go on to do. It seems likely that the Supreme Court case will have implications for all of these state laws, though *Locke v. Davey* leaves the meaning of "theology" totally unclear.

An even greater misunderstanding lies in the popular notion, reinforced by the majority and minority in this case, that all undergraduate majors match directly to specific careers. Despite pleas from professional and graduate schools for broadly educated students and a rapidly growing rate of career changes in the workforce, many students are advised by parents and faculty to make a one-to-one link between the major and the career beyond it.

By upholding the law withholding scholarships from theology students, the Supreme Court has done more than assuage civil libertarians; it has reinforced the confusion between religious study and practice and perpetuated the caricature of higher education as vocational training.

Resource

Shapiro, Samantha M. "All God's Children." *The New York Times Magazine*. September 5, 2004. http://www.nytimes.com/2004/09/05/magazine/all-gods-children.html.

Brian Britt (PhD, University of Chicago Divinity School) is associate professor and director of the Religious Studies Program, Department of Interdisciplinary Studies, at Virginia Tech.

16. Greeley's War

January 3, 2005
By Martin E. Marty

Andrew Greeley, sociologist, novelist, columnist, and priest, asked in the Christmas Eve edition of the *Chicago Sun-Times*, "Why?" He was referring to the Iraq War in the decades ahead. His language about the adventure was incautious: It's a "cockamamie and criminally immoral war . . . planned before the Sept. 11 attack in which Iraq was not involved. . . . It has nothing to do with the war on terror. . . . [It is the product of] hallucinations by men and women [who write] long memos—. . . intellectuals with pointy heads."

Greeley would support the troops in "the best way possible: Bring them home, get them out of a war for which the planning was inadequate, the training nonexistent, the goal obscure, and the equipment . . . inferior. They are brave men and women . . . [but] sitting ducks for fanatics. Those who die are the victims of the big lie. . . . They are not the war criminals. The 'Vulcans,' as the . . . foreign policy team calls itself, are the criminals, and they ought to face indictment. . . . In fact, the war . . . has become a quagmire. . . . [T]here is no possibility of victory."

Theology from this papist (supporter of Pope John Paul II): "One of the criteria for a just war is that there be a reasonable chance of victory. Where is that reasonable chance? Each extra day of the war makes it more unjust, more criminal. The guilty people are [also] those who in the November election endorsed the war. They are also responsible for the Iraqi deaths. . . . We celebrate 'peace on Earth to men of good will.' Americans must face the fact that they can no longer claim to be men and women of good will. . . . [By the way, there is no] serious reason to believe that Sen. John Kerry would have had the courage to end the war."

Being the moderate Swiss half of the Irish-Swiss duo "Born February 5, 1928," I would have used more temperate language, but I believe Greeley raises a point we must face in 2005, the first year of the next decade of this war. What does one do if he or she becomes convinced that the "just war" criteria did not and do not "fit" this war? When the majority of the population finally came to call the Vietnam War immoral, I was counseling, among others, Lutheran "selective conscientious objectors," that is, not pure pacifists but objectors to a particular war.

Martin Luther asked, at treatise length, *Whether Soldiers, Too, Can Be Saved*. His main answer in short: Yes. But: "'Suppose my lord were wrong in going to war.' I reply: 'If you know for sure that he is wrong, then you should fear God rather than men, Acts 4 [5:29], and you should neither fight nor serve, for you cannot have a good conscience before God.'" Luther did say, give your "lord" the benefit of the doubt; "you ought not to weaken certain obedience for the sake of an uncertain justice." But otherwise, "it is better for God to call you loyal and honorable than for the world to call you loyal and honorable."

Greeley is *not* putting the onus on the troops, whom he applauds and for whom he has sympathy. He questions the citizens who support the venture. He is not the only questioner, and the hawkish Luther is not the only adviser on the morality of war. Still, in 2010 will we look back and ask whether we would not have done better at least to have given such voices a hearing earlier on?

Resources

Greeley, Andrew. "No Peace on Earth during Unjust War." *Chicago Sun-Times*. December 24, 2004.

Luther, Martin. *Luther's Works*. Vol. 46, *The Christian in Society III*. Edited by Helmut T. Lehmann and Robert C. Schultz. Minneapolis: Fortress Press, 1967.

17. The Theodicy of Everyday Life

JANUARY 17, 2005
BY MARTIN E. MARTY

Sightings was overwhelmed with more theological news clippings in the wake of the Asian tsunami than at any time since September 11, 2001. Not being free to go on here at book length, I choose this week to shift the genre from "op-ed" or "civic pedagogy" to "mini-essay." The viewpoint and interest will clearly recall my first vocational role, that of pastor (1952–63)—a job from which one never retires.

The theological theme will be theodicy, that is, "defense of God's goodness and omnipotence in view of the existence of evil." Let us leave, as I often do, the "omni-" words; we will focus on "goodness." Theodicy is every person's enterprise when bad things happen. I have never read a satisfying theodicy, and I want to "spit on the explanations"—isn't that a line from the movie *Zorba?*—when experts glibly give accounts that attempt to do justice to cases of evil and suffering. The painful death of one infant from a brain tumor creates as big a problem for theodiceans as does the death of 150,000 from earthquakes, tidal waves, or terrorism. That trio evokes the kind of explanations that reach prime time and page one. But, on varying scales of loss, they are the stuff of daily existence for hundreds of millions of people.

I will begin by rating theodicies from worst toward better—there are no bests. The worst, whether from Christian, Muslim, or Hindu sources, are those that are sure that God or the gods are punishing—yes, punishing— someone else. You probably heard the weirdest such explanation from an American who "knew" that God was killing those Asian tsunami victims because Americans practice abortion. Second worst are those that are sure God is punishing not "them" but "us." Muslims and Christians often favor this one, without explaining why some of us endure punitive suffering and not others.

More seriously, there are some genuine and intelligent struggles with the issue within the narrow confines open to Christian thinkers. We "Bible believers" are boxed in by scriptures such as Isaiah 45:7, tucked into a favored chapter: "I make weal and create woe, I the Lord do all these things" (or "I create disaster," as the New Jerusalem Bible renders the verse). Christians get around the "singled-out by God" explanation through Luke 13:4, Jesus's physics lesson: if a tower falls, and you, an innocent or a guilty person, happen to be standing under it, you get killed. So people who happened to be on shores where the wave happened to hit got killed.

With thanks to the major columnists, philosophers, and theologians for their nice tries, I come to my point: looking back over newspaper accounts from sundry locales, the best clips came from reported interactions between local pastors and their faithful. These were not the "Sunday-after-disaster" worshippers but regular strugglers and celebrators. The clerical or lay person in a sustained pastoral or chaplain-like role has been at the bedsides of innocents a thousand times, stood at the side of victims in divorce courts, grieving parents of the stillborn, citizens of communities swept away by flood or tornado, and have heard, every time, "Why?" Or—it's almost a cliché after September 11 and the recent tsunami—"Where was God in this?"

Whatever is uttered or gestured (embraces help!) by families, counselors, and pastors at such times are the relative positives shared in the face of absolute horrors—and they show that affirmation comes among those who have lived with occasions for offering theodicies and found some meaning.

18. The World House

MARCH 31, 2005
BY ROBERT M. FRANKLIN

As war rages in Iraq and as President Bush advocates a budget that many fear will further neglect the nation's poor, the writings and ministry of Martin Luther King Jr. are as relevant as ever. In particular, the urgent message of his largely ignored "final testament" merits revisiting. Indeed, I hope it will become the basis for careful study and discussion in the months to come, especially as many religious individuals and organizations continue thinking about how to respond to ongoing strife. King's testament is found in the closing chapter of his last book, *Where Do We Go from Here: Chaos or Community?*, published in 1967, the year before his assassination. It is titled "The World House."

King opens with the story of a deceased novelist whose papers include suggestions for future stories. One of the most prominently highlighted ideas is the following: "A widely separated family inherits a house in which they have to live together." King elaborates on this metaphor, suggesting that it communicates "the great new problem of humankind. We have inherited a large house, a great world house in which we have to live together—black and white, Easterner and Westerner, Gentile and Jew, Catholic and Protestant, Muslim and Hindu—a family unduly separated in ideas, culture and interest, who, because we can never again live apart, must learn somehow to live with each other in peace." In other words, "whatever affects one directly affects all indirectly."

King was at pains to communicate that humanity's interrelatedness is not simply a political and economic reality but represents a profoundly moral and theological imperative. And as such, people are obligated to exercise prudent stewardship over both the world's resources and our own status as responsible citizens and moral agents residing in what has become the world's only superpower. King's testament demands to be taken seriously by professors and students of religion, America's houses of worship, and the citizenry at large.

Let me mention three areas where, if we are to follow King's example and thought, we could flex greater moral muscle. First, King would urge us to practice our commitment to eradicating racism and its many subtle manifestations. Each of us should engage in a critical "diversity inventory" of the religious and secular organizations to which we belong and provide financial support. Are these organizations doing all they can to reverse the legacy of white-skin preference by including ethnic-racial minorities? If not, we should exercise our voices and votes.

Second, King pleads for the tolerance and understanding of others' religions. The xenophobia of the past is now a renewed danger. To the extent that we can, we should be resources for communities that need assistance in viewing other religious traditions as manifestations of a good and generous God who is capable of loving all of God's creatures, even when some of us falter in doing so.

Third, the relatively affluent folks among us should demonstrate courageous moral stewardship by identifying with our poor neighbors and doing all we can to advance policies and programs that accelerate their transition to self-sufficiency, while condemning politicians that reward the rich at the expense of the poorest.

One group of religious progressives is out to live up to these demands. The Clergy Leadership Network is jointly sponsoring a national witness against the war to be held at Riverside Church in New York City on April 4, 2005, the thirty-eighth anniversary of Dr. King's historic sermon against the Vietnam War ("Beyond Vietnam: A Time to Break Silence"). The list of fifty organizational sponsors includes the Tikkun Community, Protestants for the Common Good, the National Council of Churches, Drive Democracy, and the Sikh World Council–America Region. They will focus on alternatives to war and, in the spirit of King, expand the agenda to address poverty, racism, sexism, and other forms of social oppression. The group will also attempt to build a national movement for peace and justice inspired by King's concept of the "Beloved Community." The effort aims to gather one million signatures and launch a national bus tour on April 4. Following music from a youth choir, speakers on the evening roster will include many old and new activist voices, among them Riverside senior minister Dr. James Forbes, Rev. Jesse Jackson, Dr. Susannah Heschel, and Imam Feisal Rauf.

Their hope is that these efforts and others like them will echo and reinvigorate King's message of interrelatedness, finding receptive ears within the corridors of power in this nation and throughout the world house.

Resource

King, Martin Luther, Jr. *Where Do We Go from Here: Chaos or Community?* Boston: Beacon Press, 1967.

Robert M. Franklin (PhD, University of Chicago Divinity School) is professor of social ethics at Emory University.

45

19. Collisions and Doubts

MAY 16, 2005
BY MARTIN E. MARTY

Where to draw "the line of separation between the rights of religion and the Civil authority" (James Madison)? Or, less felicitously, where to maintain or breach the "wall of separation between church and state" (Thomas Jefferson)? When to make use of the line? Those questions are older than 1787, and today more than ever there are "collisions and doubts," as Madison called them. The line has always been messy, the wall has always had breaches, and this will always be so, as long as a dynamic republic shall last. Two newspapers on May 12 offered new examples of this fact.

In a *Chicago Tribune* op-ed, David McGrath, an expert on English literature and Native American affairs, complained about a 198-foot-tall crucifix towering at the junction of I-57 and I-70 ("The Art of Jamming Beliefs Down Our Throats"). It stands "as close to the highway" as the state will permit, its glistening surface serving to "shout and bully with its message of Christian morals." McGrath welcomes civil controversy but finds this uncivil. And a photo of the cross suggests that it may be just this; it is overbearing, triumphalist, and more. What would Jesus do? He'd probably call such use of his cross "tacky." But *where* it is, is perfectly legal. If it is even as close as one inch from the legal boundary, all we can do is put on our dark glasses, glower with McGrath, and take refuge in more chaste visions of the cross and expressions of piety. Why? Because the cross is on private land. On public land it would be claiming privilege for faith over non-faith, one faith over others. Where it is, "any number can play" on equal terms.

Most misplacements of the Ten Commandments and crosses occur on courthouse lawns or classroom walls. Are these about religion? Since religion can be expressed on most private lawns and on church, home, and store walls, aren't these courthouse and classroom placements saying something political and primeval? "We belong, and you don't! We set the terms and you are marginal, unpatriotic, or wrong!" Such forms of "shouting and bullying" may be detrimental to faith and civic life.

As for the "when": *The New York Times* and then the Associated Press (on May 14) ran stories about Air Force Academy personnel, programs, and privileges, as well as pressures against most religions that do not focus on the "born-again" experience and orthodoxy. Details remain controversial, but charges are that anti-Semitism and anti-other-religion mark some of the teaching on the premises of the Academy (the wrong "where") and during classroom and other teaching and publicizing time (the wrong "when"). Air Force Academy chaplain Melina Morton—who has to be trusted because she's a fellow Lutheran—says, "I realize this is the end of my Air Force career" because she protested and pointed to wrongs. In fairness, we have to hear more from Major General Charles Baldwin, Air Force chief of chaplains, who said the higher-ups merely sent Morton to Japan, far from Colorado Springs, and changed her duties, assigning her to serve there in her final chaplaincy days.

The Pentagon is looking into more than fifty recent complaints of religious intolerance at the Academy and is assessing a report by Yale Divinity School professor Kristen Leslie. Leslie quoted an Air Force chaplain during basic training who warned that "those [cadets] who are not born again will burn in the fires of hell." Off premises and off time he can say that. On premises? Wrong.

Resources

Goodstein, Laurie. "Air Force Chaplain Tells of Academy Proselytizing." *The New York Times*. May 12, 2005. http://www.nytimes.com/2005/05/12/education /air-force-chaplain-tells-of-academy-proselytizing.html.

McGrath, David. "The Art of Jamming Beliefs Down Our Throats." *Chicago Tribune*. May 12, 2005. http://articles.chicagotribune.com/2005-05-12/news /0505120038_1_crosses-pharmacists-beliefs.

20. Billy Graham's Final Crusade

July 7, 2005
By James L. Evans

Two weekends ago, Billy Graham preached what has been predicted to be his final American evangelistic campaign—perhaps his last campaign ever. If this proves to be true, his career will have concluded where it began, in New York. His first nationally recognized crusade was held at Madison Square Garden in 1957. In 2005, however, Madison Square Garden was far too small to accommodate crowds that approached ninety thousand on the evening of the event, which was held at Flushing Meadows–Corona Park, in Queens.

Billy Graham, now eighty-six, has served as America's unofficial preacher-at-large for over six decades. His life and ministry have tracked alongside some of our country's most dramatic moments. And in more than a few instances, Graham was a player in the drama.

He rose to national prominence during the height of the Cold War, preaching vigorously against the evils of "godless communism." In fact, it was his staunch anti-Communist message that brought him to the attention of newspaper publisher William Randolph Hearst. Impressed with Graham's message, Hearst ordered his editors to "puff Graham." That puff ignited the preacher's national identity.

Apart from communism, however, Graham was reluctant to speak directly to social issues. For instance, the 1957 crusade at Madison Square Garden took place the year after the Montgomery Bus Boycott. Dr. Martin Luther King Jr. had gained a national reputation for his leadership, and the civil rights movement was building momentum. Rather than address the issue of segregation directly, Graham invited Dr. King to lead in prayer during one of the services. Some Christian leaders criticized Graham for what they saw as his failure to use his own national reputation to help advance the cause of civil rights. But sympathetic historians argue that Graham's willingness to reach out to Dr. King sent a clear signal of support, and Graham was reported to have said that a Christian racist is an oxymoron.

During the Vietnam era, Graham did not speak out against the war. In fact, there is reason to believe he was in favor of the conflict. One reason for his support, at least initially, was related to his strong anti-Communist sentiments. Vietnam was sold as a war against Communism, and Graham considered Communism to be the antithesis of Christianity.

But critics also point out that during this time Graham gained unprecedented access to the Johnson, and later the Nixon, White House. These close connections may have affected Graham's willingness to criticize administration policies. The experience of Watergate, however, and the revelations of Nixon's corruption were sobering epiphanies for Graham. Indeed, during the early days of the rise of the Moral Majority—the early flagship venture of the Religious Right—Graham warned of the dangers of linking faith's reputation to political parties.

But politics has always had a way of finding Graham. During the first night of this most recent crusade, Graham was introduced by former president Bill Clinton. Senator Hillary Clinton was also present on the platform. After the introduction, Graham quipped that he always thought that Bill Clinton should have been an evangelist. After citing the many gifts that would allow Clinton to become a successful evangelist, Graham then said, "And Hillary could stay home and run the country."

Several conservative Christian leaders took serious offense at this remark, accusing Graham of endorsing Senator Clinton for a presidential run in 2008. That was not the only time Graham ran afoul of members from his conservative base. In an interview just prior to this most recent evangelistic campaign, Graham said he would not preach about any of the political issues important to evangelical conservatives, including abortion, homosexuality, and stem cell research. "I'm just going to preach the gospel and am not going to get off on these hot-button issues," Graham told *The New York Times*. "If I get on these other subjects, it divides the audience."

This desire for unity has been an important theme for Graham. Three years ago, taped conversations emerged with Graham and Nixon engaging in anti-Semitic banter in the White House. After the revelation, Graham quickly met with Jewish leaders and apologized to the Jewish community. In preparation for the present evangelistic campaign, Graham again met with Jewish leaders and pledged anew his opposition to all forms of prejudice.

For the most part, Graham has traveled a middle course between liberal and conservative evangelicals, with a focus on changing people by means of a unifying message rather than changing laws to reflect evangelical social concerns. Over the years, this middle course has brought criticism from all sides. But in a time of shrill and divisive religious rhetoric, Graham's simple message of faith rings with refreshing authenticity.

Resource

Goodstein, Laurie. "Spirit Willing, One More Trip Down Mountain for Graham."
The New York Times. June 12, 2005. http://www.nytimes.com/2005/06/12/us
/spirit-willing-one-more-trip-down-mountain-for-graham.html.

James L. Evans is pastor of Auburn First Baptist Church in Auburn, Alabama.

21. Black Theology and Womanist Theology in Conversation

OCTOBER 27, 2005
BY DWIGHT N. HOPKINS

Black theology originated when African American male pastors and ecclesial administrators began reflecting on the black church's role in providing religious understandings of the major developments in America during the 1960s and '70s. Womanist theology, created twenty years later out of black and feminist theologies, emerged with black Christian women embracing the positive relation between their faith and their creative, God-given female and African American identities.

Black and womanist theologies maintain their ties to the black church; they share similar theoretical methodologies, developing doctrines on the basis of the Christian experiences of people in churches. Each claims liberation and survival for marginalized communities as essential to ministry, the message of Jesus, and ecclesial mission. Each now proclaims inclusive gender leadership. And as religious movements, black and womanist disciplines have found voices within the academy.

Next week, black theology and womanist theology will be in conversation for the first time on a national platform, at the University of Chicago Divinity School and the Lutheran School of Theology in Chicago. The twenty-two speakers at "Black Theology and Womanist Theology in Dialogue: Which Way Forward for the Church and the Academy?" comprise an equal number of men and women. Half of the speakers are pastors and half are professors, with Protestants and Catholics lecturing along with African American gay and lesbian speakers.

An innovative format will foster in-depth debate: male speakers will reflect on subjects typically associated with womanists, while women will engage themes usually linked to black theology. Topics under discussion include liberation, survival and quality of life, patriarchy in the family, human sexuality, black males as an endangered species, Jesus the Man, Christ as a Woman, global missions, and the future of black theology–womanist theology dialogue in church and academy.

An important principle underlies this conference: all parties—black and womanist academics as well as female and male clergy—agree that the discipline of theology entails critical reflection on the message and witness of the church. Theology tests whether or not the church is faithful to what it has been called to believe, say, and do. And the church provides the religious community for whose benefit academics develop theology. Mutual account-ability thus obtains: theology serves the church, while the church opens itself for ongoing theological inspection.

Before now, a conference of this sort has been impossible, as African American women required the space and time to develop their own voices, apart from the dominating and agenda-setting tendencies of earlier male scholars. And previously there did not exist a sufficient number of black women professors to offset some of the earlier, often arrogant, positions of men. In the last ten years, however, womanist scholars and black male theologians, each in their separate gatherings, have spoken of the need for a venue for critical and collaborative dialogue.

Womanist theologians and ethicists have edited volumes calling for African American female thinkers to develop a methodology that starts with the religious beliefs and practices of women, while also embrac-ing the entire constituency of the church (i.e., men and boys as well). Varieties of womanists' syllabi in various academic institutions cite the same concern. Womanist methodology seeks to be inclusive of the entire community.

Similarly, while the first generation of black theologians wrote as if Af-rican American women were invisible in the church and academy or, worse, simply spoke for women, today's black (male) theologians express concern and a yearning for interaction with womanists. A growing cohort of second- and third-generation black male theologians is recognizing that partnerships with black female religious scholars and pastors are crucial for church vitality and empowering theological curricula. Black theologians realize that what it means to be a male theological scholar or church pastor hinges on perceiving one's own humanity as tied to the humanity of African American women thinkers and preachers.

In fact, black male scholars are reinterpreting the gospel message itself as focusing on the plight of, and prospects for, women. Next week's con-ference affirms a sacred vision that had formerly been rejected: the right of women to reflect critically on their own unique and independent relation to God.

Men's and women's beliefs and theological rationales continue to evolve. With increased openness and a growing desire to forge dialogue and collaboration, the time has come for a conference facilitating conversation between two vital and important movements in contemporary theology.

Dwight N. Hopkins is professor of theology at the University of Chicago Divinity School.

22. Multiple Choices from the Founders

OCTOBER 31, 2005
BY MARTIN E. MARTY

The "Founding Fathers," or "Founders," are getting worked over in public affairs, and especially in religious matters, more than ever before. With courts wrestling with issues of church and state, educators fighting over ways to treat faith and faiths in public institutions, and communities battling over the place of religious symbols on "everybody's spaces" like courthouse lawns and walls, we often find citations from figures like Washington, Jefferson, Adams, Madison, and so many others. These figures were writing in the context of their own times and are easily misrepresented out of that context, but we can still draw some signals from their works.

Fortunately, a new collection of snippets from their writings is available in *The Founders on Religion: A Book of Quotations*, edited by James H. Hutson. I first came across Hutson during the bicentennials of the Declaration and the Constitution, about which he had so many sane things to say. He is chief of the Manuscript Division at the Library of Congress, and a scholar friendly to religion—one who shows little bias in his writings and in this current work. Thus, since the Founders differed so much from each other, Hutson offers some conflicting and contradictory comments by these leaders.

I used his book while preparing a lecture on Founders' types. First, let it be noted that this whole cast of characters was concerned with "virtue" and "morality" in the young republic, and all were favorable to the influences of religion on these. The differences came in on the question of what public institutions should do to privilege and promote religion and its practice.

Type one was John Jay, author of Federalist Paper No. 2, who spoke of "the privilege and interest of our Christian nation." He thought citizens of such a nation should elect only Christian rulers and not vote for the infidels, the ungodly. He was nearly alone, and his view, popular as it is in some circles today, did not win out among constitutionalists in his day. He wanted uniformity in faith.

Type two was Thomas Jefferson, who thought that legal privileging and promotion was harmful to church and state. "Truth can stand by itself. Subject opinion to coercion: whom will you make your inquisitors? Fallible men.

. . . And why subject it to coercion? To produce uniformity. . . . Is uniformity attainable? Millions of innocent men, women, and children, since the introduction of Christianity, have been burnt, tortured, fined, imprisoned; yet we have not advanced one inch towards uniformity."

Type three found its voice in James Madison, who had the most influence on the Constitution. He famously wrote that "in matters of Religion, no man's [*sic*] right is abridged by the institution of Civil Society and that Religion is wholly exempt from its cognizance," while the Civil Magistrate was not a "competent Judge of Religious Truth" or a good user of it "as an engine of Civil policy." Christians ought to be most concerned, since the Christian religion was never to show "dependence on the powers of this world." Privilege Christianity, and you have "pride and indolence," ignorance, servility, superstition, bigotry, and persecution.

It's our choice which direction to go in, which type to favor.

Resource

Hutson, James H., ed. *The Founders on Religion: A Book of Quotations*. Princeton: Princeton University Press, 2005.

23. Buddhists on the Brain

NOVEMBER 3, 2005
BY DAN ARNOLD

To regular readers of mainstream newsweeklies like *Time* and *Newsweek*, stories on the latest interface between Buddhism and neuroscience are familiar; every few months there is at least a brief notice on, say, a study of MRI data from Tibetan Buddhist meditators or on the Dalai Lama's addressing cognitive scientists at MIT. These dispatches from the frontiers of science and "spirituality" are common enough that some readers might have been taken aback by the note of controversy sounded in a recent *New York Times* piece on the subject (Benedict Carey, "Scientists Bridle at Lecture Plan for Dalai Lama").

Not all members of the Society for Neuroscience, it seems, are enthusiastic about the Dalai Lama's scheduled address at next month's annual meeting; more than five hundred brain researchers have signed a petition calling for the talk's cancelation. To complicate matters, eyebrows have been raised by the fact that many of the signatories are Chinese (or of Chinese descent), possibly raising the sensitive political issue of China's occupation of Tibet. There is, however, no shortage of scientists willing to go on record as questioning the scientific merit of studies in this vein; one scientist, dismayed by creeping credulity, worried about this professional organization looking increasingly like the "Flat Earth Society."

The *Times*'s coverage of this flap chiefly concerned debates internal to the scientific community—debates, for example, about whether scientific objectivity is compromised by the fact that some scholars engaged in this research are themselves practitioners of Buddhist meditation and about what kind of phenomena are suitable for properly scientific study. One signatory to the petition (Dr. Zvani Rossetti of Italy's University of Cagliari) rightly noted that "neuroscience more than other disciplines is the science at the interface between modern philosophy and science"—whence he concluded that "no opportunity should be given to anybody to use neuroscience for supporting transcendent views of the world."

The latter remark is not only something of a non sequitur, but a little strange since chief among the philosophical questions at stake here is what kind of relation (if any) there is between studies of the *brain* and the phenomena of the *mind*—and such questions at least arguably involve recourse to something like "transcendent views of the world" (depending, of course, on what *that* means).

But the controversy in question should take into account some of the contestation internal to the Buddhist side of the story: there is a history behind the peculiarly high-profile relations that various Buddhist traditions have to science. This history dates at least to the late nineteenth century, when Sinhalese Buddhists in Sri Lanka—reacting against Christian missionaries, and encouraged by sympathetic Westerners from the Theosophical Society—developed what many modern scholars have come to call "Protestant Buddhism": Buddhist movements that sought (among other things) to detach the "pure" or "original" Buddhist doctrine from the forms of life and practice that an English-educated Buddhist of the late nineteenth century might find disadvantageous to have to defend before Christian missionaries.

Buddhists like Anagarika Dharmapala (an emissary to the 1893 World Parliament of Religions) in this way advanced the idea that it is Buddhism (and not Christianity) that is most compatible with the deliverances of science. I would urge that this idea—which reflects perhaps the chief apologetic strategy of "Protestant Buddhism"—lives on in a statement that you have all likely heard or even uttered: "Buddhism isn't a religion, it's a philosophy (or way of life, etc.)."

This commonplace statement advances the idea of the peculiarly rational and empiricist character of Buddhist thought (specifically as contra the unscientific "faith" that presumably defines "religion")—and hence the unique extent of Buddhism's supposed amenability to scientific explanation. The contemporary version of the same idea would have it that Buddhism isn't a religion, it is (to use the title of one recent book in this vein) "mind science."

While certain trajectories of Buddhist thought might indeed be suggestively comparable with the philosophical projects of cognitive science, it is important to ask what is at stake (and for whom) when it is urged that Buddhism is uniquely compatible (if not coextensive) with science. In particular, we should ask which tradition's *authority* is meant to be advanced by such claims—a question that becomes all the more complex when it is further asked why either of these traditions should be thought to benefit from the borrowed authority of the other.

Resource

Carey, Benedict. "Scientists Bridle at Lecture Plan for Dalai Lama." *The New York Times*. October 19, 2005. http://www.nytimes.com/2005/10/19/us/scientists -bridle-at-lecture-plan-for-dalai-lama.html.

Dan Arnold (PhD, University of Chicago Divinity School) is assistant professor of philosophy of religions at the University of Chicago Divinity School.

24. The Future of New Orleans

DECEMBER 22, 2005
BY JAMES B. BENNETT

Religious institutions will play an important role in New Orleans's move from recovery to rebuilding, as a recent *New York Times* article describing the re-opening of the St. Joan of Arc parish school reminds us. In the immediate aftermath of Hurricane Katrina, national and regional religious agencies provided crucial assistance to both evacuees and those stranded in the city (their success all the more noteworthy in light of the horrifying inadequacy of federal efforts). While these agencies will continue to provide significant resources, local churches will be an increasingly determinant factor in shaping New Orleans's recovery. That influence will extend to the crux of the social divisions that outsiders learned about when Katrina exposed them for the nation and the world to see.

Churches and schools, and the relationships between them, have long been part of the complex racial and residential patterns in New Orleans. When New Orleans briefly experimented with interracial public schools during Reconstruction, racially exclusive parochial schools were a common retreat for white parents trying to keep their children out of an integrated environment. Soon, the interracial public schools disbanded, and the city's black communities were left with few educational options for their children.

Thirty-five years later, the school featured in the *Times* article was opened. In a city where racially mixed parishes had been the norm for nearly two centuries, St. Joan of Arc (originally named St. Dominic's) would become the city's second parish created exclusively for black Catholics. In 1909, the then-integrated congregation had completed a magnificent new church at a nearby but more prominent location. On the Sunday before the move, however, the parish priest announced that only the white members would relocate; the black members would remain behind to form a new separate black parish in the old building.

As was typical, a school also opened. Church leaders hoped that black families who would otherwise reject segregated congregations might compromise to secure an education for their children. At St. Joan of Arc, the hand-me-down building was destroyed by a hurricane in 1916, while the new white church a few blocks away escaped unscathed.

Over the next few decades a pattern emerged, as numerous separate black Catholic churches and schools opened throughout the city, leading to a thoroughly segregated Christian population. (Most Protestants had separated decades earlier.) In some cases, the separate facilities opened in predominantly black neighborhoods; other times the reliance on buildings cast off by white congregations led to a black religious presence in mixed or even predominantly white neighborhoods—but not for long: residential patterns followed religious ones, creating increasingly homogeneous communities in a city long characterized by its racially mixed neighborhoods.

In this context, parish schools played an increasingly important role in expanding the limited educational options for black children, even though these classrooms could not overcome the pervasive segregation in religious and public institutions alike. At the same time, religiously affiliated colleges (the predecessors to the now heavily damaged Dillard and Xavier universities), offered the best opportunities for higher education, training nearly all of the region's black professionals, including teachers, doctors, lawyers, and pharmacists.

And now a new opportunity arises. The religious dynamics that once contributed to separation can help restore a devastated city. With the future of most of the city's public schools still unknown, religious institutions that a century earlier had reinforced divisions may now present a key reason for families to return and create a renewed sense of communality. The determination of parish schools like St. Joan of Arc will be an important element in the effort of Mayor Ray Nagin and his recently appointed commission to "bring back New Orleans."

The city's racial dynamics have changed considerably in the century since St. Joan of Arc opened. Hispanic and Vietnamese immigrants, among many others, have swelled church ranks alongside longstanding communities of African Americans and Creoles of color. As churches and the Archdiocese continue the cutbacks already under way, they face difficult decisions as to which churches and schools will remain, which will close, and which resources might be consolidated or relocated.

The lessons of the past are instructive; religious institutions will once again make choices that shape New Orleans for the century to come. May they choose wisely.

Resource

Levy, Clifford J. "In New Orleans, Doors Start to Open at Catholic Schools." *The New York Times*. November 6, 2005. http://www.nytimes.com/2005/11/06 /us/nationalspecial/in-new-orleans-doors-start-to-open-at-catholic-schools. html.

James B. Bennett is assistant professor of religious studies at Santa Clara University.

25. The Changing Faces of Islam

January 19, 2006
By Malika Zeghal

Since September 11, 2001, the issue of the connection between Islam and violence has been raised repeatedly. An adequate response lies not in positing some allegedly "violent" nature of Islam, nor is it even about Islam as such, but rather about how Muslim individuals interpret Islam and relate these interpretations to their political perspectives. These representations of Islam are diverse, and in constant evolution and interaction with other religious, cultural, and political influences.

While the traditional Orientalist paradigm, in convergence with the "clash of civilizations" thesis as well as some contemporary political Islamist doctrines, views Islam as a phenomenon with fixed features that produces a homogeneous, anti-democratic, and anti-pluralistic political culture, it is obvious that today, in the Muslim world and in the West, many public interpretations and manifestations of Islam contradict this notion. Islamist political parties in Algeria, Morocco, and Jordan have participated in relatively open electoral competitive processes that remain fragile but show these groups' abilities to coexist in peaceful political competition.

These instances are elements in a vast and diverse array of practices and interpretations of Islam that must be considered—along with the question of violence—to understand Islam today. Violence emerged in tight relation to Islam in the 1970s, giving rise to a pervasive dichotomy opposing "violent" to "nonviolent" Islam. This dichotomy is partly the result of a colonial enterprise in which those in power in Muslim nations and in the West have co-opted, disciplined, and praised the "good" Muslims and vilified the "bad" ones. But beyond politics, violence has also recently provoked important intellectual transformations.

In the very country where the September 11 disaster occurred, some Muslim intellectuals resist the categories of "good" and "bad" Muslims, while at the same time radically redefining, through their practices or their theologies, the meanings of Islam. A new generation of American Muslims, born and educated in the United States, is questioning Islamic apologetics and literalism in order to grant more complexity, context, and historicity to their religious experiences and theologies. They contest the "West vs. Islam" divide and thus the clash of civilizations thesis. They argue that violence used by Muslims is the result of mistaken interpretations of Islam. Muslims, they believe, must work from their own rich heritage to condemn and dissolve violence, while avoiding apologetics. They must also rewrite the gender logic, starting from the Qur'an: in their practices, women should be the equals of men, standing in the same room in prayer and even leading men in prayer.

Very different figures characterize this trend. Asma Gull Hasan—a pro-Bush, media-savvy graduate of New York University's law school, and "self-proclaimed Muslim feminist cowgirl"—writes, "I don't think the Qur'an and God are asking me to wear *hijab*. I could be wrong, but I believe modesty comes from the inside-out, not the outside-in."

Also in the US, Islamic studies scholar Omid Safi, political scientist Muqtedar Khan, poet Mohja Kahf, and novelist Asra Nomani are among a diverse, intellectual, and often caustic group of new voices that have reverberated on a global scale since September 11. Amina Wadud, a female African American Muslim professor of Islamic studies at Virginia Commonwealth University, publicly implemented her theological reform by leading, as an *imam*, a gender-mixed prayer in New York this past March.

Beyond North America, both self-proclaimed and institutionalized Muslim authorities have sought to discuss, accept, or confront these new practices, making new national and transnational spaces for debate on race, ethnicity, and gender. Religious freedom, doubt, transgression, and even sexual satire are some of the themes with which "progressive Muslims" deal, as one sees from the website Muslim Wakeup!, Islam is defined as an individually and freely (re)discovered "repertoire," where certainty and righteousness are often mocked. The Muslim repertoire is thus expanded along the lines and languages of Western liberalism, but not without internal and external conflicts and differences.

Progressive local and national US organizations have tentatively emerged, trying—with difficulty—to institutionalize these diverse trends into an organized movement. But the very nature of a trend that claims religious freedom, complexity, and diversity contradicts the possibility of a unified institutionalization, as made clear by the recent defections from the Progressive Muslim Union.

In some sense, such difficulties do not matter; what is new, unique, and consequential here is that these interpretations of Islam are publicly exposed and not defined from outside Islam but from within it. Before September 11, these voices remained implicit, silent, or isolated. They felt that conservative immigrant mosques and organizations were too hegemonic to let them offer their own definitions of Islam and mobilize a new audience. The violence of September 11 propelled these voices into the public arena. It remains to be seen if they can truly find their place in America and beyond.

Resource

Hasan, Asma Gull. *American Muslims: The New Generation.* New York: Continuum, 2002.

Malika Zeghal is associate professor of the anthropology and sociology of religion at the University of Chicago Divinity School.

26. Reflections on Chicago's *Cloud Gate*

April 20, 2006
By Jeremy Biles

April 22 will mark the twentieth anniversary of the death of Mircea Eliade, prodigious writer of novels, articles, journals, and numerous scholarly books in comparative religion. Eliade was also a "founding father" of the history of religions discipline at the University of Chicago Divinity School, where he taught from 1956 until his death in 1986. From his and his colleagues' vision emerged what came to be known as the "Chicago School" of the study of religion.

Eliade's work came under fire in the years leading up to his death, and it has been vigorously criticized in the decades since. He has been accused of being methodologically unsound and at times prone to conceptual inconsistency. Moreover, his endorsement, while still a young man in his native Romania, of the Iron Guard (a far-right, fascistic political group) has given rise to serious concerns regarding his early political sensibilities and their possible reverberations in his scholarship.

Notwithstanding these very real challenges—and I have no interest in apologetics here—Eliade remains, as Jonathan Z. Smith has suggested, the giant upon whose shoulders subsequent students of comparative religion stand.

Eliade is perhaps best known for his obsessively revisited insights into the relations between "the sacred and the profane." In his book of that title, Eliade builds on Rudolf Otto's famous formulation of the "holy," asserting that humans become "aware of the sacred because it manifests itself, shows itself, as something wholly different from the profane." He terms this irruption of the sacred into the profane a "hierophany"—a manifestation saturated with numinous power.

While Eliade believed that "archaic" peoples were and are particularly attuned to hierophanies, he also insisted that religious myths and symbols, though often obscured or distorted, remain alive in the contemporary world; he repeatedly drew attention to the presence of religion in popular culture, claiming that the sacred "haunts our novels as well as our films."

Indeed, the sacred haunts much art, even contemporary art apparently devoid of religious images and forces. Among the vast array of hierophanies

Eliade treated in his scholarly works, the "omphalos" ("navel") and related images and objects—sacred stones and such—enjoy a position of privilege. The omphalos constitutes a center, or "axis mundi," around which a community can be built; it manifests a kind of sacred centripetal force, bringing order to chaos and ensuring felicitous intercourse between the heavens and the earth. Jacob's ladder, the Kaaba of Mecca, a cosmic tree, the omphalos at Delphi, the altar of a Christian church, or a Hindu temple: each of these indicates a site where, Eliade claims, divine power can "come to earth, the point at which the transcendent might enter the immanent."

A spectacular contemporary example of an omphalos can be found in the heart of Chicago. Within the surreal expanse of Millennium Park— with its metallic serpentine bridge, the extraterrestrial architecture of the Frank Gehry-designed pavilion, the gigantic and ever-changing LED faces of *Crown Fountain*, and the mysterious, almost labyrinthine garden—is an eye-catching and crowd-pleasing sculpture called *Cloud Gate*. This massive, elliptical structure, designed by British artist Anish Kapoor, is made of highly polished stainless steel that reflects the city surrounding it.

Kapoor's ingenious use of reflection may usefully be submitted to an Eliadean interpretation. Not only is Chicago literally gathered, or centered, in the surface of this centric sculpture; the mirrors of this artifact, as its title suggests, also bring the sky down to earth—a fine symbol of connection between the transcendent and the immanent.

The religious resonances do not end there. Kapoor, whose works frequently allude to mythic imagery, has designated the concave underbelly of his sculpture an omphalos. Why this peculiar reference? When passing beneath the gate, visitors can look up into the reflective vault of the chamber, and there gaze upon their own images. Seeing themselves in the curving space of this omphalos, they are part of a celestial constellation— transformed, transcendent, often in giddy communion. This piece of contemporary art gathers the city, centering visitors around it, with a magnetism that verges on divine.

"Cloud Gate" thus attests to Eliade's continuing applicability, while demonstrating his claim that humans thirst for holiness, for experiences that lie beyond the everyday, for the irruption of the sacred into profane life. And this desire for the extraordinary finds its counterpart in modern life, which still swarms with "half-forgotten myths," elusive symbols, and disguised hierophanies—evidence of what Eliade called "the persistence of the sacred."

I suspect that Eliade would have delighted in the mythic resonances of *Cloud Gate*, here in this city where he did so much of his significant work—

for both the scholar and the sculpture put humans in touch with the sacred, drawing down the heavens to touch the earth.

Resource

Eliade, Mircea. *The Sacred and the Profane: The Nature of Religion*. Translated by Willard R. Trask. New York: Harcourt, 1959.

Jeremy Biles holds a PhD from the University of Chicago Divinity School and is the managing editor of Sightings.

27. Intelligent Watches

JUNE 1, 2006
BY RICHARD A. ROSENGARTEN

While Cardinal Schönborn and the Roman Catholic Church's astronomer have officially indicated that it is possible to accept the science of evolution while remaining in good standing with the church, the idea of intelligent design persists in at least this nation's conversation, as a challenge to that claim. And there is less clarity in those discussions than in official pronouncements from a cardinal and his church.

In Kansas City, Missouri, earlier this year, a talk about intelligent design drew, among others, an attentive cohort of backbench listeners who serve as teaching assistants in introductory biology courses at the University of Kansas in Lawrence. They had driven approximately one hundred miles to hear how a theologian would talk about evolution and intelligent design. During the ensuing discussion they explained that "we get asked about this all the time in class, and we don't really know what to say." Their undergraduate charges want to know why the class does not include discussion of intelligent design as an alternative theory of the origins of life. The teaching assistants—PhD students in biology—report that citing the series of decisive court decisions to the contrary is insufficient to the challenge.

In part, this is simply a tribute to the cleverness of the Discovery Institute, the prominent think tank largely responsible for shifting the terminology around this ongoing discussion from "creationism" to "intelligent design." In doing so, the institute implies that its position is identical with one of the oldest and most popular arguments in the Christian tradition for the existence of God. And while creationism was decisively discredited by the courts in the 1980s, intelligent design retains a tenacious hold on the discourse, despite Judge John Jones's opinion in the 2005 *Dover* case.

Intelligent design will maintain this hold until more theologians become involved in the discussion. Exemplary precedent in this regard can be found in Langdon Gilkey's testimony in the 1981 creationism trial *McLean et al. v. Arkansas Board of Education*, the case that reviewed Act 590 of the Arkansas State Legislature, which mandated the co-teaching of "creation science" and "evolution science" in the public schools. Judge William Overton's decision in *McLean* to invalidate Act 590 on grounds quite similar to those of Judge Jones—the Act constituted an establishment of religion and thus violated the separation of church and state—drew centrally from Gilkey's distinction during the trial between questions of our ultimate origins, which are theological, and questions of our proximate origins, which are scientific.

Gilkey's testimony addressed the creationist position, but his distinction can usefully be extended to the debates about intelligent design, as follows: scientists can opine about religion, and religious believers can opine about science—but each needs to recognize that in doing so, the grounds of the discussion shift. So when the eminent biologist Richard Dawkins argues, on the grounds of his exemplary science, that no thinking person can reasonably maintain that God exists, he is confusing scientific demonstration for theological claim. Similarly, when creationists argue that Genesis 1 and 2 should be included in the biology curriculum of public schools as an alternative scientific theory of origins, they are confusing theological claim with scientific theory.

Behind this distinction is a fact inconvenient to the proponents of intelligent design: their term takes its basis from what is the most popularly recognized but philosophically dubious formulation of the teleological argument for the existence of God. This is the presentation of William Paley, who argued in his *Natural Theology* (1802) that a hiker who came upon a watch on the ground and opened it would discover its intricate mechanism and conclude that the watch's design reflected a designer. By analogy, Paley argued, we can look at the world and see evidence of a Designer who is God. The difficulty here, perhaps most trenchantly formulated by David Hume, is that an argument from experience cannot explain something—in this case, God—which is beyond experience and thus beyond causation.

The elegance of Gilkey's distinction is that it inserts an intellectual traffic cop at the hectic public intersection where science and religion meet. This intersection has the potential to be an interesting, busy, and important place, and it is regrettable that first "creationism" and now "intelligent design" have caused such traffic jams there.

Richard A. Rosengarten (PhD, University of Chicago Divinity School) is dean and associate professor of religion and literature at the University of Chicago Divinity School.

28. Sanctuary or Spectacle?

August 31, 2006
By Cynthia Gano Lindner

Two weeks ago, Elvira Arellano and her seven-year-old son sought sanctuary in the Adalberto United Methodist Church of Humboldt Park, Chicago, instead of reporting to the Department of Homeland Security for deportation. Arellano, a thirty-one-year-old Mexican woman, was working as a cleaning woman at O'Hare airport in 2002 when she was arrested during the immigration sweep that followed the September 11 attacks; it was discovered then that she had been deported previously and had re-entered the country illegally. Fighting to stay in the US with her son—himself a US citizen—who was receiving medical treatment, Arellano was granted three stays of deportation beginning in 2003.

Though initially sympathetic to the mother's concern for her child, some supporters find Arellano's continued claims against deportation harder to justify. "It is an unfortunate truth that scores of people are in the same situation as Elvira and her family," Illinois senator Dick Durbin said in a statement recently. "We cannot fix the injustices of this system with private bills. Only comprehensive immigration reform can permanently remedy this situation." Though the debate around immigration has become increasingly polarized of late, there is widespread agreement with the sense of Sen. Durbin's statement: US immigration policies and procedures have failed US citizens and immigrants, legal and illegal alike; reform is necessary. But such reform will not come easily or quickly—and so what of the current reality of the countless parents and children who find themselves caught in the punishing gears of immigration's badly broken machinery?

Taking up residence in the church was her last resort, Arellano asserts, since she does not intend to return to Mexico. She and her supporters invoke a tradition attributed to the early Greeks which allowed a fugitive to seek sanctuary from prosecution by installing himself in a temple or designated sacred space, affording the lawbreaker a limited reprieve from the punishment meted out by an often imperfect justice system and time to consider his next move. Historically, while a fugitive resided in sanctuary, the community was responsible for his or her nourishment and safety; otherwise, the individual was not to be hindered or harassed.

This practice received elaborate codification in medieval England. In more recent times, it has been employed as a strategy of direct peaceful action—most notably during the 1980s, when dozens of US congregations sheltered Central Americans fleeing war in their homelands. There is no legal protection for the practice of sanctuary in American law; several ministers were convicted for their participation in the Central American sanctuary movement, though their actions did secure new lives for hundreds of refugees and ultimately led to revised US policies concerning Central American immigration.

From its ancient beginnings, the appeal of a "time out" for lawbreakers has consistently relied on a twofold sensibility which exceeds any single religious tradition, but which resonates with much classical religious anthropology. The practice of sanctuary embodies compassion for the human condition, which transcends citizenship or legal status, while maintaining skepticism about the adequacy of human applications of justice. This dual perspective is surprisingly relevant to our culture's current situation, suggesting that while we, as human beings, must rely on the human community to ensure even our most basic needs, one of those needs may well be for protection against the community's own life and institutions, which, unrestrained, can threaten our humanity.

In the relentless local media coverage of the Arellano case these past two weeks, there has been very little talk about the meaning or utility of sanctuary as either a religious or a deeply human practice. The storefront church has become a stage for political rhetoric and spectacle, including candlelight vigils by the family's supporters and staged television sound bites by activists who oppose broader immigration laws. These appeals are most often made on behalf of the "rights" of the speaker's own constituencies; religious language is invoked to enlist God's imprimatur for "our side." Rather than observing sanctuary's mandates of space and time for human healing and human decision-making to occur, partisan interests and institutions have continued their machinations.

Occasionally, though, the relentless media eye is startled by a glimpse of the human at the heart of this issue—the sadly serious face of the bewildered child, an early report that Arellano had been suffering from the flu, a more recent one revealing that she has moved upstairs to get a bit more distance from the din of the demonstrations on the street. As a human being caught between the rock of broken immigration law and the hard place of making a sustainable life for herself and her son, Arellano is entitled to sanctuary—compassion, respect, and noninterference—as she chooses her next course of action. Instead, her bid for safety threatens to become yet another spectacle in the noisy public theater that has replaced serious dialogue about renewing social policy for a plural America.

We would do well as a community and a culture to insist on that respectful space not only for Arellano but for all of us. Perhaps it is time to visit the practice of sanctuary again, at least in our imaginations—to revive our richer theological and humanist sensibilities about the complexity of human existence, the fragility of human life, and the provisional nature of human decision-making, and to extend to one another the possibility of time and space—free of noise, threat, or manipulation—in which to choose to do the right thing.

Cynthia Gano Lindner (DMin, University of Chicago Divinity School) is director of ministry studies and clinical faculty for preaching and pastoral care at the University of Chicago Divinity School, and associate staff at the Center for Religion and Psychotherapy in Chicago.

29. Allah's Trailblazer

SEPTEMBER 21, 2006
BY R. JONATHAN MOORE

Minnesota's fifth congressional district is about to make some history.

This past week, Keith Ellison defeated three challengers to receive the Democrat-Farmer-Labor Party's nomination for the US House of Representatives. Given the district's Democratic leanings, Ellison is virtually assured a spot in the 110th Congress.

Ellison will become the first African American to represent Minnesota in Washington. That might be enough history for one district, which includes Minneapolis and some suburbs, and is around 70 percent white. But in Ellison, Fifth District voters will also be sending to Congress the nation's very first Muslim representative.

During the primary campaign, the forty-three-year-old Ellison, a college convert to Islam, had to respond to charges of associating with Nation of Islam leader Louis Farrakhan. While in law school, writing as "Keith Hakim," Ellison contributed school newspaper columns defending Farrakhan against charges of anti-Semitism and criticizing affirmative action as a "sneaky" substitute for reparations. And in the mid-1990s, Ellison helped organize Minnesota's delegation to Farrakhan's Million Man March.

However, Ellison has denied ever belonging to the Nation of Islam, and he has directly renounced anti-Semitism in public and in letters to Jewish community organizations. Though some Jewish leaders remain unconvinced, a Minneapolis Jewish newspaper endorsed him in the primary, and several high-profile Jewish Democrats have supported him publicly and financially.

So far, for most Democrats, what matters has not been Ellison's religion but his political similarity to former senator Paul Wellstone (who died in 2002). Ellison has marked himself as a passionate progressive by calling for the withdrawal of troops from Iraq, for strong support of labor, and for universal health care. The charismatic candidate even adopted Wellstone's familiar green for his campaign posters.

In winning the backing of longtime Wellstone advocates Sam and Sylvia Kaplan, the particularities of his faith mattered less than the commonality of their politics. "What came through to us," said Sylvia, "was he believes in social justice and the common good, which is a Jewish tradition."

At a recent campaign stop, Ellison again addressed the religion issue. "I'm a Muslim. I'm proud to be a Muslim," he said. "But I'm not running as a Muslim candidate." Although he has not hesitated to greet the burgeoning Somali population in Minnesota with a heartfelt "Salaam Alaikum," he would rather talk about Iraq and health care than about religion.

Not surprisingly, Ellison's opponents don't plan to forgive his partial flirtation with black separatism. Republican Alan Fine has signaled that he'll be painting his competitor with a broad brush in coming weeks. "The voters of the Fifth District have a clear choice," he said recently. They can vote Republican, or "they can choose to elect an extremist candidate who has associated himself with the likes of Louis Farrakhan, Khalid Abdul Muhammed [who once called Jews "the bloodsuckers of the black nation"], Kwame Ture [Black Panther leader Stokely Carmichael], Sharif Willis [former Vice Lords gang leader] and others."

The chairman of the state Republican Party, Ron Carey, has made a similar argument: "By supporting Louis Farrakhan . . . Ellison has become a national embarrassment for his radical views." And when terrorist leader Abu Musab al-Zarqawi was killed in Iraq, one blogger recommended that "condolences should be sent to Ellison HQ."

In spite of—or perhaps because of—his opponents' guilt-by-association strategy, Ellison will soon belong to the congressional class of 2006. So it's worth asking, What difference might a Muslim representative make?

Ellison may serve as much more than a role model for American Muslims. A spokesman for the Council on American-Islamic Relations has said that Ellison's election would "be a tremendous assertion of the fact that we're Americans and we're just as interested in public service as anyone else, and here's the proof—we have somebody in Congress." In other words, Ellison may not only show American Muslims who they can become; he might also show suspicious fellow citizens who their Muslim neighbors already are.

Ellison has tried to downplay the political significance of his faith. "The focus on my religion doesn't bother me, but I feel that it's a distraction from what we need to be talking about," he says. "My faith informs me. My faith helps me to remember to be gentle, kind, considerate, fair, respectful. But I don't make my faith something that other people have to deal with."

Other people, however, have made and will continue to make his faith something that he must deal with. News of Ellison's primary victory was picked up by media outlets from as far away as Somalia and Qatar, and his

American profile will only grow as November nears. E pluribus unum? Another test awaits.

R. Jonathan Moore (PhD, University of Chicago Divinity School), a long-ago Sightings *editor, is visiting scholar in the Department of Religious Studies at Grinnell College.*

30. Watch Your Language

NOVEMBER 13, 2006
BY MARTIN E. MARTY

With regard to the recent election—was it a seismic or glacial change?—I want to make one observation or suggestion. It's in the "watch your language" category. Ever since my article "The New Christian Right" appeared in the 1981 *Encyclopedia Britannica* yearbook, I've quietly argued that in political contexts the term "the New Christian Right" should be used in place of "evangelicals," which is what the public media have chosen to use—and which they regularly misuse. The "Christian Right," then as now, I wrote, spoke only for "a minority of evangelical, fundamentalist, and Pentecostal Protestantism" and included some "Roman Catholics, who shared some of the New Christian Right's viewpoint," especially against abortion. That "minority," of course, has since grown.

If these together do not make up all of "evangelicalism," many evangelicals also are not fully at home on the political right. That was clear back when many took up the "it's the economy, stupid" theme in the Clinton years. Columnist Andrew Greeley and Michael Hout, in their important little book *The Truth about Conservative Christians*, provide ample sociological data to show that class, region, party, and self-interest also go into the mix of "evangelical" voting patterns, and only a minority of evangelicals are hard right. Reviewing the 2004 elections, they wrote that religion remained the story "because it suits both the interests that want to further the influence of their brand of religion . . . and those who want to raise money to stop them." Each spooks out the other, most media, as well as many of us in the public.

The 2006 election was a partial de-spooker. Many in the Christian Right showed their frustration before, during, and after the election, feeling that their candidates and party did not deliver. On Greeley lines, we can read more declarations of independence from the Christian Right by many evangelicals, especially as they now put energies into other issues that they find religiously important (e.g., the environment, immigration policies, et cetera). In 2004, had a couple tens of thousands of Ohioans voted differently, commentators would likely have said that the Christian Right had met its limits and would fade. Instead, reporters had only asked voters in exit polls whether they had voted their values. Many said "Yes." But who wouldn't, and who didn't, vote their values? That question was a blunt instrument. Now we shall look to John Green, Greeley and Hout, and Chris Smith, among others, to sharpen the tools of measurement and focus our lenses.

My take: The Christian Right took shape in the 1980s with the motives of the "politics of resentment," its members having long felt, and been, disdained. In the years of the Reagan charm, they found it easy to gain power, so they moved to the "politics of will-to-power," still voicing resentment. Many sounded as if they should and maybe could "win it all" and "run the show."

They have now begun to learn what mainline Protestants and mainline evangelicals, Catholics, Jews, and humanists know: no one is simply going to "run the show" in the American pluralist mix, as we watch shifting powers face off against other shifting powers, which is what happened again last Tuesday.

Resources

Greeley, Andrew. "Iraq Disaster Finally Caught Up with Bush." *Chicago Sun-Times*. November 10, 2006.

Greeley, Andrew, and Michael Hout. *The Truth about Conservative Christians: What They Think and What They Believe*. Chicago: The University of Chicago Press, 2006.

Marty, Martin E. "The New Christian Right." *1981 Britannica Book of the Year*. Chicago: Encyclopedia Britannica, 1981.

31. On the Migration of Religious Ideas

FEBRUARY 8, 2007
BY W. CLARK GILPIN

The current issue of *The New York Review of Books* (February 15, 2007) contains a probing article by the noted author and columnist on international relations, William Pfaff. Entitled "Manifest Destiny: A New Direction for America," Pfaff's essay excoriates the Bush administration for pursuing its international economic and political goals "by means of internationally illegal, unilateralist, and preemptive attacks on other countries, accompanied by arbitrary imprisonments and the practice of torture, and by making the claim that the United States possesses an exceptional status among nations that confers upon it special international responsibilities, and exceptional privileges in meeting those responsibilities." Increasingly, the American public is joining the international community in criticizing the catastrophic folly of President Bush's violent efforts to impose his vision of democratic virtue. "A claim to preeminent political virtue is a claim to power," Pfaff rightly observes, "a demand that other countries yield to what Washington asserts as universal interests."

For *Sightings*, however, with its mandate to identify and assess the role of religion in public affairs, another aspect of Pfaff's essay holds particular interest. How is it, Pfaff wants to know, that President Bush's political, journalistic, and foreign policy critics find themselves "hostage to past support of his policy and to their failure to question the political and ideological assumptions upon which it was built?" The ideological assumptions, Pfaff recognizes, have deep roots in an American religious history that has generated a national myth of exceptional mission and destiny. Pfaff locates the origins of this national myth in the religious beliefs of the New England Puritans and synoptically observes its later appearances in nineteenth-century ideas of manifest destiny, Woodrow Wilson's idealism regarding the League of Nations, and the Cold War rationale for American international involvement, "interpreted in quasi-theological terms by John Foster Dulles."

The myth-building energies of religious ideas are a perennial source of hope in a world all too frequently cruel and difficult. Simultaneously, these energies combine with the human will to power to generate many of these very cruelties and difficulties. Theologians through the centuries have therefore constrained and counterbalanced visions of future possibility with more austere spiritual norms. Among the New England Puritans, for instance, the first governor of Massachusetts Bay, John Winthrop, did not simply announce that the colony would be "as a city upon a hill" but immediately followed with the warning that the people's failure to observe their covenant with God would invite the wider world to "speak evil of the ways of God, and all professors for God's sake." Embarking on their mission, these Puritans insisted that humility was the "fundamental grace" and the gateway to all the virtues, and they agreed completely with the great Puritan poet John Milton that the primordial sin was pride.

The "failure to question the political and ideological assumptions" of the Bush administration, therefore, lies not only with Congress, the media, and the foreign policy community. In addition, the public responsibility of the theologian entails appraisal of the role of religious ideas in the formation of ideological assumptions. When religious vision migrates from its theological context, amidst the constraining and countervailing spiritual norms of responsible humility and wariness of pride as the deepest fault, its hope-engendering powers become perilous indeed.

Resource

Pfaff, William. "Manifest Destiny: A New Direction for America." *The New York Review of Books*. February 15, 2007. http://www.nybooks.com/articles/19879.

W. Clark Gilpin (PhD, University of Chicago Divinity School) is Margaret E. Burton Professor of the History of Christianity and Theology at the University of Chicago Divinity School.

32. Religion and Redemption in *Black Snake Moan*

MARCH 29, 2007
BY KRISTEN TOBEY

While many reviews describe Craig Brewer's *Black Snake Moan* as a movie about religion, the immediate impression one gets from the trailers and posters is more accurate: the film is primarily about a barely clad woman named Rae (Christina Ricci) chained to a radiator. Some have argued that the religious elements serve only to disguise the film's pornographic nature, but there are deeper implications for the relationship between sex and religion, not only as plot elements but also as tools of filmmaking.

We in the audience know we're supposed to feel bad about watching a portrayal of utterly degraded femininity, but we feel better because the film deals with religion—which presumably will lead to redemption, as the character of Lazarus (Samuel L. Jackson) sets out to "cure" Rae's nymphomania with a Bible in hand. At the same time, we know we're supposed to feel just as bad about being titillated by portrayals of crazed religiosity, because being titillated by someone else's religion (fire-and-brimstone preachers are among those to whom this film is decidedly not marketed) implies objectification, much as pornography does.

We're not supposed to gawk at religion, or at a naked woman beaten and in chains. But Brewer gives us license to gawk at them in tandem by making us think that we're gawking at the other one, each in turn. And in the battle for thematic supremacy, we end up taking neither wild sexuality nor wild religiosity seriously. The film sets itself up to present sex and religion as pervasive and powerful forces, responsible for who people are and who they become—but ultimately *Black Snake Moan* deals with an ambiguous, tenuous kind of redemption that has little to do with either.

The movie's religious aspects initially seem intended to appeal on the same prurient level as its sexual content. This is nothing new; a recent spate of religious films have portrayed religion provocatively. However, the early hints of crazed religiosity don't bear on the plot. More significantly, they don't bear out atmospherically. Religion starts out intense and threatening, with Lazarus hissing to his estranged wife, "You best pray, girl." Her response, "Don't you lay a curse on me," suggests a deep and dark power to religion.

But from there the religion portrayed is humdrum. Perhaps the director felt he had to live up to his tagline, "Everything is hotter down south": sexuality is more desperate, the music is more trance-inducing, and the religion is more dodgy. But after a few scenes, Brewer presents religion as the stuff of everyday life—not unimportant but tame, a social institution that compels one to ask after churchgoers who are missing from the pew on Sunday. And this might make for a disappointingly boring film, if not for the woman chained to the radiator—which would be appalling, if not for the soothing religion in the background.

In the one overtly theological scene, a local reverend instructs Rae in a kinder, gentler version of Christianity, more quiet and prayerful than the fire-and-brimstone variety with which she has been raised. But in the film, redemption comes not from prayer but from action: for Lazarus, in making blues music, a form of spiritual fulfillment; for Rae, in putting on a dress and making scrambled eggs, marks of her integration into conventionally moral domestic life.

The "message" preached by the film, then, is platitudinous: pull yourself together, live your life, bond with someone. It would be rather dismal to identify this as particularly "religious." Indeed, this mild portrayal of redemption mirrors a conspicuously tepid portrayal of religion.

While audiences know how to be outraged or annoyed at some depictions, or even suggestions, of religion in film—consider reactions to *The Passion of the Christ*, *The DaVinci Code*, or *The Lion, the Witch and the Wardrobe*—in *Black Snake Moan* religion is, despite early suggestions to the contrary, neither particularly scandalous nor potent. In a film that is ultimately about redemption, religion neither brings about that redemption nor stands in its way.

But when the picture of redemption is such a tentative one, the disconnect between redemption and religion, though it counters the film's set-up, may actually be comforting—for Brewer's unwillingness to show the viewer the potential power of religion is also an unwillingness to show its potential ineffectuality. And while this may be less titillating, it is also rather less depressing.

Resource

Scott, A. O. "Chained to the Radiator? It's for Her Own Good." *The New York Times*. March 2, 2007. http://movies2.nytimes.com/2007/03/02/movies/02blac .html.

Kristen Tobey is a PhD student in anthropology and sociology of religion at the University of Chicago Divinity School.

33. Mother Teresa's Agony

SEPTEMBER 24, 2007
BY MARTIN E. MARTY

Once when Mormon origins were being radically questioned by a man who turned out to be a forger, I asked Jan Shipps, foremost Gentile scholar of Latter-day Saints, what if the publicized fake documents turned out to be authentic? Wouldn't such shaking of the foundations bring down the whole edifice? No, she reminded me: the faithful have ways, indefinite and maybe infinite, of responding with new explanations. Without cynicism, Shipps noted that religions do not get killed by surprises that would seem to necessitate revision.

I thought of Shipps's dictum this month when a beautifully sad or sadly beautiful book by the late Mother Teresa, *Come Be My Light*, saw the light of day and met the glare of publicity. Aha! was the instant and general response of well-selling a-theists: this shows that a character on the way to sainthood was inauthentic, and her failure to experience God "proves" God's non-existence.

Not to worry, was the main literate Catholics' response. Catholic apologists and experts on mysticism addressed Teresa's agony over her non-experience of God and her disappointment in the Jesus in whom she believed but whom she did not experience. They scrambled to show how her story would more likely lead people to the search for faith than it would disappoint them and drive them away. But if Mother Teresa had trouble feeling the presence of God, wrote critics, the old hypocrite should not have hung in there as a model, a self-sacrificing but not always easy to applaud rigorist. We were told that she would be a challenge to every right-thinking and right-experiencing Catholic.

Wrong. Her published diary is likely to sell as well as those attacking her. From what I have read, it is a cry of the heart to a heaven evidently empty and silent to her: "Lord, my God, who am I that You should forsake me?" In response, historically informed commentators reached back to the Psalms or medieval precedent for analogies. Those familiar with mysticism were ready with "Is this the first time you've heard of this?" or "Let's make this a teaching opportunity." Eileen Markey in September 14's *National Catholic*

Reporter laid it out well, as did colleagues in most weekly Catholic and many Protestant papers. Most asked what any of this had to do with the existence of God.

Then followed, in most accounts, learned revisitations of believers who had doubts or were victims of what medievalists called *accidie* or, deeper than that, "The Dark Night of the Soul." While few who value the experience of God's presence would envy Mother Teresa, most expressed sympathy for a now-deceased figure who always offered compassion but did not always receive it. The Jan Shipps dictum did not even have to be put to work. Catholics and other Christians did not need to reinvent the faith—austere, threatening experiences like Teresa's are as old as faith itself. It was asked: if there are bright sides to this darkness or palpitations to replace the numbnesses of spirit, so that the darkness can be, conditionally, a boon, why don't believers put more energy into preparing their fellow devotionalists, showing that such silence may be in store for them, and then telling them not to fear?

Resources

Markey, Eileen. "Mother Teresa's Silence." *National Catholic Reporter*. September 14, 2007.

Mother Teresa. *Come Be My Light: The Private Writings of the "Saint of Calcutta."* Edited by Brian Kolodiejchuk. New York: Doubleday, 2007.

34. *The Economist* on Religion

NOVEMBER 12, 2007
BY MARTIN E. MARTY

The Economist, our favorite weekly (still-)news magazine, published a keeper on November 3 in the form of a sixteen-page "special report on religion and public life." As many of you know, our Center's early "public religion" efforts presumed that we would have to squint when searching for tiny, fine-print media references to religion. This week again, however, we are nearly blinded by the coverage. The editors drew on substantial figures, from old-pro sociologist Peter Berger, who provided the liveliest lines, to younger-pro Philip Jenkins, currently the most notable interpreter of what global Christianity means for the US.

A key Berger line: "We made a category mistake. We thought that the relationship was between modernisation and secularisation. In fact it was between modernisation and pluralism." Because pluralism implies "choice," it becomes a major theme. The editors and the people they quote depict religious offerings almost on the model of a cafeteria line. It's a buyer's market, and both growth and vitality patterns pretty much follow the lines of those who package the most attractive offerings. Scriptures of the faiths discuss such approaches as threatening to spiritual integrity, but those who resist tend to be left behind.

A reader seeking balance might fault *The Economist* for featuring "religious wars" on the cover, when it set out to cover "religion." Inevitable distortion results when the accent is on "wars of religion," "religious politics at its worst," how "the world's most religious country is still battling with its demons," et cetera. One does not learn from topics like these why so many people remain religiously involved in a time when religious forces are so lethal. There's not much here on the spiritual side of raising children or on what faith means when one is in doubt, on a deathbed, or seeking comfort. But, admit it: the religions that come out of hiding and present themselves in the public fray are often violent and unfair.

One can note that most coverage of religion occurs when "in God's name" people take advantage of religion for malign purposes. The editors here are engrossed in surveying the awesome varieties of religion that are in

84

the public eye, and they do some justice to them. Unsurprisingly, given the UK base of their magazine, the editors spend time on Europe and offer "a heretical thought" about it—namely that there is a potential for recovery on a continent with largely empty churches.

An alert from the editors: "If you gather together a group of self-professed foreign-policy experts—whether they be neoconservatives, real-politickers or urbane European diplomats—you can count on a sneer if you mention 'inter-faith dialogue.' At best, they say, it is liberal waffle; at worst it is naive appeasement. But who is being naive?" And then *The Economist* comes out swinging against the sneerers, pointing to the fruits of tough inter-faith interactions around the world. The sneers will continue, and so will mis-portrayals of the enemy.

What this weekly magazine does is go against the grain of sophisticated opinion, as it discerns how much anti-waffle strength characterizes those who take the risk of not contributing to the climate in which religious groups have to be absolutist, sure of themselves, ready to shoot—and shooting.

Resource

"In God's Name: A Special Report on Religion and Public Life." *The Economist*. November 3, 2007. http://www.economist.com/sites/default/files/special -reports-pdfs/10015148.pdf.

35. Baptism by Torture

NOVEMBER 29, 2007
BY WILLIAM SCHWEIKER

Religious practices have often been tied to violence and torture, but this connection is often hidden within public discourse. That is the situation now in the United States with the debate about waterboarding, the religious meanings of which have yet to be articulated and explored.

The candidates in the current presidential campaign have taken starkly different stances on the practice of waterboarding. Some condemn the practice as outright torture; others have refused to condemn the practice if in an extreme case it could save millions of American lives. The topic has been divided into two separate but related questions: Is waterboarding a form of torture? and, However torture is defined, are there situations in which waterboarding and other practices are justified?

The argument for possible justification turns on several assumptions: that we could infallibly know that someone had vital information that would in fact save millions; that torture would extract this information without distortion; and, finally, that if the information were secured truthfully and infallibly, it could be put to use in good time. None of these assumptions is warranted. Expert opinion and empirical evidence concur that torture is an ineffective means to gain reliable information. The scenario of the lone knower of the facts whose torture would save millions of lives is the stuff of bad spy movies and bad exam questions in ethics courses. In terms of the question of definition, matters are both legal and visceral. International conventions provide ample guidelines, and, as more than one commentator has noted, if waterboarding is not torture, it is not clear what else to call it, the Bush administration's penchant to alter definitions notwithstanding.

Less often observed is that the practice of waterboarding has roots in the Spanish Inquisition and parallels the persecution of Anabaptists during the Protestant Reformation and the Roman Catholic Counter-Reformation. Why did practices similar to waterboarding develop as a way to torture heretics—whether the heretics were Anabaptists or, in the Inquisition, Protestants of any stripe as well as Jews and witches and others?

Roman Catholics and Protestants alike persecuted the Anabaptists or "re-baptizers" since these people denied infant baptism in favor of adult baptism. The use of torture and physical abuse was meant to stem the movement and also to bring salvation to heretics. It had been held—at least since St. Augustine—that punishment, even lethal in form, could be an act of mercy meant to keep a sinner from continuing in sin, either by repentance of heresy or by death. King Ferdinand declared that drowning—called the third baptism—was a suitable response to Anabaptists. Water as a form of torture was an inversion of the waters of baptism under the (grotesque) belief that it could deliver the heretic from his or her sins.

In the Inquisition, the practice was not drowning as such, but the threat of drowning, and the symbolic threat of baptism. The *tortura del agua* or *toca* entailed forcing the victim to ingest water poured into a cloth stuffed into the mouth in order to give the impression of drowning. Because of the wide symbolic meaning of "water" in the Christian and Jewish traditions (creation, the great flood, the parting of the Red Sea in the Exodus and drowning of the Egyptians[!], Christ's walking on the water, and, centrally for Christians, baptism as a symbolic death that gives life), the practice takes on profound religious significance. Torture has many forms, but torture by water as it arose in the Roman Catholic and Protestant Reformations seemingly drew some of its power and inspiration from theological convictions about repentance and salvation. It was, we must now surely say, a horrific inversion of the best spirit of Christian faith and symbolism. Is it the purpose of the United States nowadays to seek the conversion, repentance, and purity of supposed terrorists and thus to take on the trappings of a religious rite? The question is so buried behind public discourse that its full import is hardly recognized.

In the light of these religious meanings and background to waterboarding, US citizens can decide to reject any claim by the government to have the right to use this or other forms of torture, especially given connections to the most woeful expressions of Christianity; conversely, they can fall prey to fear and questionable reasoning and thus continue to support an unjust and vile practice that demeans the nation's highest political and moral ideals even as it desecrates one of the most important practices and symbols of Christian faith.

I judge that it is time for repentance, the affirmation of new life, and the humane expression of religious convictions.

William Schweiker (PhD, University of Chicago Divinity School) is the Edward L. Ryerson Distinguished Service Professor of Theological Ethics at the University of Chicago Divinity School, and director of the Martin Marty Center.

36. How to Bury a Prophet

February 7, 2008
By Kathleen Flake

The Latter-day Saints buried their prophet on Saturday. Thousands attended the service in person and millions of the faithful watched in chapels around the globe, as well as on the internet. What they saw was an unusually personal ceremony for a very public man who led and to a large degree defined the contemporary Church of Jesus Christ of Latter-day Saints. Notwithstanding the numbers and titles of participants, Gordon Hinckley's funeral was a family affair both in word and sacrament. It was an extraordinary display of what makes Mormonism tick.

Gordon Hinckley died at the age of ninety-seven, having been in the church's leading councils since 1958 and serving as its fifteenth president since 1995. He shaped the church through a half century of growth in 170 countries. A third of its present membership joined during his tenure as president. Displaying remarkable vigor late in life, he met with church members on every continent, responding to their needs with curricular, welfare, and building programs whose costs are impossible to imagine and no one will admit. He met the press to a degree unequaled and with an openness heretofore unknown among Mormonism's leadership. This effort too was largely successful. No less a cynic than CBS's Mike Wallace admitted that Hinckley "fully deserves the almost universal admiration that he gets." He was, as *Newsweek*'s Jon Meacham said, "a charming and engaging man, an unlikely prelate—and all the more impressive for that." The same could be said of his funeral.

Hinckley's funeral was an unlikely but impressive mix of the sacramental and the mundane, in large part because it observed Mormonism's custom that families bury their dead. The family designs the memorial program, participates actively in it, and performs the ordinances that send their loved ones off to the next life. Yes, the chapel in this case was the LDS Conference Center that held 21,000 mourners; the lay pastor who conducted the meeting was Thomas Monson, Hinckley's presumptive successor as "prophet, seer, and revelator"; and the music was provided by the three-hundred-plus-member Mormon Tabernacle Choir. But, in all other essentials, the service was performed by the family. A son gave the invocation. Monson conducted at the request of the family, he said, not by ecclesiastical right. The eulogy was given by a daughter who described her father's life as a halfway point in the now seven-generation story of sacrifice, death, and survival that is the Mormon saga. Explicitly gathering the millions watching into that story, she declared, "We are one family sharing an inheritance of faith." Friends with high titles spoke next. Though the requisite list of Hinckley's ecclesiastical accomplishments was given, it was subordinated to his success as a courageous and amusing friend and a successful husband and father. Another daughter gave the benediction: "We are buoyed by the knowledge that we will see him again as family, as friends."

Hinckley's sons and daughters with their spouses led the casket out of the hall and between an honor guard of church authorities. Cameras followed the mourners, focusing on his five children, twenty-five grandchildren, and sixty-two great-grandchildren who formed the cortege to the cemetery. There, possibly most surprisingly, the eldest son dedicated the grave without fanfare. Notwithstanding the presence of the entire church hierarchy, the son stepped forward to pronounce: "By the authority of the Melchizedek Priesthood, I dedicate this grave for the remains of Gordon B. Hinckley, until such time as thou shall call him forth." Then, church leaders were "dismissed," as Monson put it. As the church teaches is the case in the afterlife, only the family remained.

Families are, as Latter-day Saints like to say, forever. What they don't say is that the church is not forever. It is only the instrument for endowing families with the right and duty to mediate the gifts of the gospel to their members, thereby sealing the willing among them as families in the life to come. This was Hinckley's message as a prophet. As he would have it and as the best Mormon funerals do, his message was embodied and enacted by his family who blessed him in death, no less than in life. This is how the Latter-day Saints, at least, bury a prophet.

Kathleen Flake (PhD, University of Chicago Divinity School) is an associate professor of American religious history at Vanderbilt University Divinity School and Graduate Department of Religion.

37. E Pluribus Obama

NOVEMBER 13, 2008
BY M. COOPER HARRISS

In the November 6 *New York Times*, photographer Matt Mendelsohn describes a restlessness that overcame him on election night, leading him to drive across the Potomac to the Lincoln Memorial in Washington, DC, "expecting to find a crowd and some news." Instead he found roughly twenty-five people huddled around a transistor radio, a crowd so relatively small and quiet that they were unmolested by camera crews who, like Mendelsohn, expected numbers and bombast more in keeping with the throng in Grant Park, Chicago, not quite forty-score miles away.

Mendelsohn's instincts upon the election of our first president of color resound for evident reasons (Lincoln as "Great Emancipator" and the Memorial's steps as the location of Martin Luther King's "I Have a Dream" speech). They also respond to signals manufactured by Obama's campaign, ranging from the announcement of his candidacy at the site of Lincoln's "House Divided" speech to his invocation of the man and his words last Tuesday night. But to ascribe this rhetoric simply to matters of race overlooks a broader religious move that the president-elect and his handlers appear to understand, and which surely has contributed to their success.

Abraham Lincoln is the patron saint of the American civil religion, a category that Robert Bellah codified in 1967 as "a genuine apprehension of universal and transcendent religious reality as seen in or . . . as revealed through the experience of the American people." That Bellah's definition coincided with discernible fractures in a singular American mythology is significant. Commentators including our own Martin Marty have noted that the past four decades have witnessed a shift from "the one" to "the many" in national discourse. Marty's formulation in the third volume of *Modern American Religion* marks a movement from "centripetal" to "centrifugal," from a strong, centrally unified national identity to one thrust away from a center, multivalent. Within this context, "Americanness" has become a competitive hermeneutic, recently evident in the debates surrounding the nature of patriotism and the responsibilities of liberty and citizenship.

Similarly, Abraham Lincoln finds himself created, like Albert Schweitzer said of Jesus, by "each individual . . . in accordance with his own character." Consequently, how should we read the Obama candidacy and these earliest phases of his presidency? Is "change" skin deep or does it extend further? Might we also read a return to a centripetal orientation of American national identity, a new validation of a civil religion lost for nearly two generations? Should we even aspire for a sense of "one" over the pluralistic diversity of "the many," given the very real hegemonic potential that such a homogenous orientation raises? These are questions to bear in mind and questions to which we shall, no doubt, return.

But in the hopeful interim, we might remember Ralph Ellison, another antecedent of the president-elect. In a recent article for *The New Republic*, David Samuels remarks on the evident influence Ellison's *Invisible Man* (1952) exerts on Obama's autobiography *Dreams from My Father* (1995) and, thereby, "as a major influence on his personal evolution." I would argue that another portion of Ellison's work resonates with Obama's candidacy— especially with his centripetal understanding of American civil religion: the second novel that Ellison wrote from 1952 until his death in 1994 and never completed, though excerpts were published as *Juneteenth* in 1999. In *Juneteenth* we find Adam Sunraider, a race-baiting, white New England senator, engaged in deathbed conversations with Rev. Hickman, an African American preacher. The reader learns that Sunraider was once known as "Bliss," a child of ambiguous racial origins who, though he could pass for white, was adopted by Hickman, raised and loved by his congregants, and trained in the homiletical arts of the black church. Indeed, Sunraider's hateful "white" eloquence was fostered by Bliss's "black" rhetorical apprenticeship—evincing Ellison's profound understanding of the irony of American history.

At a pivotal moment in the novel's disjointed chronology, Hickman stands at the Lincoln Memorial, considering "some cord of kinship stronger and deeper than blood, hate or heartbreak." His admiration for Lincoln conflates with Bliss's betrayal. Yet, ironically, it is the racist Sunraider, speaking on the Senate floor, who invokes the one and the many: "History has put to us three fatal questions, has written them across our sky in accents of accusation. . . . How can the many be as one? How can the future deny the Past? And how can the light deny the dark?"

Now that the remarkable feat that many believed they would not live to see is accomplished, these questions, which invoke the mystery of American faith, should occupy our concern and the new president's. May we rejoice in this remarkable moment, yet not blind ourselves in tragic self-satisfaction to the challenges and complexities of what lies ahead.

Resources

Bellah, Robert. "Civil Religion in America." *Daedalus: Journal of the American Academy of Arts & Sciences* 96, no. 1 (Winter 1967): 1–21.

Ellison, Ralph. *Juneteenth.* New York: Random House, 1999.

Marty, Martin E. *Modern American Religion.* Vol. 3, *Under God, Indivisible, 1941–1960.* Chicago: The University of Chicago Press, 1996.

Mendelsohn, Matt. "Memorial Day." *The New York Times.* November 5, 2008. http://www.nytimes.com/2008/11/06/opinion/06mendelsohn.html.

Samuels, David. "Invisible Man." *The New Republic.* October 21, 2008. https://newrepublic.com/article/62148/invisible-man.

M. Cooper Harriss, a junior fellow in the Martin Marty Center, is a PhD candidate in religion and literature at the University of Chicago Divinity School.

38. God and Man at Yale

December 4, 2008
By Eboo Patel

The Commons at Yale University looked like a cross between Hogwarts and Medina. Over five hundred students, staff, and faculty had gathered for a university-wide *iftar*, the meal where Muslims break their dawn-to-dusk fast during the month of Ramadan. Linda Lorimer, Yale's vice president, gave an opening talk, expressing the university's commitment to religious inclusivity and interfaith activity. Omar Bajwa, the university's recently hired coordinator of Muslim life, thanked Yale for its efforts to accommodate the unique dietary and prayer needs of Muslim students. And when the Muslims left the dining area for the evening prayer, most of the seats were still occupied. Hundreds of Jews, Sikhs, Christians, Hindus, agnostics, Unitarian Universalists, and others had come to support their fellow Muslim students, partake in some excellent South Asian food, and celebrate the religious devotion and diversity that are increasingly a part of campus life at Yale.

It is a remarkable shift from when I was a student fifteen years ago. Identity politics were all the rage then, but they were almost always about race, class, gender, and sexuality. Academic departments, leadership programs, and residence halls—prompted by the Rodney King incident—put on hundreds of diversity programs every year intended to create a more inclusive campus environment. Late-night student discussions typically focused on the new Spike Lee film or bell hooks book. Religion was something that the InterVarsity kids did at their song circles on Wednesday evenings. The rest of us didn't sneer at it; we just shrugged and went on our way. Faith might play a role in some people's private lives, we figured, but it barely registered in our campus discourse. Even as newspapers told of strife in the Balkans, Northern Ireland, South Asia, the Middle East, West Africa, the multicultural movement hardly turned its head. As Harvard professor Diana Eck wrote in *Encountering God*, "Religion (was) the missing 'r' word in the diversity discussion" at universities.

This is the result of what I call secularization theory hangover, a condition that afflicted universities long after the rest of society recovered. Secularization theory emerged from lecture halls in the 1960s, advanced by scholars like Peter Berger and Harvey Cox who stated that as societies modernized they would necessarily secularize. Such scholars revised their theories a long time ago. But many of the intellectuals who came of age during that era, and who are now running the universities where they once read such books, continued to believe that religion, if it persisted at all, would do so in the privacy of a handful of homes and at the furthest margins of our public life.

But an important segment of student life on college campuses was actually heading in the opposite direction. Groups like InterVarsity Christian Fellowship and Campus Crusade for Christ continued to grow, bolstered by a powerful evangelical movement in the broader society. Additionally, as Dr. Alyssa Bryant of "Spirituality on Campus" observes, "There is increasing interest among today's college students, faculty, and administrators in the inner life of spiritual reflection, contemplation, and meaning-making." Finally, the past two decades have seen the American-born children of the 1965-era immigrants arrive on campus in significant numbers and bring their Muslim, Hindu, and Buddhist faiths with them. Sharon Kugler, the chaplain at Yale, told me that the number of religious organizations at her previous post, Johns Hopkins, skyrocketed from eight to twenty-seven during her fourteen years there.

This combination of devotion and diversity occurred on campus just as religion emerged as a central force in the broader culture. 9/11 has done to religion what Rodney King did to race—put it front and center on the campus agenda. One way that universities are responding is by hiring leaders like Sharon Kugler—the first lay, Catholic woman in her position at Yale—to transform their historically liberal Protestant chaplaincies into full-fledged multifaith programs. This means working with the existing Jewish, Catholic, and Protestant (both evangelical and mainline) ministries; hiring new staff to work with Muslim, Buddhist, and Hindu students; and organizing interfaith service projects and multifaith student councils.

We live in a society starkly polarized around religion. A 2007 Pew survey found that twice the number of respondents had a negative view of Muslims than a positive view. If the color line was the problem of the twentieth century, as Du Bois famously observed, it appears that the faith line will be the challenge of the twenty-first. And just as decades of campus activism on the issue of the color line have helped to produce a more racially inclusive society, so will initiatives like Yale's Ramadan banquet ultimately produce one characterized by religious pluralism.

Resource

Eck, Diana L. *Encountering God: A Spiritual Journey from Bozeman to Banaras.* Boston: Beacon Press, 1993.

Eboo Patel is executive director of the Interfaith Youth Core.

39. On Trust

DECEMBER 22, 2008
BY MARTIN E. MARTY

For the next fortnight the University of Chicago and the Martin Marty Center close down; so, while I rarely visit either of them except electronically, I'll close down, to return in 2009. This end-of-year and holiday-greeting issue differs from the other fifty columns of the past year in that they all focus on a specific "sighting" of religion in public life, usually in print media and sometimes in electronic ones. We then cite chapter and verse, date of issue, and the like.

This week I could reference Saturday, December 20, *The New York Times*, *The Wall Street Journal*, our Chicago papers, and dates on the covers of newsmagazines, "public religion" expressions in religious outlets, and so on. But this week I won't zero in on one. Instead I will editorialize on the basis of virtually all news and opinion media of the past months. The theme: trust. Typical is the Madoff scandal, in which one network of trusters, many of them relying on connections and handshakes, saw a criminal breakdown of trust. In our state of Illinois, wiretaps confirmed what millions already knew: that our governor corruptly broke trust with the public in myriad ways.

Meanwhile, the media tell of the breakdown of trust in the entire financial sector, and of the difficulty of recovering there unless and until some measures of trust are restored. An old administration in Washington fades away, one of its main legacies being stories of broken trust in the highest counsels. Scandals, sexual and fiscal, in religious organizations have led many in the public to stop trusting clergy, evangelists, and fund-raisers who use the name of God to misuse others, often horribly. A new administration takes shape, and the main issue is: who can be trusted, before and after appointment? I am almost embarrassed to speak in terms so familiar and broad that they can sound banal, like clichés. Yet the witness to broken trust is so vast and deep that to avoid it would be irresponsible. People in many disciplines need to speak up, and they are doing so.

Now I am going to venture with brief comments. I hope and trust that they are rare intrusions in *Sightings* about my own project. "Trust" is a centrally central, focally focal theme in Christian (as in Jewish and other) theo-

logical discourse and in the language of prayer and action. It shows up in titles of two small books I edited some years ago, mentioned here only to show
that I am not a newcomer to the field but still one who has much to learn. It
happens that during the past year I did several commutes to SUNY Stony
Brook, New York, and its "Trust Institute," to lecture and lead little semi-
nars. Out of reading for it, I am finishing a book probably to be called *Building
Cultures of Trust*. Talking about such projects in detail awaits another day and
other media than this.

When I started writing the book, I thought I had to spend many pages
discussing why "trust" and "broken trust" were relevant themes. During
these months the public media have incessantly shrieked, in effect: dealing
with trust is not only relevant; it is desperately crucial! Stony Brook, its institute, and people like me can do little more than add a brick or stone or trowel
full of intellectual mortar into the efforts of many who would work toward
some restoration of trust. By the way, if ever there was front-page or prime-
time moral and ethical discussion about a theme which has theological dimensions, this is it. Many economists, writers, and thinkers in general used
to sound as if economics, political science, and the like, exhausted efforts to
address the grand themes. But "trust" is a grand theme, whose biblical and
theological ties are coming to the fore. I trust.

40. News from the Religion and Science Front

JANUARY 8, 2009
BY DOUGLAS ANDERSON

In the scientific community, there has been a significant increase in "sightings" of articles and studies on the "science" of religion. Various points of view, and occasionally overt agendas, emerge from the research. If a Templeton-like foundation is funding the study, for instance, the perspective seems to be a test of the hypothesis: God is up there, and we will prove it to you (at least insofar as measured by statistically significant outcomes) with the following randomized, double-blind clinical trial. Several years ago there appeared "A Randomized, Controlled Trial of the Effects of Remote, Intercessory Prayer on Outcomes in Patients Admitted to the Coronary Care Unit." The study showed that "prayer may be an effective adjunct to standard medical care." However, the critical reader was also warned that there were several limitations to the study. One problem was that there was no way to determine whether others might have been praying for the control group, those not supposed to be the beneficiaries of intercessory prayer. Another problem was that the main result of the study was a rather meager "10 percent improvement" in the short-term cardiac health for those in the group for whom prayer was offered, as measured by a score that was "an estimate of the overall CCU (cardiac care unit) course."

One wonders what God was thinking while deciding how to weigh in on this exercise. If I sound cynical, it's because clinical randomized trials are notoriously expensive and difficult and yet can be very influential in the definition and direction of clinical practice. I am both a Christian and a clinical scientist/neurosurgeon who silently prays before and sometimes during surgery. I'm also struggling to obtain funding for a clinical trial of a brain tumor vaccine to supplement the inadequate therapies we presently have. I'm not suggesting that studies of religion's intersections with science shouldn't be done or are not important, but attempting to put God on the witness stand, demanding an accounting, and then suggesting that something has been learned, is, in my opinion, wasteful of resources that might better be employed elsewhere.

A different type of scientific analysis appeared recently in the widely read journal *Science*: "The Origin and Evolution of Religious Prosociality." Religious prosociality is "the idea that religions facilitate acts that benefit others at a personal cost." In this review and synthesis of nearly fifty articles, we learn that there is "an association between self reports of religiosity and prosociality" but that the association "emerges primarily in contexts where reputational concerns are heightened." Further, behavioral studies searching for a "good Samaritan" effect in an anonymous encounter experiment document that "unobtrusively recorded offers of help showed no relation with religiosity in this anonymous context." It is telling from the article that only one variable produced a change in the behavior of study participants: "Whether participants were told to rush or take their time—produced differences in helping rates." We may have learned something there: religious variables aside, we all respond to the rush of modern life and sometimes lose our sensitivity to be an empathic and caring community—all of us.

That "active members of modern secular organizations are at least as likely to report donating to charity as active members of religious ones" should not be a surprise. For what and for whom this information might be useful is open to question. Clearly, more generosity is needed from all of us. The authors suggest that more research is needed to "establish the specific conditions under which costly religious commitment could evolve as a stable individual strategy and whether these models need to take into account intergroup competition." They also suggest that "the extent to which religion is implicated in human cooperation, and the precise sequence of evolutionary developments in religious prosociality" are important questions. These research interests might well be interesting for the fields of theology, psychology, and sociology among others, and as the authors note, "This is an area of no small debate, but scientific attention is needed to examine precisely how individuals and groups determine who are the beneficiaries of religious prosociality and who its victims." On the other hand, after reading samples of research on the nature of religious experience, examining the design of experiments and techniques used to probe these complex questions, one wonders, what do we really learn? The concern of scientists that "the same mechanisms involved in ingroup altruism may facilitate outgroup antagonism" may just as well apply to the scientific community as the religious.

Resources

Harris, William S. et al. "A Randomized, Controlled Trial of the Effects of Remote, Intercessory Prayer on Outcomes in Patients Admitted to the Coronary Care Unit." *Archives of Internal Medicine* 159, no. 19 (October 25, 1999): 2273-78.

Norenzayan, Ara, and Azim F. Shariff. "The Origin and Evolution of Religious Prosociality." *Science* 322, no. 5898 (October 3, 2008): 58–62.

Douglas Anderson is a neurological surgeon and associate professor of neurological surgery at Loyola University Medical Center.

41. An Inner Life with New Meaning

JANUARY 22, 2009
BY KRISTA TIPPETT

As the indicators by which we've measured our collective well-being in recent years continue to plummet, I found a conversation with Parker Palmer echoing in my head. He and I spoke years ago on the radio program *Speaking of Faith* about his mid-life experience of clinical depression, about which he has written searchingly and made rich sense in later life. He told me about a psychiatrist who helped him move to a new level of healing by asking him, "Could you begin to imagine your depression not as an enemy that is crushing you—but as a friend pressing you down to ground on which it is safe to stand?" His description of the unrealistically elevated heights of ego and freneticism that preceded his psychological depression—an unsustainable, inflated sense of what is normal—was startlingly analogous with our economic present.

And of the "economic terrors that now engulf us," Parker Palmer makes this plain but startling observation: "At some level most of us knew they were coming." We know that we can't live forever beyond our means, that unregulated greed cannot end well, that a cycle of prosperity that brings unparalleled wealth while simultaneously impoverishing an ever-wider population will eventually yield to that imbalance. In recent years many of us have suspended this knowledge in favor of optimism and opportunities based on facts and figures—"the numbers," as my colleagues at *Marketplace* say—that we began to collectively accept as a surer reality.

The knowledge we need to reckon morally and spiritually with the place we're in now—the commonplace knowledge that might have shielded us from some of the human wreckage that is being wrought—comes, Parker Palmer says, "from a place deeper than our intellects." During a bull market, such talk might sound sentimental, fanciful, and irrelevant. Yet as the numbers betrayed us, the ubiquitous talk even among economists has been of a loss of "faith" in the market. We are given to realize anew that, even in the realm of commerce and finance, human emotion and desire shape our most concrete endeavors. Fear and greed, for example, helped create the illusions behind hedge funds, subprime mortgages, and derivatives that we accepted, for a time, as the contours of solid economic reality.

This kind of truth-telling—this correction, if you will—is sobering, but it is also good news. The numbers don't become irrelevant now, but we can see their limits more clearly, and give due attention to other modes of analysis that complete and anchor our humanity. We can tap more seriously into the practical resources that religious and spiritual traditions have mined for centuries. They offer wisdom that can invigorate and refresh our common reflection. They speak about abundance and scarcity in nonmaterial terms, about violence and nonviolence in everyday life, and about acknowledging fear without being consumed and guided by it.

Dr. Rachel Naomi Remen, a pioneer in exploring the overlap between spiritual and physical health, points out that the questions we're pondering in our financial and family lives now are essentially spiritual questions. What does it mean to live a worthy, if not wealthy, life? What is genuinely important, and what can I genuinely live without? What are my children learning from this moment? Whom and what do I trust in, and why? And how, in my immediate world, will I respond to and take responsibility for the consequences of human and societal wreckage that we are about to experience?

I'm well aware of the ease—the danger—of making lofty observations on the virtue that might emerge from economic crisis, when human beings are falling through the cracks all around us. I believe that as we learn to speak about the important questions in our lives in new, fresh, and vivid ways, we can also live them differently together. In the new conversations that this moment makes possible, we must summon practical wisdom and collective courage.

Krista Tippett is the host of American Public Media's Speaking of Faith.

42. Economics

MARCH 16, 2009
BY MARTIN E. MARTY

Virtually every church newsletter, denominational website, religious periodical, or other medium, disseminated in print or electronically, makes some reference to the economic situation in which all classes of Americans find themselves today. Local congregations' offers of spiritual sustenance, community-sharing burdens, and hopes are still among the main and best things they do, as well as providing counseling, tips, and sometimes guidance to non-church organizations and experts who may be of help. These concern issues of joblessness, home foreclosures, and other devastating realities in 2009.

When religious commentators or commentators on religion look at the theme, their observations tend to follow one of three lines. Those who are instinctive and ideological supporters of "unfettered" free markets report on and predict trends that will deprive churches of part of their mission as government is increasingly involved in health, education, and welfare programs. Churches (and synagogues, et cetera) will be worse off than before the crunch and the crash. A second set advocates to religious organizations that they do more and better than before with works of mercy (and justice), taking initiatives to help make the best use of enhanced governmental initiatives. In a sense, they say, thank God for government, secular organizations, and others who help feed and heal. The third set takes a long view, asking churches to re-explore their traditions (e.g., Catholic social teachings which support the common good).

It is too soon to know how this recession-depression will work out for religious institutions and ideas. While watching and waiting, I decided to do what so many do: compare today to the Great Depression of the 1930s. I had explored religious roles and responses in my *The Noise of Conflict: 1919–1941*, the second volume in my *Modern American Religion*. If we repeat in any way—but who says we will, or must?—what happened then, there is not a lot of cheer to be spread. I particularly relied on Samuel C. Kincheloe's 1937 *Research Memorandum on Religion in the Depression*, an extensive, judicious, realistic survey done for the Social Science Research Council by a Chicago

Theological Seminary (then Congregational) professor. Like so many other secular and mainstream Protestant analysts, he did not pay much attention to what was prospering when nothing else was: fundamentalism.

Some leaders hoped and prayed for religious revivals, none of which erupted. "There has been much emphasis on the belief that what society needs is religion," Kincheloe reported, and I observed, "but society evidently did not think so." Money problems limited church efforts to serve the poor, whose numbers grew exponentially. At the same time, deep believers within all congregations and denominations "did not fall away from faith merely because of economic trauma." *The Christian Century* editorialized, with a view on the past: "Did people not address this Depression religiously because for once they did not think it occurred under the providence of God?" The editorial conclusion: this may have been "the first time men have not blamed God for hard times." If that was true in 1935, it seems to be true today, too. There are accusers, accused, and commentators on all hands today, but one seldom hears that all the dealings, many of them now seen as greedy at best and criminal at worst, were anything but the results of individual and corporate folly and corruption. This time again citizens can't blame God for getting them into this and are trying to find God-ly ways to get out of it . . . together.

Resource
Marty, Martin E. *Modern American Religion.* Vol. 2, *The Noise of Conflict, 1919–1941.* Chicago: The University of Chicago Press, 1991.

43. Back to the Twelfth Century: Peter the Venerable and Pope Benedict XVI

OCTOBER 29, 2009
BY LUCY K. PICK

In his general audience in St. Peter's Square on October 14, Pope Benedict gave an address in which he held up the twelfth-century monk and abbot of Cluny, Peter the Venerable, as a model for contemporary Christians, lay and monastic, praising him for his ability to balance both contemplative spirituality and the demands and pressures of the world. Peter was an unusual choice. Though the pope associated him with the abbey's canonized abbots, quoting his papal predecessor Gregory VII that at Cluny "there was not a single abbot who was not a saint," Peter in fact was never canonized. Why select him as a model over other Benedictine contemplative administrators, not least Saint Benedict himself, who could provide the same example of tranquility in the face of turmoil? What makes Peter stand out from his brethren at this moment in time?

Pope Benedict praised Peter in part because "he showed care and solicitude even for those who were outside the Church, in particular for the Jews and Muslims: to foster knowledge of the latter he had the Quran translated." His admiration for Peter's interest in Jews and Muslims was important enough that the pope repeated it in the much shorter English paraphrase that followed the address. Peter is indeed well known for his strong and passionate belief in the power of reason to convert Jews and Muslims to Christianity; for his efforts to translate Islamic texts; for his treatises against Jews, Muslims, and heretics—and for his conclusion that those who did not convert when approached with reason were not rational and thus not fully human.

When I read this recent address, I immediately recalled the famous, or infamous, address the pope gave three years ago, at the University of Regensburg. His quotation in this speech of a Christian anti-Islamic polemic that argued that Christianity persuades by reason, while Islam converts only through violence, enraged the Muslim world. But just as disturbing were the broader claims his speech made about the correct nature of reason. Benedict presented a model of right reason and right faith as both intrinsically united and intrinsically Christian. "Not to act reasonably, not to act with logos, is contrary to the nature of God," he proclaimed, quoting his medieval Christian polemicist. Though the address was framed as an invitation to dialogue with those of other religions, it is necessarily a dialogue of a very particular kind—not dialogue as a free exchange between equal partners but a dialogue in which Christian reason sets the parameters and limits of the discussion. It is medieval dialogue, very familiar to Peter the Venerable, used both as a pedagogical genre in which a master instructs a student and as a way of showing the truth of Christianity in contrast with other religions.

The dangers of a dialogue in which its parameters predict its outcome should be evident. Arguments like these were made in the Middle Ages with horrendous results when Muslims and especially Jews continued in their own paths despite being faced with the "rational" arguments of medieval polemicists. Convicted of irrationality, non-Christians could easily then be labeled as less than human. Peter the Venerable himself points the way to this tragic history in his treatise against the Jews in a passage addressing an imagined Jewish interlocutor that is typical, not exceptional: "It seems to me, Jew, that I have satisfied every man about the questions put to me with many authorities, and much reasoned argument. And if I have satisfied every man, then also you too, if you are a man. For I do not dare to call you a man, lest perhaps I lie, since I know that reason, which separates man from the other beasts, is extinguished, nay buried in you. . . . Why should I not call you a brute animal? Why not a beast, why not an ox?"

This is not dialogue that seeks to widen channels of communication between those of different faiths; this is not even dialogue that seeks to convert. This is a discourse that uses the form of dialogue as a means to define non-Christians and distance them from the community of the faithful. It may be exactly what the pope wants, especially if Ross Douthat's *New York Times* opinion column of October 25 is correct that the pope's recent gesture towards disaffected Anglicans was motivated by his desire to present a united Christian front against the Islamic world. But it is a radical departure from the way the Roman Catholic Church has approached interreligious dialogue for decades and a return to a mode of Catholic self-understanding with a very unhappy past.

Resources

Benedict XVI. "On Peter the Venerable, Abbot of Cluny." October 14, 2009. https://zenit.org/articles/on-peter-the-venerable-abbot-of-cluny.
———. "Papal Address at the University of Regensburg." September 17, 2006. http://www.catholic.org/featured/headline.php?ID=3650.

Douthat, Ross. "Benedict's Gamble." *The New York Times*. October 25, 2009. http://www.nytimes.com/2009/10/26/opinion/26douthat.html.

Peter the Venerable. *Adversus Iudeorum inveteratam duritiem*. Edited by Yvonne Friedman. Corpus Christianorum, Continuatio Medievalis 58. Turnhout, 1985.

Lucy K. Pick is senior lecturer in the history of Christianity and director of undergraduate studies at the University of Chicago Divinity School.

44. Religion-Based Arguments in Juvenile Life without Parole Cases

NOVEMBER 12, 2009
BY JOAN GOTTSCHALL

Those interested in the intersection of religious values and public policy, and particularly criminal justice policy, should take note of a brief filed this past summer in the Supreme Court of the United States in the joined cases of *Graham v. Florida*, No. 08-7412, and *Sullivan v. Florida*, No. 08-7621, on behalf of approximately twenty religious organizations as *amici curiae* or friends of the Court (see below for a full list of organizations). These two cases present the issue of whether the Eighth Amendment to the Constitution's ban on cruel and unusual punishment proscribes the sentencing of juveniles convicted of non-homicide offenses to life imprisonment without the possibility of parole, as occurred in these two cases. Oral argument for the cases took place on Monday, November 9.

The brief is noteworthy for a number of reasons. First, it represents an effort by the diverse religious groups involved to speak in one voice on a matter of faith and conviction. Second, the brief locates as central to each of these faith traditions the values of mercy, forgiveness, and compassion, and the link between these values and concepts of justice and charity: "In short," the brief states, "religious texts make clear that each of these three values—mercy, forgiveness, and compassion—must guide interpersonal and societal relations, and are to serve as the bedrock principles for a just and fair society." Third, *amici* make the claim, rarely heard in contemporary culture, that the duty of a judge, and of a society imposing judgment, is to make adequate provision for these values.

The legal position advanced by the brief is also remarkable, for *amici* argue that their shared religious values require the Supreme Court to reverse the Florida judgments and to hold that it is a violation of the Eighth Amendment to sentence juveniles convicted of non-homicide offenses to life without the possibility of parole. The brief reasons are as follows: First, it reviews traditional religious recognition of the distinction between children and adults, both in religious teachings regarding crime and punishment and in other aspects of religious law. It then summarizes the growing scientific support for this distinction and reviews the widespread cultural recognition that "the physical and mental immaturity of youth requires special treatment." Third, it argues that ignoring the special status of youth and condemning juveniles to die in prison contravenes the fundamental religious values of mercy, forgiveness, and compassion. The brief points out that all individuals are entitled to these but that the weak and vulnerable (such as children) have a special entitlement to compassionate treatment. Indeed, it states that "juveniles who commit serious crimes often come from disadvantaged backgrounds: many are poor, and frequently they have been the victims of abuse and neglect. These are exactly the type of children *amici*'s faith traditions stress are most deserving of kindness and compassion."

Finally, the brief discusses the religious problem posed by a natural life sentence imposed on a juvenile offender. Such a sentence is unjust, the brief argues, because it fails to recognize the potential of juveniles to grow, develop, and be rehabilitated; it thus contravenes the foundational concept of rehabilitation within each of the *amici*'s faith traditions. The brief quotes the Florida judge who sentenced Terrance Jamar Graham (sixteen years old when he committed the crime for which he was sentenced) to life imprisonment without the possibility of parole. The judge noted Graham's "escalating pattern of criminal conduct" and concluded, "there is nothing we can do for you." This "nihilistic view," the brief argues, "is antithetical to the perspectives of *amici*'s faith traditions and of American society at large."

The *amici* observe that their religious traditions recognize that "just punishment must allow for the offender to be rehabilitated and restored to the community when possible." Each of their traditions, they write, embraces the principle of "restorative justice," which involves establishing a system of justice that, in the words of Michael L. Hadley, "moves from punishment to reconciliation, from vengeance against offenders to healing for victims, from alienation and harshness to community and wholeness, from negativity and destructiveness to healing, forgiveness, and mercy." The brief describes with detailed examples how the concept of restorative justice is rooted in the faith traditions of the *amici*.

Anyone who has read the news of the last several months is aware of the controversy ignited by the president's remark that among his criteria in selecting judges was empathy. As the pundits are fond of pointing out, on this issue, even his Supreme Court nominee "threw him under the bus." In the context of our contemporary public discourse, the importance of the argument of these *amici curiae* cannot be overstated. Their insistence on the religious centrality of mercy, forgiveness, compassion, and rehabilitation, and the relevance of these values to our system of justice, is a message rarely heard.

Note: The religious organizations joining in the *amicus curiae* brief include the American Association of Jewish Lawyers and Jurists, the American Catholic Correctional Chaplains Association, the American Friends Service Committee, the Buddhist Peace Fellowship, the Engaged Zen Foundation, the General Synod of the United Church of Christ, the Islamic Shura Council of Southern California, the Mormons for Equality and Social Justice, the National Council of the Churches of Christ in the United States of America, the Office of Restorative Justice of the Archdiocese of Los Angeles, Prison Fellowship Ministries, and the General Board of Church and Society of the United Methodist Church, among others. The brief was prepared by lawyers at the law firm of Fried, Frank, Harris, Shriver & Jacobson LLP, led by Michael B. de Leeuw.

Resource

Hadley, Michael L. "Multifaith Reflection on Criminal Justice." Introduction to *The Spiritual Roots of Restorative Justice.* Edited by Michael L. Hadley, 1–29. Albany: State University of New York Press, 2001.

Joan Gottschall is a United States District Judge for the Northern District of Illinois, a member of the Visiting Committee to the University of Chicago Divinity School, and a member of the Martin Marty Center Advisory Board.

45. The Sacred and the Sartorial

JANUARY 14, 2010
BY COURTNEY WILDER

At first blush, the blog *Beauty Tips for Ministers* does not seem like a hotbed of feminist theology of the body. Written primarily, though not exclusively, for women, the blog includes posts on a wide range of topics related to clergy and their professional dress, including how to discern between attractive, trendy shoes and those that are too sexy for ministry, the difficulties of achieving professional-looking hair, what constitutes good makeup, and how clergy should dress for weddings. The advice is practical, the commentary is very funny, and the images are consistently good.

As one reads more posts, and reads them more deeply, a distinctive pastoral theology begins to emerge, a theology that embraces the physical presence of women in ministry. The author, whose *nomme de blog* is PeaceBang, is otherwise known as Rev. Victoria Weinstein, the Harvard-educated pastor of First Parish Unitarian Church in Norwell, Massachusetts. She addresses her readers with a range of endearments, including "darlings," "my revered pigeons," "kittens," and "my pets." Blog posts include examples of especially good fashion choices on the part of clergy, images of garments that would be appropriate in clergy wardrobes, critiques of dowdy or inappropriate ministerial outfits, and answers to readers' questions.

What keeps the blog from being either frivolous or harsh is Weinstein's consistent recognition that female clergy occupy a professional and theological space that requires them to respond to a long and often critical tradition. In a post titled "Too 'Hot' for Ministry?" Weinstein offers advice for young, female members of the clergy who have been instructed to tone down their attire because someone, perhaps the senior pastor, considers them too attractive. She writes, "Document EVERY word you can remember from that first meeting and before you do a thing about shopping, call in another pair of eyes to assess your wardrobe and appearance. It may, in fact be that you DO need some sprucing up. It may also be that your supervisor is trying to shame you for being a hottie. Don't fly off the handle; walk carefully and govern your angry thoughts. We serve a monumentally sex-phobic institution, my darlings—this should neither surprise nor enrage you. Be ye wise as a serpent and . . . you know the rest." In the remainder of the post, Weinstein offers practical advice on how to navigate this especially thorny situation.

The purpose of the blog becomes clear when Weinstein reflects on the connection between professional appearance and what it means for congregants to have their pastor present in the room. She writes, "I guess what I am trying to say is that in some way, our ministerial bodies are not just personal but are also communal. This may be neither rational nor fair, chickens, but that's just how it is. When one of our beloveds is dying, it's not just anybody who shows up who can represent the church. It's when your particular body shows up that the Church is there at bedside. You know it, I know it and God knows it. When you become a 'Rev.,' your body isn't just your body anymore. Maybe not fair or rational, but I think that's how it works." *Beauty Tips for Ministers* is not only about how the pastor ought to look, but about why it matters.

Thus what separates Weinstein's approach from secular guides to professional dress are, first, her ability to exercise pastoral care in guiding her readers and, second, her clear conviction that having (and dressing) a female body does not interfere with a pastor's vocation. Indeed, Weinstein argues that for female clergy dressing one's body ought to reflect both affirmation of one's gender and acknowledgment of the leadership role of clergy within the community. She identifies the tendency of some female clergy to efface their gender and/or sexuality in their professional attire and argues that this approach does no one any favors; instead, she advocates for a model of religious womanhood that is frankly feminine, and simultaneously highly professional and even sartorially conservative. In so doing, Weinstein presents a deeply feminist view of religious vocation: she holds not only that women are suitable to be clergy but also that women can most powerfully embody their vocational calling when also attending to the care of their own bodies.

Courtney Wilder (PhD, University of Chicago Divinity School) teaches in the Religion and Philosophy Department of Midland Lutheran College, an ELCA institution in Fremont, Nebraska. She is a past junior fellow at the Martin Marty Center.

46. Jim Wallis on Morals and Values

FEBRUARY 1, 2010
BY MARTIN E. MARTY

In 1957, young Harvard-bred historian Timothy Smith, of the Church of the Nazarene, knocked a lot of us budding ordinary historians—secular, "mainstream," and whatnot—off our library stools with his book *Revivalism and Social Reform*. We had been trained to look for the roots of American social Christianity in the liberal Protestant Social Gospel (post-1907) and progressive Catholicism (post-1919). Smith backdated such movements by a half-century, to revivals around 1857, which, he argued, added concern for morality and ethics in the social order to the private-and-personal moral agenda of older evangelicalism. Having fought against dueling, profanity, Sunday mails, et cetera, these revivalists found new ways to address slavery, poverty, and inequality. Imperfect, they did chart a course.

Smith died in 1997, but historians in his train often remind us of how things were back when evangelicals were evangelical and not Evangelical, as if a quasi-political party. These years their ancient cause—dated from the eighth century before Christ, among the Hebrew prophets—is revived on many fronts. This week we will sight one of them, Jim Wallis's *Sojourners,* which we have been reading for two-score years. This is not a blurb for the magazine—*Sightings* sights, it does not blurb—but it is time we put into print (or online) some notice of the kind of concern it's shown through the decades. Jim and a colleague dropped by the other day for a chat, in the week when he'd made a repeat visit to *The Daily Show* with Jon Stewart, and we made up a bit for lost time.

The Martys welcome all kinds of company, even someone like Wallis, whom Christian anti-Communist Crusaders (there are still such) call "pro-Marxist, pro-Communist, even pro-Socialist," the third of which is a term applied to anyone to the left of Genghis Khan these days. Wallis was on a book tour for his new *Rediscovering Values on Wall Street, Main Street, and Your Street: A Moral Compass for the New Economy*. This is not a blurb for the book—*Sightings* sights, it does not blurb—but he gave us a theme for the week, as did a chapter from the book in the February *Sojourners*. His choice of words like "values" and "morals" instead of "biblical" or "Christian" may enlarge the zone of discourse, but he has not left his evangelicalism behind.

Wallis has always been puzzled by the way some Evangelicals specialize in quoting the six biblical verses which refer or may refer to homosexuality, but consider it out of bounds for believers to notice the six hundred or six thousand that reference Mammon, money, riches-and-poverty. Like the ancient prophets, he names names: not Edom and Moab, Assyria and Babylon, but Goldman Sachs, Bank of America, and Citigroup, which, bailed out with the public's money, had rewarded themselves at the time he wrote with $8.66 billion (that's $8,660 million) in bonuses, while, Wallis adds, "the average bank teller at Bank of America makes only $10.73 an hour, or just over $22,000 a year."

He notices that the financial services industry spent $223 million lobbying Congress to fight any regulations or restrictions. (He wrote that before the recent Supreme Court decision that will allow the banking industry and others to advertise and lobby and influence Congress in amounts that will make that $223 million look like peanuts.) You get the idea. Next week *Sightings* may be back to appraising our moral framework from a crypto-capitalist viewpoint. After all, we'll now have to do something compensatory lest this column get typed as—gasp!—not "prophetic" but—sh-h-h-h!—populist.

Resource

Wallis, Jim. *Rediscovering Values on Wall Street, Main Street, and Your Street: A Moral Compass for the New Economy*. New York: Howard Books, 2010.

47. Keeping on the Sunny Side: Southern Traditionalism's Bid for Academic Respectability and Tolerance

FEBRUARY 4, 2010
BY JOHN HOWELL

According to a December 6, 2009, article for *The Chronicle of Higher Education*, entitled "Scholars Nostalgic for the Old South Study the Virtues of Secession, Quietly," genteel Southern traditionalism is having a coming-out party. In the article, writer Ben Terris calls the attention of the *Chronicle*'s readership to the upcoming annual conference of the Abbeville Institute—"an association of scholars in higher education devoted to a critical study of what is true and valuable in the Southern tradition"—which will convene in early February 2010 and focus on the issues of secession and nullification. Importantly, Terris notes, the institute is for the first time choosing to advertise its annual meeting, heretofore a closeted affair, publicly.

Any Southern traditionalist organization resides somewhere on a continuum with proponents of a white-supremacy-tinted political secessionism at one end; and, at the other, expositors of an Old South ideal that they see as cleft from the inessential legacies of race hatred, chattel slavery, and direct political action. The Abbeville Institute places itself at the latter end of this continuum: they claim a work that is "philosophic in nature, namely to explore the metaphysical image of things human and divine to which the Southern tradition bears witness." While most Southern traditionalist organizations are legatees of the Lost Cause—a civil religious discourse extant during the post–Civil War epoch in American history (roughly 1865-1920) that figures the American South as an embattled redeemer nation—the Abbeville Institute chooses to retrieve from the Lost Cause only the notion that the Old South ideal furnishes a spiritual principle, and an aesthetic sensibility, that ought to be missionary in American society writ large. It claims to leave behind both the hope of a future political secession and Southern traditionalism's historical association with white supremacy.

But despite Abbeville's insistent language concerning its relationship to the Old South ideal, Terris's article suggests that there is no small amount of anxiety concerning its debut in a broader academic public. Terris reports that Donald Livingston, the institute's founding father and professor of philosophy at Emory University in Atlanta, declined to publish a complete group roster out of a concern for the potential professional implications of being on such a list, and Livingston himself was chary of sitting for the interview. One can read this anxiety on Livingston's own face: Billy Howard's photograph of Livingston, which appears atop the article, has Livingston breaching the window-framed boundary between the public, sunlit foreground of a weather-beaten barn wall and the dark background of the building's interior (where the majority of his body, unseen, resides). He's unsure of his hands. He appears discomfited, threatened, by the auditor's gaze.

Interestingly, there is tension between the language Livingston uses in the article to describe the institute's position relative to the wider academic world and the language used on the institute's website to describe its mission. The website spurns the "ideologies of multiculturalism and political correctness," which are quick to suspect any attempt to retrieve a Southern tradition as an apologetic for slavery or racism, but in Terris's article, Livingston leverages the very logic of multiculturalism in his bid for legitimacy and respectability. What the institute wants, it seems, is a seat at the table of cultural pluralism. It wants the heritors of a Southern tradition to be permitted to speak in their own voices, to control their own narrative. Livingston figures Southern traditionalism as the constitutive outside of a multicultural universal that fails on its own terms because it judges the perspective of Southern traditionalists as unfit (unsafe?) for self-representation: "The Southern tradition as taught in the academy today, if taught at all, is studied mainly as a function of the ideological needs of others. . . . It is not examined in terms of its own inner light. It is as if you had programs of Jewish studies explored from the point of view of Catholics, or worse, of Nazis." When Livingston speaks of the Southern tradition's "inner light," however, he evokes a notion of culture that harkens back to Matthew Arnold's in *Culture and Anarchy*—wherein *culture* is a generic descriptor and *Culture* signifies a better-than-yours master culture, graced as it is with "sweetness and light"—thereby threatening the institute's capacity to participate in, or to leverage, a logic that refuses the gradated arrangement of cultures.

It will be interesting to see the fruits of the Abbeville Institute's new-found publicity—whether the fears of professional retribution will prove to have been warranted or whether the advance publication of those fears will shame what the institute sees as multiculturalism's hypocrisy. And it will be interesting to see whether the institute will regret forsaking the insular comfort of relatively private conferences with a camp meeting atmosphere for the chance at wider purchase.

Resources

Arnold, Matthew. *Culture and Anarchy*. New Haven: Yale University Press, 1994.

Terris, Ben. "Scholars Nostalgic for the Old South Study the Virtues of Secession, Quietly." *The Chronicle of Higher Education*. December 9, 2009. https://www.chronicle.com/article/Secretive-Scholars-of-the-Old/49337.

Wilson, Charles Reagan. *Baptized in Blood: The Religion of the Lost Cause, 1868–1920*. Athens, GA: University of Georgia Press, 1980.

John Howell is a PhD candidate in religion and literature at the University of Chicago Divinity School writing a dissertation on the proper signification of the generic epithet, "Civil War literature."

48. Cuts in the Humanities

MAY 10, 2010
BY MARTIN E. MARTY

"Why cuts in humanities teaching pose a threat to democracy itself" is the subhead for an article titled "Skills for life" in the April 30 *Times Literary Supplement*, authored by the University of Chicago's (and the world's) Martha Nussbaum. Such headlines can evoke everything from an "Oh, come now!" to a yawn among those who are not professionals in the humanities, or those who are oblivious of them, who often seem to be "almost everybody." And they raise the question: What does that have to do with "public religion," which we keep in our sights for *Sightings*? In a world of religion-connected explosions and conflicts, why sit back for a week and take on such a quiet, scholarly subject?

"Humanities" have officially belonged in our scope since 1965 when President Johnson signed into law a bill creating the National Endowment for the Humanities, in which Congress listed "literature, history, languages, archaeology, philosophy," et cetera, including "comparative religion." We were not all sure what that two-word discipline included, recalling Archbishop William Temple's quip that "there is no such thing as comparative religion"; there are only people who are "comparatively religious." Still, we all snuggled under the tent-roof of the humanities, seeing religious studies prosper a little bit and religion find some place in public programs nationally and in all fifty states. And now?

"We are in the midst of a crisis of massive proportions and grave global significance. I do not mean the global economic crisis.... I mean a crisis that goes largely unnoticed, but is likely to be, in the long run, far more damaging to the future of democratic self-government, a worldwide crisis in education," which hits the humanities hardest. A crisis worse than the economic one? Again, "Oh, come now, Professor Nussbaum!" Is she crying wolf? I was on the Commission on the Humanities between 1978 and 1980, and got used to seeing the words "Crisis in ..." always connected with the noun "the Humanities." This time is it worse, is it scarier? Nussbaum makes her case.

Part of the crisis is *within* the humanities, as critics among the disciplines question the turns some of them have taken toward postmodern nihilism and anti-humanism. But while the professors are fighting among themselves over such, colleges and universities are cutting back hiring, budgets, curricula, and set-priorities in them globally. As Nussbaum shows, much of the higher academic redirection is motivated by societal interest in developing nothing but market-ready professions, to prepare citizenries for soulless if techno-logically adept and sophisticated cultures. There is a low premium placed on wider and deeper forms of knowledge. Nussbaum: "Knowledge is no guaran-tee of good behavior, but ignorance is a virtual guarantee of bad behavior."

Relevant to our subject, she adds: "Responsible citizenship . . . re-quires the ability . . . to appreciate the complexities of the major world re-ligions." Some Americans talk a good line about such matters, and others find it opportune to dis-appreciate such complexities in all religions but one's own—attacking one or another of them as "evil" and wicked, from top to bottom, thus promoting ignorance and hatred, which exacerbate con-flict. "Today we still maintain that we like democracy and self-governance, and we also think that we like freedom of speech, respect for difference, and understanding of others. We give these values lip service, but we think far too little about what we need to do in order to transmit them to the next generation and ensure their survival." Time to hug your English teachers or philosophers, and support them, against all odds? Yes.

Resource

Nussbaum, Martha. "Skills for Life: Why Cuts in Humanities Teaching Pose a Threat to Democracy Itself." *Times Literary Supplement*. April 30, 2010. [Ed. Note: this article consists of an edited excerpt from Nussbaum's book *Not for Profit: Why Democracy Needs the Humanities* (Princeton: Princeton University Press, 2010).]

49. The Persecution of Religious Minorities in Iraq

JUNE 10, 2010
BY SHATHA ALMUTAWA

About a thousand years ago, a group of Iraqi philosophers in Basra wrote a dialogue between a Muslim in hell and a Muslim in heaven. The Muslim in heaven asked the Muslim in hell what he had done that led him to hell. The Muslim in hell responded that he tried to convert people who did not believe in what he believed, and if they did not agree, he used force against them, killing those who did not yield.

It was the Muslim in hell who waged war against those who didn't follow his creed, not the Muslim in heaven. The story shows that even a thousand years ago, tolerance and peace were valued by Muslims, even though there were always those who chose violence. The philosophical encyclopedia in which this story appears, *Rasa'il Ikhwan al-Safa'*, or the *Epistles of the Brethren of Purity*, was read by Muslims, Christians, and Jews not only in Iraq but throughout the medieval Muslim world, valued especially by the Arab-speaking Jews of Muslim Spain.

But the Iraq of the tenth century is not the Iraq of 2010, a country that is overrun by violent militias, where more than 1,200 suicide bombings have taken place since 2003. Despite the tyranny of Saddam Hussein's rule and the violence following the 2003 US invasion, Iraq still remains a cradle of many religions, but a rather dangerous one. Besides Sunni and Shia Muslims, today's Iraq boasts at least six denominations of Christianity, a small Jewish population, and several lesser-known religious groups such as the Yazidis, Shabaks, and Sabean-Mandaeans.

After the Coalition Provisional Authority dissolved the Iraqi military and police force in 2003, militias took over the streets of Iraq, persecuting minorities. With the withdrawal of the US military from Iraqi cities last June, violence intensified in some regions, such as the Nineveh province. Suicide bombings targeted Shabaks and Yazidis, whose religion is influenced by Sufism and Christianity and who are considered heretics by some Muslims.

According to a Human Rights Watch report, the Chaldean Archbishop Paulus Faraj Rahho was kidnapped and later killed in Mosul in 2008. A year earlier Friar Ragheed Ganni and three deacons were shot, and Friar Mundhir Al-Dayr of the Protestant Church was killed in 2006.

But it is not only religious leaders who are targeted. Graffiti on walls tells Christians to leave, loudspeakers from cars spout death threats, and individuals are approached on the street or in their homes, asked what their religion is, and then shot if they give the "wrong" answer. Christians have been fleeing Iraq ever since, their numbers decreasing from one million in 2003 to about half a million now.

What could be causing this violence? Surely there are many factors, including a lack of transparency on the part of the Iraqi government that allows vigilante crimes to take place without consequence; corruption in the same government; as well as abject poverty and a lack of jobs, causing young, unemployed men to be lured by extremists.

With a new government forming in Iraq, new leaders must take steps to protect religious minorities. In addition to addressing the circumstances above, they can stop printing religious affiliation on identity cards, disarm militias, investigate the murders and kidnappings of religious minorities, and do more to bring perpetrators to justice, for the safety and dignity of all citizens.

Resources

Corn, David. "Secret Report: Corruption Is 'Norm' within Iraqi Government." *The Nation.* August 30, 2007. https://www.thenation.com/article/secret -report-corruption-norm-within-iraqi-government.

Elliott, Debbie, and Corey Flintoff. "Report Reveals Corruption in Iraqi Government." NPR. September 1, 2007. http://www.npr.org/templates/story/story .php?storyId=14117853.

Fisk, Robert. "The Cult of the Suicide Bomber." *The Independent.* March 14, 2008. http://www.independent.co.uk/opinion/commentators/fisk/robert -fisk-the-cult-of-the-suicide-bomber-795649.html.

"Iraq: Civilians under Fire." Amnesty International. 2010. https://www.amnesty usa.org/iraq-civilians-under-fire.

"Iraq Corruption 'Costs Billions.'" BBC News. November 9, 2006. http://news .bbc.co.uk/2/hi/6131290.stm.

"On Vulnerable Ground: Violence against Minority Community in Nineveh Province's Disputed Territories." Human Rights Watch. November 10, 2009. http://www.hrw.org/en/reports/2009/11/10/vulnerable-ground.

Shatha Almutawa is Iraq country specialist for Amnesty International USA. She is a PhD candidate at the University of Chicago Divinity School, where she studies Muslim and Jewish intellectual history.

50. Franklin Graham on Islam and Violence

September 13, 2010
By Martin E. Marty

Aestas horribilis, Queen Elizabeth might call the summer just past, or those who care about civility in religious discourse and interfaith relations might judge it to have been. While *Sightings* took August off, forces, agencies, and voices of prejudice, and, frankly, hate-mongering, did not. "Protest mosques," "Restore America," "Burn Qur'ans," and many more are keywords in our internet memory. One set of these keywords is so illuminating and nearly normative that it merits comment before we enter a new but not necessarily more promising season. I refer to the pronouncements of evangelist Franklin Graham on Muslim genetics, competition for souls, Islam as killer, and scriptures.

Genetics first: There is no need to repeat Graham's bizarre charge that Islam is passed through the genes of a father to a son. Scholars of Islam find that idea nowhere in its teachings. Conversion expert Graham should understand that one becomes a Muslim the way the born-again in Graham's tradition become Christians: by making a profession of faith and a commitment through word and action. We won't go into the political dimension of this issue with reference to Graham's subject, the president of the United States, because, as long-time readers know, Monday *Sightings* does not "do" presidents.

Competition for souls, second: Graham's work is often positioned along lines crossed in Africa, where Muslims kill Christians and Christians kill Muslims. There is little point in going into "Who fired first?" or "Who killed most?" In religion-based warfare, there is never really a first and a second; there are only debates about first and second. Graham has chosen to attempt conversion in the second-most-tense area known to the two faith communities. Without doubt, there is ugliness and murder, but we picture militant Muslims speaking of Christians the way Graham speaks of Muslims. Call it a draw. (By the way, "the undersigned" is a Christian who sees a place for evangelism.)

Islam as killer of Christians, third: Graham has repeatedly charged this year that Islam, which he frequently calls "a very wicked and evil religion," is mandated to kill and that it kills. He does not qualify his remarks, as the word "very" suggests and even though he is often cautioned about the possible lethal consequences for Christians and Muslims if things get more heated. Historians have no difficulty finding Muslims in killing mode. The problem is that historians also find Christians in killing mode, from most years of Christendom, when the sword advanced Christianity, down into our own time. Think of the Christian justifications in World War I. Think Christians killing Christians in Rwanda, Northern Ireland, and elsewhere.

Fourth, scriptures: It is easy to find passages in the Qur'an and other classic Muslim texts in which Allah's people may or should kill to advance God's cause. Isolating these chunks of the Qur'an which are by now most familiar to Americans calls for overlooking Islam's many peace-promoting texts. And it also means overlooking parallel biblical texts. There are far more pictures in the biblical texts of a warrior God licensing and, yes, commanding "omnicide," the killing of men and women and children who stand in the path of God's people. Yes, all that was long ago. Now, you will never (at least I never) find Jews or Christians who think that killing people of another faith is a scriptured mandate for them.

Let's hope and work for a less horrifying autumn.

51. The Shtetl Strongman

December 9, 2010
By Sarah Imhoff

Nothing telegraphs nostalgia quite like sepia tones. The new children's book *Zishe the Strongman* paints the life of an early twentieth-century Jewish entertainer with equal parts longing and joy. Based on the real-life strong-man Siegmund Breitbart, Zishe grows from a child who can snap chains and bend iron bars with his bare hands into an internationally renowned circus performer who pulls a cart of ten men down Broadway using his teeth. "But," the tale goes, "Zishe was also quite gentle." As a child, "he loved small animals. He would hold tiny mice in his hands." (The accompanying illustration shows a smiling mouse proudly flexing his biceps for Zishe.) It is no surprise that *Zishe* appears on many lists of the best gifts for Hanukkah—the celebration of the Maccabees, those other historical paragons of Jewish strength.

What is it about Zishe that appeals to American Jewish parents? Is it nostalgia for the shtetl? The kippah-adorned blacksmith and joyous countenances of the children of Łódź indicate that the shtetl's prominent place in the American Jewish imagination remains intact. But the tale also suggests the romanticization of a simpler time of uncomplicated masculinity. Zishe embodies a strength utterly devoid of ties to violence or even competition. He "used his strength to haul and carry things for others" and then used the money for cello lessons. As an entertainer, he tossed children in the air and used his chest to support boards that elephants would plod across.

In real life, Siegmund Breitbart was an ardent Zionist. He looked up not only to the biblical Samson but also to the militant Bar Kokhba, who led a heroic and bloody revolt against Roman rule in 132 CE. Before his death in 1925, Breitbart planned an international sports league for Jews but one that had much broader political implications: he imagined that it would incorporate military training and ultimately facilitate the creation of a Jewish army which could conquer Palestine. He was outspoken in his admiration for Vladimir Jabotinsky, the militant Zionist and former British officer who famously advocated, "Jewish youth, learn to shoot!"

But the only traces of this Zishe are relegated to a text-filled informational back page of the book; it emphasizes a 1924 *New York Times* article that claimed he wouldn't hurt a worm, but nowhere mentions Bar Kokhba,

Jabotinsky, or the goal of seizing Palestine by force. The story and illustrations prefer the gentle mouse-holding, cello-playing specimen of manhood.

Hanukkah toys and gifts have not always shied away from celebrating military victory and physical dominance. Our Zishe is not the Hanukkah games of earlier decades like "Valor against Oppression" featuring "latter-day Maccabee" Moshe Dayan; he is not even the Monopoly-esque "Race Dreidel" that promised that "every Jewish boy and girl thrills to hear the heroic story of the Maccabees." Although *Zishe the Strongman* is not explicitly Hanukkah-themed (or, perhaps, because it is not Hanukkah-themed), it can present an American model of historical Jewish masculinity for boys to emulate. Books aimed at young boys so often make obvious otherwise implicit goals of masculinity, and *Zishe* suggests that American Jewish parents sought a romanticized shtetl masculinity: simple, strong, and gentle. American Hanukkah celebrations often emphasize the miracle of the oil while de-emphasizing the Israeli military, especially given the current conditions of occupation and the gorier parts of the Maccabean victory, both of which offer a much more complex version of what it means to become a Jewish man.

American parents today, despite widespread support for Israel, may feel ambivalence about teaching their boys to emulate Dayan. But the experience of besiegement and the necessity of military action also fail to resonate with the majority of American Jews. Mainstream Zionism in America lacks the David versus Goliath quality of the Maccabees or even the early state of Israel. *Zishe the Strongman*, on the other hand, represents a world of moral clarity. For Zishe, there is no fight at all: no David, no Goliath, no Maccabees, no Egypt or Syria. He demonstrates his strength through entertainment and brings joy to "his fellow Jews" everywhere. In many ways, even with its romance and nostalgia, then, this tale of Zishe resonates with American Jewish life. And it certainly represents a desire for a world with a simpler legacy of Jewish masculinity, one where every boy can grow up to be like Zishe: "His heart was as great as his strength."

Resources

Gillerman, Sharon. "Samson in Vienna: The Theatrics of Jewish Masculinity." *Jewish Social Studies* 9, no. 2 (January 2003): 65–98.

Joselit, Jenna Weisman. *The Wonders of America: Reinventing Jewish Culture, 1880–1950*. New York: Henry Holt, 1994.

Rubinstein, Robert. *Zishe the Strongman*. Minneapolis: Kar-Ben, 2010.

Sarah Imhoff (PhD, University of Chicago Divinity School) is visiting assistant professor in the Borns Jewish Studies Program at Indiana University Bloomington.

52. Good Sufi, Bad Muslims

January 27, 2011
By Omid Safi

One of the lower points in the Park51 Center controversy was the comment by New York governor David Paterson: "This group who has put this mosque together, they are known as the Sufi Muslims. This is not like the Shiites. . . . They're almost like a hybrid, almost westernized. They are not really what I would classify in the sort of mainland Muslim practice."

In a few short sentences, the governor managed to offend Sufis, Shi'i Muslims, as well as westernized Muslims, non-westernized Muslims, and "mainland Muslims" (whoever they are). Paterson overlooked the fact that some Shi'i Muslims are mystically inclined, and that six million American citizens are Muslims; thus there is no question of "westernizing" or "almost westernizing" for them. There is a more disturbing implication hiding in his assertion: the ongoing way in which the general demonization of Muslims, of the kind now routine on Fox News, is accompanied by an equally pernicious game of Good Muslim, Bad Muslims.

There are many versions of this game, but the basic contour stays the same: the assertion that the general masses of Muslims are evil, terrorist supporters, anti-Western, patriarchal, misogynist, undemocratic, and anti-Semitic; and that these masses are set off and defined against the solitary, lone good Muslim woman or man. The "good Muslim" is usually an individual, or at most a small circle, because to admit that the larger group of Muslims could be on the right side of the human rights divide is to have the house of cards of the Muslim demonization game collapse on itself.

There are endless scenarios of this fictitious bifurcation: *Reading Lolita in Tehran* is "good Muslim"; unspoken, nameless, faceless masses of Muslims are patriarchal, bad Muslims. Irshad Manji is an Israel-loving "good Muslim" who suggests that Muslims could be blamed for the Holocaust, while the majority of Muslims are bad Muslims. Salman Rushdie and Orhan Pamuk are "good" secular or ex-Muslims, defined against the masses of Muslims. It is worth noting how easily and how frequently the "good Muslim" solitary figure ends up being prominently featured on the op-ed pages of *The New York Times*.

Sarah Palin famously addressed "Peace-seeking Muslims" on Twitter: "pls understand, Ground Zero mosque is UNNECESSARY provocation; it stabs hearts. Pls reject it in interest of healing." In her inarticulate bifurcation, supporters of Park51 were defined as being outside the "peace-seeking" Muslim category.

The latest version of this bifurcation game of Good Muslim, Bad Muslims is that of pitting Muslim mystics (Sufis) as the "good Muslims" against the majority of Muslims cast as villains. Sufi tradition offers incredible reservoirs for mercy, love, and pluralism. Yet it is inaccurate, and politically appropriative, to present Sufism as disconnected from politics or wider social concerns at best and as agents of the Empire at worst.

This type of presentation was prominent in the discussion about Imam Feisal Abdul Rauf, the visionary American Muslim leader behind Park51. Time and again in the presentation of Imam Feisal and his wife Daisy Khan, we were reminded by *The New York Times* that they represented Sufi Islam, a gentle kind of Islam, nothing like the scary monster of political Islam: "He [Abdul Rauf] was asked to lead a Sufi mosque." Daisy Khan is described as "looking for a gentler Islam than the politicized version she rejected after Iran's revolution." Another *New York Times* article was even more explicit in marking the couple as worthy "good Muslims": "They founded a Sufi organization advocating melding Islamic observance with women's rights and modernity."

The suggestion that Sufi teachings are somehow immune to politics, that Sufis have been unconcerned with social issues and questions of justice and politics, is problematic. Historically speaking, Sufis have been fully engaged in both challenging political powers and alternately legitimizing political power throughout their history. The legacy of prominent Sufis like Abu Sa'id Abi 'l-Khayr has been used in legitimizing political powers, and Sufis such as 'Ayn al-Qudat Hamadani and Abd al-Qadir al-Jaza'iri have spoken truth to power. In both cases, Sufis have not remained aloof from politics.

The Park51 controversy exposes many underlying assumptions about religion in the public space and politics, particularly in the case of Muslims, who are given two options in this superficial bifurcation game: to be politically destructive in the manner of terrorists or "Islamists," or to be politically quietist, acquiescing in the face of power. In this "Good Sufi, Bad Muslims" dichotomy, Sufis are asked to line up in the politically quietist camp, so that they can be validated.

This dichotomy ignores a third group of Muslims: those who, whether mystically inclined or not, want neither to destroy the world nor to acquiesce to the wishes of the Empire, but rather seek to redeem the world by speaking truth to power. This group speaks out of the love of God and cries out for the suffering of humanity, defiantly and prophetically standing up for justice and liberation.

And here is where the canard of "moderate Muslims" comes into play. Ever since 9/11, we have been asked time and again where the "moderate Muslims" are and why they are silent. No matter how often, and how loudly, Muslim organizations and individuals condemn terrorism, the likes of Thomas Friedman can still famously, and inaccurately, state: "The Muslim village has been derelict in condemning the madness of jihadist attacks. . . . To this day—to this day—no major Muslim cleric or religious body has ever issued a fatwa condemning Osama bin Laden." No presentation of factual data seems to persuade these critics that Muslims did, do, and will continue to speak out loudly and officially against terrorism. The reason their critics do not hear the moderate Muslims is because they are not listening.

Moving beyond the question of Muslims condemning terrorism, there is the larger question of what exactly makes someone a "moderate" Muslim? In its current usage, the term "moderate Muslim" is as meaningful as a purple polka dot unicorn. If the term "moderate" implies a balancing point between two extremes, it is a hopelessly vague term in the post-9/11 landscape. If one of the two extremes away from the "moderate Muslims" is easy to imagine (terrorism, bin Laden, et cetera), the other extreme is ill-defined. What are moderate Muslims moderating? If one extreme is terrorism, then what is the other extreme?

"Moderate Muslims" are often defined, and confined, to be supporters of US foreign policy, vis-à-vis some important issues, such as supporting US global military presence, the wars in Iraq and Afghanistan, and the Palestinian-Israeli conflict. To dare suggest that the United States is today the world's only military empire with hundreds of military bases in other countries, or that we have in fact become the military-industrial complex that Eisenhower warned us about, or heaven forbid, that the Palestinians suffer from decades-long, unbearable occupation and violations of human rights, is to define one outside the safe (and lucrative) zone of "moderate Muslim." Sadly, even the safe zone is not so safe. Imam Feisal has been sent on political missions abroad by the State Department, yet even he was not safe from being branded by Fox News as a terrorist sympathizer.

If our public discourse about religion and politics is to evolve to a more subtle, and accurate, space, it must get to the point where religious voices that speak from the depths and heights of all spiritual traditions can do more than simply acquiesce in the face of the Empire. They can, and should, speak for the weak and give voice to the voiceless.

Resources

Friedman, Thomas L. "If It's a Muslim Problem, It Needs a Muslim Solution." *The New York Times*. July 8, 2005. http://www.nytimes.com/2005/07/08/opinion /if-its-a-muslim-problem-it-needs-a-muslim-solution.html.

Grynbaum, Michael M. "Daisy Khan, an Eloquent Face of Islam." *The New York Times*. November 12, 2010. http://www.nytimes.com/2010/11/14/fashion /14khan.html.

Keshavarz, Fatemeh. *Jasmine and Stars: Reading More Than "Lolita" in Tehran.* Chapel Hill: University of North Carolina Press, 2008.

Kurzman, Charles. "Islamic Statements against Terrorism." Personal website at the University of North Carolina. http://kurzman.unc.edu/islamic -statements-against-terrorism.

Mamdani, Mahmood. *Good Muslim, Bad Muslim: America, the Cold War, and the Roots of Terror.* New York: Three Rivers Press, 2005.

"Paterson: Mosque Developers 'Hybrid, Almost Westernized' Muslims." CBS New York. August 26, 2010. http://newyork.cbslocal.com/2010/08/26 /paterson-mosque-developers-hybrid-almost-westernized-muslims.

Safi, Omid. *The Politics of Knowledge in Premodern Islam.* Chapel Hill: University of North Carolina Press, 2006.

Omid Safi is professor of religious studies at the University of North Carolina. He served as the chair of the Study of Islam Section at the American Academy of Religion from 2002 to 2009.

53. The Chinese House Church Goes Public

MAY 12, 2011
BY FENGGANG YANG

On Easter Sunday, Shouwang (show-won) Church in Beijing planned to hold an outdoor worship service in a plaza amid high-rise office and commercial buildings. However, the police sealed off the plaza and dispelled gathering congregants, as they had done twice before. Thirty-six of the congregants were taken to police stations for interrogation.

Two Sundays earlier, 159 church members were rounded up in police buses and taken to police stations. While in custody, these Christians sang hymns together and shared the "good news" with the policemen when they were not being interrogated. The quiet confrontations between Shouwang Church and the Chinese government have received much media attention in the United States, Canada, and Europe, but so far the media have offered little to understand the burgeoning "house church" phenomenon in China.

Shouwang's confrontation with the government is not a political protest. It represents a spiritual revolution that has been sweeping the vast land of China. Shouwang is one of the large "house churches" in Beijing with about a thousand members, a majority of whom are college-educated young professionals who have converted to Christianity within the last two decades. Until the end of the 1980s, Christianity in China was very much a rural phenomenon and most Christians were old and feeble and had little formal education.

The phenomenon of "house churches" has mushroomed in urban areas since 1989, a fateful year that marks a turning point in Chinese history. The student-led pro-democracy movement was violently crushed by the Communist authorities who sent tanks rolling into Tiananmen Square on June 4, 1989. The 6·4 Tiananmen Incident, as it is commonly remembered by the Chinese, triggered a spiritual exodus from the Communist orthodoxy. Since then, while Chinese society has been transitioning to a market economy, many individuals have converted to Christianity. The founding pastor of Shouwang Church, Jin Tianming, was a college student at Tsinghua University from 1986 to 1991. After graduating, Tianming has dedicated himself to evangelism.

Like hundreds of "house churches" in Beijing that were formed in the 1990s, Shouwang started at Jin's apartment in 1993. When the Bible study and fellowship group grew to over two or three dozen people, it split into two groups, which in turn split further to accommodate the growth of the congregation. As a growing number of fellowship members got married and had children, it was no longer feasible to hold gatherings only at people's homes. Therefore, in 2005, a dozen or so fellowship groups conglomerated into one congregation and rented a large hall in an office building to hold Sunday School and worship services.

In 2006, Shouwang sought to register with the government as an independent church. However, the Religious Affairs Bureau of Beijing refused the registration unless Shouwang joined the Three-Self Patriotic Movement Committee (TSPM), the government-sanctioned body to oversee all Christian congregations. The literal meaning of "three-selfs" is "self-governance, self-support, and self-propagation." In reality, however, the TSPM was established as part of the control apparatus of the Communist authorities.

After TSPM forced all churches to cut off ties with Western churches, it further disbanded all denominations in 1957. This means that one could be a Christian in China, but it is illegal to be a Baptist, an Episcopalian, a Lutheran, a Presbyterian, or a Methodist. As a reaction to the forced "union service" under TSPM, some Christian leaders and believers simply stopped attending church and began to worship at home. The "house church" was born, and the "house church Christians" held steadfast in the political turmoil from the 1950s to the 1970s and have led Christian revivals since the 1970s. Shouwang leaders consider themselves spiritual heirs of the "house churches" and thus will not compromise the church's independence to join the TSPM.

On the other hand, the Chinese Communist authorities continue to cling to the religious policy that was initially formulated in the 1950s. Since 2008, the government has made multiple attempts to break down Shouwang and other large "house churches." Three weeks ago, the church was evicted from their rental place. As the last hope to win back their constitutional right of religious belief, Shouwang has gone public. But as of now, the plaza has been off limits to the Shouwang Church on Sundays. This and other "public squares" have been sealed off under Communist rule in China.

Resources

Yang, Fenggang. *Chinese Christians in America: Conversion, Assimilation, and Adhesive Identities*. University Park: Penn State University Press, 1999.

———. "Lost in the Market, Saved at McDonald's: Conversion to Christianity in Urban China." *Journal for the Scientific Study of Religion* 44, no. 4 (2005): 423–41.

Fenggang Yang is professor of sociology and director of the Center on Religion and Chinese Society at Purdue University.

54. Shrine Destruction in Bahrain

JUNE 9, 2011
BY MICHAEL SELLS

Governments and non-government forces destroy houses of worship in order to marginalize, silence, or eliminate peoples associated with the shrines and to efface visual and tangible reminders of the targeted traditions. Although shrine destruction is meant to silence the people associated with the targeted shrines, the destruction itself can also witness to the repressive activities even after arrests, secret courts, disappearances, and killings have muted human testimonies. It is relatively easy—at least in the short term—to mask the extent of human repression or to justify politically motivated arrests or killings as a response to violent attacks; but shrines do not carry out violent acts and their destruction leaves a gaping hole in the landscape that is difficult to conceal. The absent presence of houses of worship discredits the denials by responsible authorities regarding other aspects of repression. In Tibet, the Balkans, Pakistan, Afghanistan, and the Gujarat province of India—to mention a few notorious examples of the past half century—brutality against houses of worship was accompanied by equal brutality against human beings associated with them.

In recent weeks, dozens of Shi'ite mosques have fallen to a shrine-destruction campaign in the Gulf island kingdom of Bahrain. The Bahraini government and its supporters in Saudi Arabia and the United Arab Emirates have some explaining to do.

Bahrain experienced a premature end to its "Arab Spring" democracy movement. After witnesses sustained protests on behalf of electoral transparency, fairer parliamentary and government participation, and the inclusion of Bahrain's majority-Shi'ite population within the political process, Bahrain's government cracked down hard.

On March 14, the Gulf Cooperation Council—made up of Bahrain, Saudi Arabia, Kuwait, Oman, Qatar, and the United Arab Emirates—responded to Bahrain's request for military and police reinforcements by sending more than a thousand Saudi troops and several hundred UAE police. The next day, King Hamad bin Isa Al Khalifa declared a state of emergency in the island kingdom.

Roy Gutman, whose groundbreaking reports on human rights violations in Bosnia and North Alliance–controlled Afghanistan were subsequently vindicated, has reported from the Bahraini capital of Manama on what took place in the aftermath of the March 14 GCC intervention.

"Authorities have held secret trials where protesters have been sentenced to death," Gutman writes, "arrested prominent mainstream opposition politicians, jailed nurses and doctors who treated injured protesters, seized the health care system that had been run primarily by Shiites, fired 1,000 Shiite professionals and canceled their pensions, detained students and teachers who took part in the protests, beat and arrested journalists, and forced the closure of the only opposition newspaper."

Gutman's report also details some of the Shi'ite mosques that were targeted. They include the four-centuries-old Amir Mohammed Barbaghi mosque and the Momen mosque in the town of Nwaidrat, which appears in photos as "a handsome, square building neatly painted in ochre, with white and green trim, and a short portico in dark gray forming the main entrance."

Bahraini officials have denied charges of human rights violations, and they also deny targeting Shi'ite mosques for destruction. "These are not mosques. These are illegal buildings," the justice and Islamic affairs minister, Sheikh Khalid bin Ali bin Abdulla Al Khalifa, stated. "The mosques that have been demolished, most of them are not mosques. Very few numbers of mosques, which are illegally built, have been demolished," added Adel Al-Moawda, deputy chairman of the Bahraini parliament.

The Bahrain destruction carries some disturbingly regional traits. For several decades, authorities in Saudi Arabia, the Bahraini government's powerful supporter, have worked to obliterate Shi'ite heritage, particularly in the area around Medina. Mosques, cemeteries, and other sites held dear by Shi'ite citizens of Saudi Arabia or by Shi'ite pilgrims have been effaced or radically altered, and in many cases even the local street names have been changed to erase all signs that the shrines had once existed.

The elimination of monuments associated with Shi'ite piety ties into a wider, long-range policy in Saudi Arabia that has seen the elimination of all religious structures (or structures that might become places of veneration) viewed as unauthorized or forbidden by Islamic tradition or law as it has been interpreted by Saudi religious scholars. The program of shrine and potential shrine elimination has been ongoing throughout much of the nineteenth and twentieth centuries within areas on the Arabian peninsula under Saudi control, and—through Saudi aid agencies and through *dawa* (religious propagation) programs—other areas from the Balkans to Central Asia.

The Al Khalifa dynasty in Bahrain apparently felt itself in position to act with impunity. Bahrain, which hosts the US Fifth Fleet, occupies a strategic place within the decades-long and ruinous proxy conflicts between Saudi Arabia and Iran and between the United States and Iran, conflicts that have stoked violence across the Middle East. The NATO nations, already committed to a war in Libya and to economic support for Tunisia and Egypt, are not likely to exert public pressure on Bahrain. And the turmoil in the larger nations of Yemen and Syria drove Bahrain out of mainstream media coverage. For weeks, the pro-government *Gulf Daily News* has been content to complain that accusations of misconduct by Bahrain's authorities were unfair and to call for a major public relations campaign to improve Bahrain's image abroad, to assure the international business community that Bahrain remained a good investment, and even to persuade Formula 1 racing officials to allow Bahrain to host future events.

In his May 19 State Department address on the Middle East, Barack Obama apparently surprised Bahraini officials by condemning the mass arrests and mosque destructions they had authorized. Bahraini leaders quickly promised to rebuild the mosques they had insisted had never been destroyed in the first place.

The credibility of Bahrain's government will depend on whether and how they fulfill that promise and upon a transparent investigation into the charges of human rights abuses within the kingdom. The credibility of those who claim to support freedom of religion, expression, and public participation in the Arab world will rest in part on whether or not they return to business as usual in a Bahrain that, in the words of one columnist, has "toppled its own people." The viability of United States policy in the Middle East remains in part hostage, as it has for five decades, to its energy and security dependence upon the Kingdom of Saudi Arabia whose role in supporting the Bahraini government crackdown was not mentioned in Obama's address.

Resources

"Bahrain Targets Shia Religious Sites." Al-Jazeera. May 14, 2011. http://www.al jazeera.com/video/middleeast/2011/05/2011513112016389348.html.

Escobar, Pepe. "Bahrain Topples Its Own People." *Asia Times*. May 11, 2011. http://www.atimes.com/atimes/Middle_East/ME11Ak01.html.

Fleishman, Jeffrey. "Bahrain Is Accused of Targeting Shiites." *Los Angeles Times*. May 12, 2011.

"Full Text: Obama Speech." Al-Jazeera. May 19, 2011. http://english.aljazeera .net/news/americas/2011/05/2011519174053886277.html.

Gutman, Roy. "While Bahrain Demolishes Mosques, U.S. Stays Silent." Mc-Clatchy Newspapers. May 8, 2011.

Michael Sells is the John Henry Barrows Professor of Islamic History and Literature at the University of Chicago Divinity School.

55. *Machine Gun Preacher*

OCTOBER 3, 2011
BY MARTIN E. MARTY

Preachers, pastors, priests, rabbis, and imams number in the hundreds of thousands in the United States. They minister at the borders between what get tabbed "sacred" and "secular" realms, and as such cannot go unnoticed in public media. Some critics in the culture wars complain that they too often do go unnoticed. But most representations of them in movies and on television evoke, in the minds of those who have positive regard for clergy, George Bernard Shaw's often-paraphrased saying that there are two tragedies in life: not getting what we want, and getting what we want. "Not getting what 'we' want," whoever "we" are, used to be represented in comments that ministers, especially Protestants, usually came across as namby-pamby and culturally marginal types as if labeled "Handle with Care." They often appeared begowned and silver-coiffed, viewed over the groom's shoulder, saying, "I now pronounce you. . . . You may kiss the bride."

Everyone who knew, or was, a full-of-life cleric, resented that cultural posture. In today's world, however, most clergy representatives on film are not suave mainline clerics, beloved Irish-American priests, or wan and thin play-it-safe rabbis. Today, with the rise of presumably Protestant born-again studs, manipulators of people, and takers-of-the-law-into-their-own-hands types, we see images of lawbreakers with macho swagger. Those observations are background comments to this week's version of the sometimes-robed swashbucklers, in a film called *Machine Gun Preacher*. It was hard to evade reviews last weekend; two which found me were in our local *Chicago Sun-Times* and *Chicago Tribune*.

We don't need to review the reviews or condense all details of the plot. The regular run of characters surrounds the Rev. Sam Childers, his ex-stripper wife here "stuck with platitudes such as 'God gave you a purpose, Sam Childers.'" The movie is based on a book which is based on a (presumably) true-life story of a convict who gets violently "born again," thoroughly baptized, and self-licensed to pick up a gun and fight in defense of children in Sudan. Childers built an orphanage there, we are told and shown, and evidently does some good things for the kids. But that's not what the movie is about. To compete today, it has to be violent, and it is.

Michael Phillips in the *Chicago Tribune* deals with the scene in Sudan, personalizing it along the way. Here is how he voices the Gospel: "Staring down an enemy, [Childers] seethes: 'The Lord I serve is the living lord Jesus. And to show you he's alive, I'm going to send you to meet him right now!' Blam! Another enemy, smote." What does the viewer get to see in a plot plotted for today's American market? Ebert in the *Sun-Times*, on the reverend gun-slinger: he "is nothing but a one-dimensional rage machine." So the preacher and the filmmaker "can't wait to get to the ass-whipping part of this inspirational story, [which] lacks any real sense of how Childers underwent his staggering transformation." Well, "he isn't the first to go to war in the name of the Lord. . . . He's born again, yes, but he seems otherwise relatively unchanged. . . . He seems fueled more by anger than by spirituality." Until next week's violence-in-religion movie comes along, *Machine Gun Preacher* invites some pondering: Is this preacher what we wanted? And, if so, who are "we"?

Resources

Ebert, Roger. "Machine Gun Preacher." *Chicago Sun-Times*. September 28, 2011. https://www.rogerebert.com/reviews/machine-gun-preacher-2011.

Phillips, Michael. "Machine Gun Preacher: Man of God, Carnage—1½ Stars." *Chicago Tribune*. September 29, 2011.

56. *Commonweal*'s "Bishops and Religious Liberty"

JUNE 11, 2012
BY MARTIN E. MARTY

"The Bishops and Religious Liberty," the cover topic in *Commonweal* this week, brings together opinion by six Catholics who know their way around and through issues of "church and state." What prompts the issue is the action by Roman Catholic bishops in the United States to declare war against government proposals and policies which the bishops declare to be a war against liberty. While all the writers find something or other to criticize in administration concepts and actions on the health-care front, they all are critical of the bishops and ask them to "cool it," not to exploit the scene for political advantage, and more. Several critics also argue that the bishops are hurting, or likely to hurt, themselves, their church, and their cause, not because they are wholly wrong but because of their stridency and refusal to deal with the government when it adjusts and compromises. It's "winner take all" for them at the moment.

Let me lift out some summary sentences by the writers and editors. "There are compelling reasons within modern states to carve out a protected space for dissenting moral voices. But in the end, the tensions between the laws of the state and the demands of faith cannot be fully resolved." Amen. We've long argued that there is no way to draw lines between religion and the civil authorities (James Madison's term) in ways that can satisfy all legitimate but necessarily conflicting interests. William A. Galston, Michael P. Moreland, Cathleen Kaveny, Douglas Laycock, Mark Silk, and Peter Steinfels, authors whose names will be familiar to anyone who reads "church-state" arguments, have sympathy for the bishops but find their present arguments of no help. Thus the "bishops cannot base their teachings on opinion polls, but if they intend to argue effectively for religious liberty, they need to acknowledge the difficult ground on which they stand."

The ground is difficult partly because the wider public and Catholic faithful are highly aware that the bishops have not convinced their own faithful of their case, certainly as it is, against birth control; less every year on same-sex marriage; though they hold their own against (most cases of) abortion. Many Catholic theologians point out, as the authors in this *Com-*

monweal insist, the bishops are not making an argument; they are not even trying to make an argument. They are merely asserting, insisting, and declaring their viewpoint when they should set out to make their case. (Some of the arguments by some of the authors in *Commonweal* provide some arguments bishops could use.)

Since regular readers know that I do not butt in on intra-church arguments, I turn such over to *Sightings* readers. However, in this case—as in so many other church-state issues—the church leaders are engaging in public sector arguments and make no secret of the fact that they want directly to influence the forthcoming election, continuing legislation, and urgent court decisions. Peter Steinfels here reminds readers that Quakers, Jehovah's Witnesses, and, come to think about it, any other thoughtful and intense religious people, won't be able to have all their interests satisfied, or their consciences quieted. That's how things are in a republic, including this one, where there is not, our writers agree, a war against religion. Instead, there are legitimate conflicts which await legitimate argumentation. *Commonweal* supplies some of that, in an argument without end. An argument which, in a healthy republic, cannot end.

Resource

"The Bishops and Religious Liberty." *Commonweal*. May 30, 2012. https://www
.commonwealmagazine.org/bishops-religious-liberty.

57. Adiaphora

June 13, 2012
By Seth Perry

At about 11 p.m. on May 27, a preacher in West Virginia named Randall "Mack" Wolford passed away from a rattlesnake bite he had sustained that afternoon. Wolford was a widely known advocate of serpent handling, practiced by a handful of Appalachian Pentecostals who believe that the phrase "they shall take up serpents" in Mark 16 means that handling poisonous snakes is a required sign of Christian faith, just like casting out devils, speaking in tongues, and laying hands on the sick (the signs that ordinary Pentecostals observe). During services people like Wolford pass poisonous snakes around, sometimes wave them about, and occasionally, per Luke 10:19, walk on them. Early in the proceedings on Sunday the 27th, Mack Wolford sat down next to a yellow timber rattler that he had placed on the floor, and it bit him on the thigh. As a sign of faith in God's protection and, ultimately, obedience to God's will, Wolford refused medical care.

Serpent handlers pride themselves on the claim that they are the rare Christians who live and practice according to the entirety of Christ's message, the entirety of the Bible. "We feed over ALL of the Lord's Will, His Word and His Way," Wolford's church's site says. "We are not side choosers that pick apart the scriptures and cross out verses we don't like." Serpent handlers, like other Christians, have chosen something to emphasize. Over the course of two thousand years, others have chosen the precise nature and identity of Christ, the proper understanding and practice of the Eucharist, the correct way to baptize, the proper way to organize a church, which day of the week to call the Sabbath, and any number of other things as the *sine qua non* of being a true Christian, and in each case some other Christians have regarded that defining center of faith as "adiaphora"—something indifferent.

The dark extremes of eccentric faith unsettle a public discourse on religion predicated on tolerance and understanding: How do we react to a faith like Wolford's? Often the law provides us with a guide—many destructive forms of religious expression are also illegal—but this was not one of those times. There are no laws against snake handling in West Virginia, and as a grownup Wolford was free to choose how he died. A photographer who had been working with Wolford was present as he lay dying, and has written about "com[ing] to peace with the fact that everyone in the crowded trailer, including myself, let Mack die as a man true to his faith." Such extreme devotion carries an air of nobility. A deliberately provocative op-ed in *The Washington Post* by a psychologist who has studied snake handlers suggests that they be "lauded for their faith."

An adult rattlesnake's venom is "hemotoxic," which means that a severe bite in the wrong place, untreated, eliminates your blood's ability to clot and begins to dissolve the tissue of your muscles and organs. The snake begins to digest you, from the inside. With some biblical resonance of her own, a young mother in San Diego bitten by a rattlesnake last year described the pain as "more horrific than giving birth."

In an important sense, respecting the depth of Wolford's faith is an essential part of avoiding easy caricature; but in another sense, avoiding caricature of a man like Wolford should make his death sadder and harder to understand, not more approachable or ennobled. Wolford's life, like his faith, had aspects other than snake handling that he might have chosen to emphasize. He was friendly and voluble, according to those who knew him; Facebook has pictures of him posing playfully with a filmmaker who is finishing a documentary about serpent handlers. A few days after his death, Wolford's widow changed the cover photo of her Facebook page to one of her late husband cuddling not a snake but a small, shaggy dog she described as his "little shadow." At forty-four, Wolford had a wife, a daughter, three step-children, and nine grandchildren, as well as at least one devoted pet, but at least compared to his faith, it seems, the other parts of his life were so much adiaphora. We are obligated to respect a faith like this, but not to laud it.

"Change in Christian thought," writes Edmund Morgan, "has usually been a matter of emphasis, of giving certain ideas a greater weight than was previously accorded them or of carrying one idea to its logical conclusion at the expense of another." "It all boils down to Mark 16:17 and 18 to be taken literally that differentiates pure believers from pale imitations," a snake-handling site says. "One man esteemeth one day above another: another esteemeth every day alike," Paul observed to the church at Rome. "Let every man be fully persuaded in his own mind."

Resources

Duin, Julia. "Serpent-Handling Pastor Profiled Earlier in Washington Post Dies from Rattlesnake Bite." *The Washington Post*. May 29, 2011. http://www.wash ingtonpost.com/lifestyle/style/serpent-handling-pastor-profiled-earlier-in

-washington-post-dies-from-rattlesnake-bite/2012/05/29/gJQAJef5zU_story
.html.

———. "In W.Va., Snake Handling Is Still Considered a Sign of Faith." *The Washington Post*. November 10, 2011. http://www.washingtonpost.com/lifestyle
/magazine/in-wva-snake-handling-is-still-considered-a-sign-of-faith/2011/10
/18/gIQAmiqL9M_story.html.

Hood, Ralph. "Mack Wolford's Death a Reminder That Serpent Handlers Should Be Lauded for Their Faith." *The Washington Post*. June 5, 2012. http://www
.washingtonpost.com/local/mack-wolfords-death-a-reminder-that-serpent
-handlers-should-be-lauded-for-their-faith/2012/06/05/gJQAWDN8FV_story
.html.

Luke, Steven, and R. Stickney. "Rattlesnake Victim: 'Pain Worse Than Childbirth.'" NBC San Diego. August 31, 2011. https://www.nbcsandiego.com/news
/local/Oside-Woman-Bitten-by-Rattlesnake-128672663.html.

Morgan, Edmund S., ed. *Puritan Political Ideas, 1558–1794*. Indianapolis: Bobbs-Merrill, 1965.

Seth Perry is a PhD candidate at the University of Chicago Divinity School and a Mellon Fellow in early American literature and material texts at the University of Pennsylvania's McNeil Center for Early American Studies.

58. A Jewish Classic for Muslims

SEPTEMBER 13, 2012
BY JAMES T. ROBINSON

In the past few months several news agencies have reported on a new publication of Judah Halevi's *Kuzari*, a classic of Jewish thought written in Judaeo-Arabic (Arabic written in Hebrew characters). Completed in 1140, the *Kuzari* is an apologetic defense of "the despised faith" framed as a dialogue about the conversion of the Kazar kingdom to Judaism. The king of the Kazars, tormented by a recurring dream, which tells him his thoughts are pleasing but his actions are not, interviews in succession a philosopher, a Christian, a Muslim, and a Jew, the latter converting him—along with his entire kingdom—to Judaism. Much of the book is focused on the dialogue between the king and the Jew, including an argument for the superiority of the Hebrew language written in fine classical Arabic! The dialogue ends with the Jew's departure from the Jewish kingdom for the Holy Land—reflecting Halevi's own migration east from Islamic Spain.

Not often does the publication of a medieval work of Judaeo-Arabic thought receive attention in the press, even if it is a classic. This publication, however, is different. It is an Arabic-script version of the work published in Beirut by an Arab-Israeli doctoral student, Nabih Bashir, for a Muslim readership. What's more, the author's copies of his new book, sent from Beirut, were prevented entry into Israel, since imports from an enemy country of Israel are illegal. The irony was certainly not lost on the reporters: a classic of Jewish thought and foundational work of Zionism was prevented entry into Israel; a work on dialogue between philosophy and the three Abrahamic religions was not allowed free distribution.

Nabih Bashir's work (which has since made it to Israel; I just bought a copy in Jerusalem), however, is more than sensation. What he accomplished is quite remarkable. Although the *Kuzari* has been published several times—in the original Judaeo-Arabic, in Hebrew translation, and in European languages—this is the first Arabic-script version. And he did much more than transcription: he translated biblical and rabbinic citations into Arabic, provided a lengthy Arabic introduction setting the work in its intellectual context, and added copious annotation. The result is an impressive

727-page tome which immediately makes a foundational work of medieval Judaism, still studied avidly by Jews today, easily accessible to millions of Arabic-speaking Muslims (and Christians) who do not know Hebrew.

To be sure, this is not the first Judaeo-Arabic work published in Arabic characters. Maimonides's *Guide of the Perplexed* circulated in Arabic characters during the Middle Ages, and an Arabic version was published in 1972 by the Turkish scholar Huseyin Atay; his version—now available online—is (I've been told by students) intensely studied by Muslims at al-Azhar in Cairo. Saadia Gaon's theological *Book of Beliefs and Opinions*, Bahya ibn Paquda's Sufistic *Duties of the Heart,* Solomon ibn Gabirol's ethical treatise *Improvement of the Moral Qualities,* and Moses ibn Ezra's work of poetics *Book of Conversation and Discussion* have also appeared in Arabic characters. Moreover, the Karaites, a non-rabbinic, often anti-rabbinic sect of Judaism, wrote many of their Arabic works in Arabic characters during the tenth and eleventh centuries—they even transcribed the Hebrew Bible into Arabic script!—and, more and more frequently, in recent years their works have been appearing in the original script. With the exception of Huseyin Atay's *Guide,* however, the others were produced by scholars for scholars. In contrast, Nabih Bashir's *Kuzari* is self-consciously directed at a popular non-Jewish audience in the Middle East.

In a region where the Jews, Christians, and Muslims have a shared religious and intellectual history, yet remain so divided politically and socially, the significance of Bashir's work should not be underestimated. One might even hope it is the beginning of a trend. As mentioned, Maimonides's (ibn Maymun's) *Guide* is studied intensely in the Muslim world, as are works by Abu al-Barakat al-Baghdadi and ibn Kammuna, two important Jewish influences on the development of Ishraqi philosophy (Illuminationism). The Talmud has recently been translated into Arabic by a team of scholars in Amman. And, in the other direction, Arabic texts are being put into Hebrew: a new rendition of the Qur'an has recently appeared, along with Hebrew translations of Sufi and philosophical texts, including writings by al-Farabi, ibn Sina (Avicenna), and ibn Tufayl. One can only hope that the work of dedicated scholars and translators like Nabih Bashir in the literary and cultural sphere will gradually break down the artificial borders that separate the communities of the Middle East, which have so much in common and so many ideas to share.

Resource

Ahren, Raphael. "The Muslim Who Wants to Teach the Arab World about Judaism." *The Times of Israel.* May 29, 2012. http://www.timesofisrael.com/the-muslim-who-wants-to-teach-the-arab-world-about-judaism.

James Robinson is associate professor of the history of Judaism at the University of Chicago Divinity School.

59. The Swift Rise and Apparent Demise of "Jesus' Wife"

OCTOBER 25, 2012
BY TREVOR W. THOMPSON AND DAVID C. KNEIP

On September 18, 2012, Professor Karen L. King of Harvard Divinity School made public the so-called "Gospel of Jesus' Wife" at a conference in Rome. The text, written in Coptic (the form of Egyptian spoken in the early Christian period), is preserved on a codex papyrus fragment (4 × 8 centimeters) with eight visible lines on one side (the other side is heavily faded). The fragment seems to come from the middle of a page, with lost text on either side of what is visible as well as above and below. King argues that the fragment is from the fourth century CE and is likely a translation of a second-century CE Greek original.

Most likely, readers will have heard of this papyrus due to the content of the fourth and fifth lines: the fourth line reads, in part, "Jesus said to them, 'My wife . . .'"; the fifth line includes, "She is able to become my disciple . . ." The texts of the New Testament make no mention of Jesus being married. The canonical Gospels do mention some women as being part of Jesus's "circle" (cf. Luke 8:1-3). The papyrus raises questions both concerning Jesus's marital status and about whether women might have been included alongside men in the group called "the disciples."

As part of her publishing the fragment, King gave an interview to reporters, provided high-resolution images and a transcription of the Coptic text (with adjoining English translation) on the HDS website, and posted a draft of her article on the papyrus scheduled to be published in *Harvard Theological Review* in January 2013. Not surprisingly, news of the fragment spread quickly as major news outlets around the globe carried the story. Bloggers both academic and popular debated various issues surrounding the papyrus; scholars posted academic papers directly to the Web; NPR covered the story on "All Things Considered"; and even YouTube videos appeared discussing various aspects of the problem.

One special difficulty has concerned the papyrus's provenance; the antiquities market in the Middle East is notoriously complex, and very little is known with certainty about this fragment's origin. But the doubts about the papyrus extend beyond this matter even to its authenticity as a whole.

As part of its standard protocol for vetting potential publications, *HTR* consulted three anonymous reviewers regarding King's essay. As she notes, one reviewer accepted the fragment as genuine, a second raised queries, and a third asked serious questions about the grammar and handwriting. This mixed response has continued: while at least one papyrologist and an expert in Coptic grammar have affirmed aspects of the fragment as genuine, others have not been so sure.

Francis Watson, from the UK's Durham University, was one of the early detractors of the fragment's authenticity; he argued that significant material in the text derives from the Gospel of Thomas, and specifically from a modern print edition of that text. Leo Depuydt of Brown University has come to similar conclusions, with his views scheduled to be published in *HTR* alongside King's publication. Finally, Andrew Bernhard, connected with Oxford University, has discovered what seems to be a "typo" in the "Gospel of Jesus' Wife" that is also present in a widely distributed electronic interlinear transcription and translation of the Gospel of Thomas. For these reasons, at the time of this writing, the tide of scholarly opinion seems to be turning decidedly against the authenticity of the fragment.

On the chance that the papyrus fragment turns out to be legitimate, we should say that Jesus's reference to "my wife" can be understood in a number of different ways. It is possible that some second- to fourth-century Christian(s) thought that Jesus was married in the way that we understand it today, but we must also remember that Gnostic groups with Christian affiliations used language of marriage and family (including the concept of "spiritual marriage") with great fluidity during those centuries. Regardless, the papyrus and its reception again demonstrate an insatiable appetite in the media for controversial "discoveries" concerning the origins of Christianity; this appetite will surely continue to manifest itself in the future.

Resources

"Gospel of Jesus' Wife." Harvard Divinity School. https://gospelofjesuswife.hds.
harvard.edu.

"Gospel of Thomas." Translated by Stephen Patterson and Marvin Meyer. In *The Complete Gospels*, edited by Robert J. Miller , 301–29. 3rd edition. Salem, OR: Polebridge Press, 1994.

Trevor W. Thompson is a PhD candidate at the University of Chicago in the Department of New Testament and Early Christian Literature. David C. Kneip is a PhD candidate at the University of Notre Dame in the Department of Theology.

60. Divorce's Toll

January 21, 2013
By Martin E. Marty

Last Wednesday the *Chicago Tribune* alerted readers to the release that day of an ambitious set of findings about the effects of divorce on children. Reporter Manya A. Brachear called the project "unprecedented." I crossed the street to the site of the release, Fourth Presbyterian Church in Chicago, 271 steps away—I once measured it. "I have an interest," as I knew well several participants in the research, two of whom, Elizabeth Marquardt and Amy Zietlow, led the session and another, the Rev. Joyce Shin of the church's pastoral staff, hosted. You may think my "interest" must be strong if and since I post my *Sightings* on the topic of divorce on the day of a presidential inauguration.

Rationale: such inaugurations occur every four years, while the effects of divorces on children are perennial, immediate, intense, and, according to the report, often misunderstood or mishandled. This is the case in mainline Protestant churches, the focus of this study, but mingle with Roman Catholics and many kinds of evangelicals on the topic and you find similar problems. Angles on such and on the larger public are features of a column by Peter Wehner, a conservative writing for *Commentary*, whose e-column appeared a day later.

Wehner quotes the late Senator Daniel Patrick Moynihan, who was asked forty years ago to discuss the biggest change he had seen in his forty-year career: "The biggest change, in my judgment, is that the family structure has come apart all over the North Atlantic world." Wehner would say, "You haven't seen anything yet," citing statistics from the recent past. The changes occurred, writes Wehner, before and alongside and independently of the current challenges offered by the gay marriage theme.

The Marquardt/Zietlow report begins with a question: "Does the Shape of Families Shape Faith? Challenging the Churches to Confront the Impact of Family Change." The language of the report is not whiny or scolding, but, armed with statistics and ethnographic scripts and personal testimonies, the document is indeed a challenge, to be faced urgently by all kinds of churches.

The authors argue that much of the often-noted decline in mainline churches results from changes in the family resulting from divorces. That is only one sign of what amounts to a crisis.

The oral presentations included comments on "shame," which keeps divorced or divorcing church members from being ready to discuss the issue in congregations, and unawareness of divorce's implications on the part of pastors, priests, and counselors in churches. When *Sightings* discusses the life of faith or drift or un-faith in intimate settings such as parishes or families, so often splitting or split, it may seem as if we are departing from our charter to deal with "public religion." Both the Wehner article and a report on which he relies, as well as the "Shape Faith" documents, demonstrate boldly just how public are the consequences of action or neglect in church and family and other institutions often shelved as "private."

The report, which issues from the Institute for American Values, is too rich and complex to be probed or expounded in a short column. Those of us exposed to the findings come away from the discussions and the reading with new reasons to look very closely at the crisis to which these point. And what the various studies turn up deserves prime attention on the agendas of those who would make a difference tomorrow.

Resources

Brachear, Manya A. "Researchers: Even Amicable Divorces Take Toll on Children and Their Religious Attendance." *Chicago Tribune*. January 16, 2013. http://www.chicagotribune.com/news/local/ct-met-divorce-study-20130116,0,4566902.story.

Marquardt, Elizabeth. *Does the Shape of Families Shape Faith?: Calling the Churches to Confront the Impact of Family Change*. New York: Broadway Publications, 2012.

Wehner, Peter. "America's Exodus from Marriage." *Commentary Magazine*. January 17, 2013. http://www.commentarymagazine.com/2013/01/17/americas-exodus-from-marriage.

61. Christian Pop

February 25, 2013
By Martin E. Marty

Commenting on "Christian pop," if one is not at home in it, is precarious and will doubtless reveal how out of it the commentator is. So I wander in with a sense of mission. If "public religion" is the field of our notice, overlooking "trendy hip-hop, dubstep, funk and synth pop beats" would be to miss some very public expressions. Allison Stewart pointed to the music styles just mentioned when commenting on rapper TobyMac, whose album *Eye On It* was only the third "Christian" product ever to have debuted at No. 1 on Billboard's "top ten" charts.

Stewart, in an interview with the artist: "The lines between Christian and secular music are so porous now—do you think the distinction even matters?" His answer: "I think the walls are coming down between genres of music in general, and especially Christian music." The rapper's responses are cogent, modest, and to the point, as when he delineates the lines between "vulgar" and "clean" versions of popular music releases. I won't pursue this further, lest my ignorance and unfamiliarity be paraded vulgarly. We move on now to comment on the "porous" lines between Christian and secular music or most anything else in the arts line.

I was drawn to this topic while researching for a forthcoming lecture before Chicago Chorale's March 24 *Passion according to Saint John* by Bach. Whenever I am called, or freed, to wander in the fields of classical sacred music, I find that sooner or later—usually sooner, now—the subject of how "Christian and secular music" interrelate comes up. I've been hearing Bach for over eighty years, having been child-sat near my father's organ bench while mother was in the small-town church choir. And I've been reading musicologists, theologians, and other Bach scholars for three fourths of those years, again and again pondering the lines and distinctions. Sections and strains from Bach's sacred cantatas can sound much like his *Coffee Cantata* and its kin, until one hears the words. What makes the music religious, Christian, or sacred, and what is "secular"?

Rather than deal with such questions musicologically, I'll turn in the few lines ahead to questions of aesthetics, politics, and culture. Try as I might,

I can't be moved by "hip-hop, dubstep, funk and synth pop beats"—even those labeled Christian. And I have to admit that my kind doesn't try very hard. Yet as in so many areas, the porousness of the line between Christian or religious and secular is welcomed. True confession: of course, sacred and secular lines are blurred or sounds blended in the fields of folk music, and many of us classics-lovers are at home with it, as are composers of choice. A step further: Where is the line between Christian and secular in jazz, and should we worry about it? I am in the company of those, dwarfed by Christian pop adherents, who cherish jazz by Mary Lou Williams, Dave Brubeck, or close-to-home-and-almost-in-the family Andy Tecson, who for years have rendered the old line porous.

What many of us are learning is that some of these choices are simply matters of taste, however rationalized. And those of us who pay attention to how religion or specific faiths like the Christian might best be furthered, fostered, and delighted in musically are learning tolerance. But, wait a minute: what's that I hear? Bach! A-a-a-a-a-h.

Resource

Stewart, Allison. "Rapper TobyMac a Hit Inside and Out of Church." *Chicago Tribune*. February 21, 2013. http://articles.chicagotribune.com/2013-02-21/enter tainment/ct-ott-0222-toby-mac-20130221_1_christian-music-hip-hop-artists -music-fans.

62. Strange Bedfellows Scapegoat Russia's Gays

SEPTEMBER 26, 2013
BY BRYCE E. RICH

It's been a busy few months for anyone paying attention to issues affecting lesbian, gay, bisexual, and transgender (LGBT) people in Russia.

This summer the Russian parliament passed a bill prohibiting the so-called "promotion of nontraditional sexual relations" in the presence of minors, a euphemistic expression replacing language in the initial bill which more explicitly prohibited "the promotion of homosexual relations." The new law gives no explicit definition of "promotion," resulting in an environment where Russia's mass media has curtailed any reporting that might portray LGBT people or their relationships in a positive light.

A companion law banning the international adoption of Russian children by citizens in countries that recognize same-sex unions quickly followed suit, while just three weeks ago, a Russian MP introduced a third bill calling for the removal of children from families in which one or both parents are gay.

Recent reports in the American media suggest that Russian president Vladimir Putin is responsible for the new rise in anti-gay sentiment. Such claims fail to take into account the wide variety of social and religious factors contributing to the situation.

The past two decades have witnessed a mass exodus of the educated classes from Russia. While acceptance of gays increased in the 1990s, a recent Pew Research poll indicates that today 74 percent of the population believes that society should not accept homosexuality.

Religion also plays a role. When the Council of Europe recently called on Russia to protect LGBT rights, Patriarch Kirill responded that the Russian Orthodox Church must remind Russians that homosexuality is a sin before God. And Vsevolod Chaplin, head of the Synodal Department for Church and Society Relations of the Russian Orthodox Church, warned that the legalization of same-sex unions could lead to the fall of Western civilization within the next fifty years.

YouTube videos and Russian newscasts document the involvement of Russian Orthodox priests and parishioners bearing holy water and icons as they protest at pro-LGBT demonstrations.

Just three weeks ago in Saint Petersburg, Russian Orthodox clergy and lay activists staged prayers and liturgical chants in response to a pro-LGBT rally timed to President Obama's meeting with Russian LGBT activists. Local police learned from an earlier confrontation in June during which Orthodox protestors physically attacked LGBT advocates and threw rotten eggs, vegetables, and rocks at their opponents. This time the police separated the two factions with barricades and a large number of officers, and the Orthodox protestors settled for throwing loose change.

Vitaly Milonov, the Saint Petersburg politician whose local anti-gay legislation has served as the model for the national law, is a Baptist-turned-Orthodox Christian. Yet, while he and some other public officials are informed by their faith commitments and the pronouncements of church officials, religion has a limited influence on Russia today. Seventy years of Soviet campaigns promoting atheism have left the country largely secular.

Another factor contributing to Russia's anti-gay sentiment is the growth of ultra-nationalist groups that target both non-ethnic Russians and gays, blaming them for the country's economic woes and population decline. These groups, which often conflate homosexuality with pedophilia, have posted videos on the internet that document the harassment and sometimes torture of men whom the groups lure into traps by arranging fake sexual encounters through social networking sites. Reaction from Russian law enforcement has been muted.

Rhetoric from America's culture wars has also found a place in Russia's anti-gay campaign. Massachusetts-based pastor Scott Lively conducted a fifty-city speaking tour of Russia in 2007 urging the criminalization of the advocacy of homosexuality. Recent right-wing media reports in the US credit Lively with helping shape Russia's new legislation.

The direct influence of US rhetoric is clearly visible in the current anti-custody bill's inclusion of data from a study published in 2012 by Mark Regnerus, an associate professor of sociology at the University of Texas at Austin. Regnerus made headlines with claims that children raised by LGBT parents suffer from a raft of social adjustment issues. Though subsequently challenged by a host of researchers and the publishing journal, his study's findings are included in an addendum to the Russian legislation.

While it's tempting to seek a single cause for anti-LGBT sentiment in Russia, the realities on the ground confound simple explanations. Indeed, multiple interests have converged to produce the current atmosphere. There is no vast conspiracy, but rather a host of players and factors, each with a contributing role in the unfolding drama.

Resources

Agence France Presse. "Vladimir Putin Signs Russia Gay Adoption Ban." *The Huffington Post*. July 3, 2013. http://www.huffingtonpost.com/2013/07/03/putin -signs-russia-gay-adoption-ban_n_3540162.html.

Fierstein, Harvey. "Russia's Anti-Gay Crackdown." *The New York Times*. July 21, 2013. http://www.nytimes.com/2013/07/22/opinion/russias-anti-gay-crack down.html.

Gessen, Masha. "When Putin Declared War on Gay Families, It Was Time for Mine to Leave Russia." *Slate*. August 26, 2013. http://www.slate.com/blogs /outward/2013/08/26/when_putin_declared_war_on_gay_families_it_was _time_for_mine_to_leave_russia.html.

"The Global Divide on Homosexuality: Greater Acceptance in More Secular and Affluent Countries." Pew Research. June 4, 2013. http://www.pewglobal .org/2013/06/04/the-global-divide-on-homosexuality.

Grekov, Inokenty (Kes). "Russia's Anti-Gay Law, Spelled Out in Plain English." August 8, 2013. https://mic.com/articles/58649/russia-s-anti-gay-law-spelled -out-in-plain-english.

"Russian MP Moves to Strip Gays of Parental Rights." *RT*. September 5, 2013. http://rt.com/politics/gay-families-no-kids-447.

Schlatter, Evelyn. "Suspect 'Science.'" Southern Poverty Law Center. May 16, 2013. https://www.splcenter.org/get-informed/intelligence-report /browse-all-issues/2013/summer/suspect-science.

"7 Villains of Russia's Gay Rights Movement (Photo Essay)." *The Moscow Times*. September 12, 2013. http://www.themoscowtimes.com/news/article/7-villains -of-russias-gay-rights-movement-photo-essay/485975.html.

Tashman, Brian. "MassResistance: Kissing 'Provoked' Violent Anti-Gay Attack in Moscow." Right Wing Watch. June 18, 2013. http://www.rightwingwatch.org /content/massresistance-kissing-provoked-violent-anti-gay-attack-moscow.

"Western Countries Will Degrade in Fifty Years at the Most If They Don't Con- demn Same-Sex Unions—Archpriest Vsevolod Chaplin." Interfax. June 5, 2013. http://www.interfax-religion.com/?act=news&div=10522.

Bryce E. Rich is a PhD student in theology at the University of Chicago Divinity School.

63. The Doniger Affair: Freedom of Scholarly Inquiry Takes an Ominous Turn in India

FEBRUARY 27, 2014
BY SUNIT SINGH

Last month, the executives on the board of directors of Penguin India made the determination that it was best to settle an anti-defamation case that names the historian of religions Wendy Doniger as one of the defendants.

The lawsuit, filed in 2011 by a hitherto obscure conservative group, the Shiksha Bachao Andolan (SBA, or the Campaign to Defend Education), insisted that Penguin India withdraw and destroy all of the available copies of Doniger's *The Hindus: An Alternative History* (2009), on account of its putatively false and lurid depiction of Hinduism. Although Doniger herself reports, in a statement released online, that Penguin India was supportive behind the scenes, eventually, the board knuckled.

To say that the news of the settlement blindsided those of us who care about the study of Indian religions is to state the obvious. While serious readers will recognize that *The Hindus* is the kind of learned book that synthesizes a lifetime of concern with translation, comparison, and interpretation, a fundamental issue remains the applicability of colonial-era libel statutes upon which the lawsuit relies.

The news nevertheless left the Indian author Arundhati Roy to ask of Penguin India, "What are we to make of this?" Another commentator referred to the settlement as the "pulping of liberal India"—although one is tempted to ask, was there ever a liberal India? For liberal thought, in its classic eighteenth-century formulation, was arguably late to arrive in India.

Part of what makes the situation so exasperating is that it is unclear whether the SBA acted alone, or whether it is a front for a national, caste-based, or local party. With national elections slated for this spring, it is difficult not to see the settlement as another omen portending the election of Narendra Modi as the candidate of the Hindu nationalist Bharatiya Janata Party. Modi, the chief minister of the western state of Gujarat, was indicted for his role in the appalling Hindu-Muslim violence witnessed in that state in 2002.

On Valentine's Day (itself an object of ire for conservative Hindus), an editorial written in the Hindi edition of the newspaper with the widest circulation in India, *Dainik Bhaskar*, criticized the Indian intellectuals who had come out in support of Doniger. The editorial's author, Ved Pratap Vaidik, linked Doniger to colonial-era Orientalists, who supposedly had a fascination with the antinomian aspects of the Hindu faith, at the expense of "the objective truth."

Vaidik, parroting arguments made in fashionable academic circles, criticized the application of "Western" categories of analysis and methods of inquiry to the study of India and compared Western academics who write about India to proselytizing Christian missionaries. Instead, Vaidik directs readers to the bourgeoisified or reformed Hinduism advocated by the late-nineteenth-century, neo-Hindu revivalist Dayanand Saraswati, and the nationalist-turned-cosmopolitan-spiritualist Aurobindo Ghose.

"Genuine freedom," Vaidik suggests, requires a balanced stance that mediates the freedom of expression and the rights of those who might take offense. While stopping short of proposing that Doniger's book be banned, Vaidik asked, "Does the right to express oneself extend to spewing opinions?"—a rhetorical flourish that, sadly, found sympathizers on Twitter.

But can there be a "balanced" stance on the issue of the right to freedom of expression and intellectual inquiry? And are scholars of religion, as Vaidik accuses, simply proffering "opinions" that can safely be ignored?

For what it is worth, the English media outlets in India are equally susceptible to equivocating about this issue of right, as is evident from their treatment of a number of similar cases going even further back than the late 1980s when a *fatwa* called upon Muslims to kill Salman Rushdie for writing *The Satanic Verses*. On the whole, by pitting sensitivity and tolerance against the right to intellectual inquiry and scholarly expression, much of the coverage on the Doniger affair obfuscates more than it clarifies.

What is significant about this case is that the board acted peremptorily, even after Doniger judiciously edited the Indian version of *The Hindus*, in an effort to fend off "hurt" sentiments. One might metaphorically refer to the creeping self-imposition of this kind of caution by the publishing industry and academics since the Rushdie affair as "the internalization of the *fatwa*."

For the right of expression that applies to Rushdie, Taslima Nasrin (the Bangladeshi novelist forced into exile by Islamist groups after publishing *Lajja* in 1993), and the conservative *Jyllands-Posten* (the Danish newspaper that ran cartoons mocking Muhammad), is surely the same one that applies to Doniger and other scholars who venture beyond what the devout might themselves think about their faith.

The erosion of this right globally signals a crisis, the effects of which are especially evident in the marked deterioration of intellectual life in India, where *The Hindus* will simply be another book lost to an audience that is itself getting ever smaller.

Resources

Devji, Faisal. "Changing Contours of Censorship." *The Hindu*. February 24, 2014. http://www.thehindu.com/todays-paper/tp-opinion/changing-contours-of-censorship/article5720626.ece.

Editorial Board. "Muzzling Speech in India." *The New York Times*. February 20, 2014. https://www.nytimes.com/2014/02/21/opinion/muzzling-speech-in-india.html.

Malik, Ashok. "Wendy Doniger Failed Most by Her Publisher." NDTV. February 12, 2014. http://www.ndtv.com/article/opinion/op-ed-wendy-doniger-failed-most-by-her-publisher-482364.

Malik, Kenan. *From Fatwa to Jihad: The Rushdie Affair and Its Legacy*. London: Atlantic Books, 2009.

Roy, Arundhati. "A Letter to Penguin India (My Publishers)." *The Times of India*. February 13, 2014. https://timesofindia.indiatimes.com/india/Wendy-Donigers-book-You-must-tell-us-what-terrified-you-Arundhati-Roy-writes-to-Penguin-India/articleshow/30306451.cms.

Shainin, Jonathan. "Why Free Speech Loses in India." *The New Yorker*. February 14, 2014. http://www.newyorker.com/online/blogs/newsdesk/2014/02/wendy-doniger-free-speech-india.html.

Vaidik, Ved Pratap. "Freedom to Write Doesn't Mean This." *Dainik Bhaskar*. February 14, 2012. http://www.bhaskar.com/article/ABH-ved-pratap-vaidik-column-on-the-hindus-an-alternative-history-4521489-NOR.html.

Williams, John. "Author Resigned to Ill Fate of Book in India." *The New York Times*. February 16, 2014. https://www.nytimes.com/2014/02/17/books/author-resigned-to-ill-fate-of-book.html.

Sunit Singh is a PhD candidate in anthropology and sociology of religion at the University of Chicago Divinity School.

64. Phone versus Online Honesty

MAY 26, 2014
BY MARTIN E. MARTY

"What fresh hell is this?" was poet Dorothy Parker's question when her phone or doorbell rang. Opinion-surveyors and telephone-pollsters may often be greeted by Parkeresque answerers, but data now suggests that many of the called choose to be nice to the phoners and to themselves.

To the point of our "public religion" business, Religion News Service (RNS) headlines Cathy Lynn Grossman's online report (May 17, 2014) with this summary: "Poll: Americans Stretch the Truth on Attending Church." In her report, Grossman quips: "You skipped church. And then nearly one in seven of you fibbed about attending."

The source of data about this sort of "fibbing" is a new survey by the Public Religion Research Institute (PRRI), which recently presented its findings at the national meeting of the American Association for Public Opinion Research. PRRI's survey was, to quote Grossman, "designed to measure the 'social desirability bias in self-reported religious behavior.' The survey finds that many Christians—and unbelievers, too—will exaggerate about attending worship in live phone interviews. However, when asked in an anonymous online questionnaire, people will answer more realistically."

When polled by phone, 36 percent report attending services weekly or more, while 30 percent say they never go. When polled online, far smaller percentages say they attended at least weekly and far more respondents said they seldom or never go.

Robert Jones, CEO of the institute, says that people who don't attend worship—but say they did—may not mean to lie. "There's an aspirational quality here. People see themselves as the kind of person who would go." So, "remove the social pressure of speaking on the phone, and people will feel less pressure to conform."

The findings and the comments, including some by Dr. Jones, who knows so much about this, do point to certain anomalies and possible contradictions. Thus "white mainline Protestants" first, and Catholics second, "lie" most. "Lie" is the term that loathers of such Protestants and Catholics use to speak of reported exaggerations.

Many factors have to enter into analyses. Aren't white mainline Protestants, for example, usually seen as caring least about being typed as pious churchgoers? If so, and if they are at best apathetic or, in other terms, critical of religious worship, why do they feel social pressure when talking to a nameless, faceless, featureless phone interviewer? And why does online transmission remove social pressure?

Among the many who show disdain for "organized religion," "the institutional church," and the practice of piety, why, when the phone rings and they answer, do they turn nicely dishonest?

Bloggers busied themselves with online, not phoned, bluster. This kind of topic brings out the self-identified "atheists" who leaped on the suggestion that religious practitioners lied or, in the critics' terms, simply were "liars."

More staid and serious commentators on the much-much-commented-upon survey and report raise significant issues. The PRRI and RNS people are experienced and sophisticated and express caution about over-interpreting findings of their surveys. They consider who in the population does not get represented in the samples of the surveyed—for example, those who never answer the phone in their effort to avoid fresh hells. The experts also take into consideration the difference between land-lined phoners and cell phone users.

Still, the new findings confirm what pollsters have known and the public surmises: there are and for a half-century have been fewer people in the pews than observers noticed or congregants claimed.

Resources

Cox, Daniel, Robert P. Jones, and Juhem Navarro-Rivera. "I Know What You Did Last Sunday: Measuring Social Desirability Bias in Self-Reported Religious Behavior, Belief, and Identity." Public Religion Research Institute. May 17, 2014. http://publicreligion.org/site/wp-content/uploads/2014/05/AAPOR -2014-Final.pdf.

Grossman, Cathy Lynn. "Poll: Americans Stretch the Truth on Attending Church." Religion News Service. May 17, 2014. http://www.religionnews.com /2014/05/17/christians-church-atheists-prri.

65. Ferguson

SEPTEMBER 1, 2014
BY MARTIN E. MARTY

I am back to "sighting" for *Sightings*, after what the editor called an August "hiatus" and this scribe called a summer "sabbatical." Pleased to hear that we were missed, we are discussing whether (or not) to publish relentlessly through all the weeks next year.

What did we miss? Frank Bruni in "Lost in America" (*The New York Times,* August 25) captures too well the spirit of a dispiriting period. America right now, Bruni writes, is "a country surrendering to a new identity and era, in which optimism is quaint and the frontier anything but endless. There's a feeling of helplessness. . . . Americans are apprehensive. . . . They're hungry for hope." No political leaders inspire hope, and institutions seem self-serving and stagnant. Et cetera. You all know all of that. The sign above my desk reads "NO WHINING," so let us move on with *Sightings*.

In a world of utter upset, one story more than any other appeared on the "religion in public life" screen, code-named "Ferguson," after the St. Louis-area site of a police shooting of an unarmed African American man and the protests, disruptions, and sometimes chaos which followed.

I knew Ferguson, and one church there, decades ago when the mainly white churchgoers had little cause for complaint except for the noise of planes taking off and landing at the not-too-far-away Lambert field. Now Ferguson is largely black, though ruled by whites. Religion on the scene? Let's look.

The Rev. Bernice King drew notice as she dialogued with and promoted nonviolence among thirty high-schoolers. Her "show your hand" poll turned up only one who, in the heat of the moment, thought her late father's nonviolent approach had much of a presence or future in Fergusonian circumstances.

Among senior leaders, the Rev. Jesse Jackson showed up, marched some, but was treated to or mistreated in a brief media encounter when some angry locals encountered him, captive in a seat belt, and subjected him to verbal attack: "Where were you?" Also, of course, the Rev. Al Sharpton was there and, no surprise, drew much media attention. Yet it was not these celebrities who left their mark. Others, somewhat later, and more quietly, appeared, served, and spoke up.

Most important during the protests were the actions of a new "Clergy United," two hundred strong, who mediated between frustrated and angry local people and police. They were organized by, among others, Rob White, pastor of Peace of Mind Church, and Bishop Edwin Bass of the Church of God in Christ.

The memorial service for the killed Michael Brown, at Friendly Temple Missionary Baptist Church in St. Louis, drew four or five thousand to hear eulogies, including from Brown's uncle, Pastor Charles Ewing, who said that his nephew's blood was "crying from the ground." (No one needed to explain the biblical references to these churchgoing citizen-mourners.)

Nationally, church leaders wrote eloquently about the need for local churches of all sorts to step up to the awesome challenges of racial prejudice, and to note that 86.3 percent of local churches in America failed to have at least 20 percent diversity in their membership. In this and all other such declarations, the "confessors" pledged new energies so that the voice of the local church might be more prominent and so that congregations would embody and exemplify more diversity.

If forty and fifty years ago evangelical-type churches, not only in the South, were seldom seen as leaders in moves to integrate and work for racial justice, let it be noted that one of the most eloquent statements of confession of guilt and resolve to change came from Mark Labberton, president of Pasadena's Fuller Theological Seminary, considered by many to be the flagship evangelical ministerial school.

A sign, among many, to hope once again?

Resources

Associated Press. "Michael Brown's Funeral Draws Thousands in Missouri." CBS News. August 25, 2014. http://www.cbsnews.com/news/michael-brown-funer al-draws-hundreds-in-ferguson-missouri.

Banks, Adelle. "Ferguson Letter from Black Clergy Becomes Interracial Call for Justice." Religion News Service. August 22, 2014. http://www.religionnews .com/2014/08/22/ferguson-letter-black-clergy-becomes-interracial-call -justice.

Bruni, Frank. "Lost in America." *The New York Times*. August 25, 2014. http:// www.nytimes.com/2014/08/26/opinion/frank-bruni-lost-in-america.html.

Crouch, Elisa. "MLK's Daughter Seeks Nonviolent Ferguson Response." Re-

ligion News Service. August 27, 2014. http://religionnews.com/2014/08/27
/mlks-daughter-seeks-nonviolent-ferguson-response.

Jervis, Rick. "Clergy and Activists Help Ferguson Protests Remain Calm."
USA Today. August 24, 2014. http://www.usatoday.com/story/news/nation
/2014/08/24/ferguson-protests-peaceful-clergy/14531429.

66. How Not to Understand ISIS

October 2, 2014
By Alireza Doostdar

The group known as the Islamic State in Iraq and the Levant or simply the Islamic State (ISIL, ISIS, or IS) has attracted much attention in the past few months with its dramatic military gains in Syria and Iraq and with the recent US decision to wage war against it.

As analysts are called to explain ISIS's ambitions, its appeal, and its brutality, they often turn to an examination of what they consider to be its religious worldview—a combination of cosmological doctrines, eschatological beliefs, and civilizational notions—usually thought to be rooted in Salafi Islam.

The Salafi tradition is a modern reformist movement critical of what it considers to be misguided accretions to Islam—such as grave visitations, saint veneration, and dreaming practices. It calls for abolishing these and returning to the ways of the original followers of Prophet Muhammad, the "salaf" or predecessors. Critics of Salafism accuse its followers of "literalism," "puritanism," or of practicing a "harsh" or "rigid" form of Islam, but none of these terms is particularly accurate, especially given the diverse range of Salafi views and the different ways in which people adhere to them.

Salafism entered American consciousness after September 11, 2001, as Al-Qaeda leaders claim to follow this school. Ever since, it has become commonplace to demonize Salafism as the primary cause of Muslim violence, even though most Salafi Muslims show no enthusiasm for jihad and often eschew political involvement, and even though many Muslims who do engage in armed struggles are not Salafi.

ISIS is only the most recent group whose behavior is explained in terms of Salafism. What makes it unique is its aspiration to form immediately a caliphate or pan-Islamic state. Even so, analysts' emphasis on Salafi thought and on the formation of a caliphate makes it easy to ignore some important aspects of the ISIS phenomenon. I would like to draw attention to some of these neglected issues and to offer a few cautions about attempts to understand ISIS purely in terms of doctrines. My argument is not that studying doctrines is useless; only that such study is limited in what it can explain.

I should begin by emphasizing that our knowledge of ISIS is extremely scant. We know close to nothing about ISIS's social base. We know little about how it made its military gains, and even less about the nature of the coalitions into which it has entered with various groups—from other Islamist rebels in Syria to secular Ba'athists in Iraq.

Sensationalist accounts of "shari'a justice" notwithstanding, we do not have much information about how ISIS administers the lives of millions of people who reside in the territories it now controls.

Information about the militants who fight for ISIS is likewise scarce. Most of what we know is gleaned from recruitment videos and propaganda, not the most reliable sources. There is little on the backgrounds and motives of those who choose to join the group, least of all the non-Western recruits who form the bulk of ISIS's fighting force. In the absence of this information, it is difficult even to say what ISIS is if we are to rely on anything beyond the group's self-representations.

Let me emphasize this last point. What we call ISIS is more than just a militant cult. At present, ISIS controls a network of large population centers with millions of residents, in addition to oil resources, military bases, and roads. It has to administer the affairs of the populations over whom it rules, and this has required compromise and coalition-building, not just brute force.

In Iraq, the group has had to work with secular Ba'athists, former army officers, tribal councils, and various Sunni opposition groups, many of whose members are in administrative positions. In Syria, it has likewise had to negotiate with other rebel factions as well as tribes, and it relies on local (non-ISIS) technical expertise to manage services such as water, electricity, public health, and bakeries.

The vast majority of ISIS's estimated 20,000–31,500 fighters are recent recruits, and it is not clear whether and how its leadership maintains ideological consistency among them. All told, our sense of ISIS's coherence as a caliphate with a clear chain of command, a solid organizational structure, and an all-encompassing ideology is a direct product of ISIS's propaganda apparatus.

We see ISIS as a unitary entity because ISIS propagandists want us to see it that way. This is why it is problematic to rely on doctrines espoused in propaganda to explain ISIS's behavior. Absent more evidence, we simply cannot know if the behaviors of the different parts of ISIS are expressions of these doctrines.

And yet, much of the analysis that we have available relies precisely on ISIS's propaganda and doctrinal statements. What does this emphasis obscure? Here I will point out several of the issues I consider most important.

First, we lack a good grasp of the motivations of those who fight for or alongside ISIS, so we assume that they are motivated by Salafism and the desire to live in a caliphate. What information we do have comes almost entirely from ISIS propaganda and recruitment videos, a few interviews, and the occasional news report about a foreign fighter killed in battle or arrested before making it to his or her destination.

Focusing on doctrinal statements would have us homogenizing the entirety of ISIS's military force as fighters motivated by an austere and virulent form of Salafi Islam. This is how ISIS wants us to see things, and it is often the view propagated by mainstream media. For example, CNN recently quoted former Iraqi national security adviser Muwaffaq al-Ruba'i as claiming that in Mosul, ISIS was recruiting "young Iraqis as young as 8 and 9 years old with AK-47s . . . and brainwashing with this evil ideology." A Pentagon spokesman is quoted in the same story as saying that the US was not intent on "simply . . . degrading and destroying . . . the 20 to 30,000 [ISIS fighters]. . . . It's about destroying their ideology."

The problem with these statements is that they seem to assume that ISIS is a *causa sui* phenomenon that has suddenly materialized out of the thin ether of an evil doctrine. But ISIS emerged from the fires of war, occupation, killing, torture, and disenfranchisement. It did not need to sell its doctrine to win recruits. It needed above all to prove itself effective against its foes.

In Iraq, the cities that are now controlled by ISIS were some of those most resistant to American control during the occupation and most recalcitrant in the face of the newly established state. The destruction that these cities endured seems only to have hardened their residents' defiance. Fallujah, the first Iraqi city to fall to ISIS, is famous for its devastation during US counterinsurgency operations in 2004. It still struggles with a legacy of rising cancer rates, genetic mutations, birth defects, and disabilities blamed on depleted uranium in American munitions.

In Mosul, many of those who joined ISIS last summer had been previously imprisoned by the Iraqi government. They numbered in the thousands and included peaceful protesters who opposed Prime Minister Nuri al-Maliki's increasingly authoritarian rule. The situation in Syria is not entirely different. ISIS emerged on the scene after a long period of strife that began with peaceful protests in 2011 and deteriorated into civil war after President Bashar al-Assad's military and security forces repeatedly deployed brutal force against the opposition.

A large number of ISIS fighters in Syria (as in Iraq) are indeed foreign, but the majority are local recruits. The emphasis on ISIS's Salafi worldview has tended to obscure the many grievances that may motivate fighters to join an increasingly efficient militant group that promises to vanquish their oppressors. Do they need to "convert" to ISIS's worldview to fight with or for them? Do they need to aspire to a caliphate, as does ISIS leadership, in order to join forces with them? These questions are never asked, and "beliefs" are made simply to fill the explanatory void.

Second, the puzzle of foreign fighters is no less obscured by an over-emphasis on the allure of Salafism. Again, the tendency here is to ignore any motivation except the overriding call of the Salafi jihadist who persuades converts of the truth of Islam and of their responsibility to wage war in de-fense of the Islamic community. In ISIS's case, the aspiration to create a ca-liphate is added to the equation. Foreign fighters must be joining ISIS, we are told, because they desire to live in a pristine Muslim utopia.

Some analysts allow the possibility that the jihadi convert is mentally unstable, a privilege usually reserved for white non-Muslim mass murderers. But rarely do they consider that sensibilities and motivations other than or in addition to mere commitment to Salafi Islam or a desire to live in a utopic state may guide their decisions.

For example, could it be that a sense of compassion for suffering fellow humans or of altruistic duty—sensibilities that are very much valued and cultivated in American society—has prefigured their receptiveness to a call to arms to aid a people they consider to be oppressed?

The novelist and journalist Michael Muhammad Knight has recently argued that his own flirting with jihad in the Chechen war of the 1990s did not grow out of his then-commitment to Salafi Islam, but from American values: "I had grown up in the Reagan '80s. I learned from G.I. Joe cartoons to (in the words of the theme song) 'fight for freedom, wherever there's trou-ble.' I assumed that individuals had the right—and the duty—to intervene anywhere on the planet where they perceived threats to freedom, justice, and equality."

Unfortunately, such first-person accounts that give us a view beyond recruiter-side doctrine are rare. The situation is even more difficult with non-Western foreign fighters, about whose conditions and motivations we know still less.

Finally, the belief that Salafi Islam is exceptional in its extremism has made it convenient to view ISIS brutality as likewise exceptional. We are variously told that ISIS's killings—especially the beheadings of victims, most recently of foreign journalists—are medieval, barbaric, pornographic, and ends in themselves (rather than means to any end). This violence is apparently counterpoised against civilized, non-gratuitous, means-end rational forms of killing, such as those practiced by the American military.

The anthropologist Talal Asad has questioned the presumptions that guide these distinctions between what we might call "humanitarian" and "gratuitous" violence and cruelty. It is not my intention to pursue that line of thought here. Instead, I want only to point out that once again, ISIS's brutality did not emerge in a vacuum; rather, it is part of a whole ecology of cruelty spread out over more than a decade.

Perhaps a decapitation is more cruel than blowing a body to bits with a high-caliber machine gun, incinerating it with a remote-controlled drone, or burning and lacerating it with a barrel bomb. But even if we limit ourselves to close-up, low-technology brutality, ISIS beheadings are hardly out of place.

The earliest videotaped decapitation of an American citizen in Iraq was conducted by ISIS's predecessors in 2004 in response, they claimed, to the photographed and video-recorded torture, rape, and murder of detainees in the Abu Ghraib prison. In 2011, it emerged that some American soldiers in Afghanistan had been hunting civilians for sport and collecting their fingers and teeth as souvenirs. In the sectarian bloodshed that engulfed Iraq after the US invasion, beheadings by Sunni insurgents turned into a morbid form of reciprocity with Shi'a militiamen who bore holes into their victims using power drills.

The point is not to identify when cruelty emerged in the long American-led Global War on Terrorism—only that the view that one particular religious doctrine is uniquely extremist will not help us understand the cycles of brutality that have fed on years of circulating narratives and images of torture, violent murder, and desecration.

Resources

Armstrong, Karen. "The Myth of Religious Violence." *The Guardian*. September 25, 2014. https://www.theguardian.com/world/2014/sep/25/-sp-karen-arm strong-religious-violence-myth-secular.

Asad, Talal. "Reflections on Violence, Law, and Humanitarianism." *Critical Inquiry*. https://criticalinquiry.uchicago.edu/reflections_on_violence_law _and_humanitarianism.

Boal, Mark. "The Kill Team: How U.S. Soldiers in Afghanistan Murdered Innocent Civilians." *Rolling Stone*. March 27, 2011. http://www.rollingstone.com /politics/news/the-kill-team-20110327.

Bonnefoy, Laurent. *Salafism in Yemen: Transnationalism and Religious Identity*. Oxford: Oxford University Press, 2012.

Caris, Charles C., and Samuel Reynolds. "ISIS Governance in Syria." *Middle East Security Report* 22. July 2014. http://www.understandingwar.org/sites/default /files/ISIS_Governance.pdf.

Dewachi, Omar. "The Toxicity of Everyday Survival in Iraq." *Jadaliyya.* August 13, 2013. http://www.jadaliyya.com/Details/29295/The-Toxicity-of-Everyday -Survival-in-Iraq.

Gilsinan, Kathy. "The Many Ways to Map the Islamic 'State.'" *The Atlantic.* August 27, 2014. https://www.theatlantic.com/international/archive/2014/08 /the-many-ways-to-map-the-islamic-state/379196.

Graeber, David. "Army of Altruists." *Harper's Magazine.* January 2007. https:// harpers.org/archive/2007/01/army-of-altruists.

Hirschkind, Charles. *The Ethical Soundscape: Cassette Sermons and Islamic Counterpublics.* New York: Columbia University Press, 2009.

"Inside Mosul: Why Iraqis Are Celebrating Islamic Extremists' Takeover of Their City." *Niqash.* June 12, 2014. https://muftah.org/why-iraqis-are-cele brating-isis-takeover-of-their-city.

Karadsheh, Jomana, Jim Sciutto, and Laura Smith-Spark. "How Foreign Fighters Are Swelling ISIS Ranks in Startling Numbers." CNN. September 14, 2014. http://www.cnn.com/2014/09/12/world/meast/isis-numbers/index.html.

Knight, Michael Muhammad. "I Understand Why Westerners Are Joining Jihadi Movements Like ISIS. I Was Almost One of Them." *The Washington Post.* September 3, 2014. https://www.washingtonpost.com/posteverything /wp/2014/09/03/i-understand-why-westerners-are-joining-the-islamic -state-i-was-almost-one-of-them.

Nichols, Bill. "Video Shows Beheading of American Captive." *USA Today.* November 5, 2004. https://usatoday30.usatoday.com/news/world/iraq/2004 -05-11-iraq-beheading_x.htm.

"Nir Rosen on 'Aftermath: Following the Bloodshed of America's Wars in the Muslim World.'" *Democracy Now!* November 10, 2010. https://www.democracy now.org/2010/11/10/nir_rosen_on_aftermath_following_the.

Sayigh, Yezid. "ISIS: Global Islamic Caliphate or Islamic Mini-State in Iraq?" Carnegie Middle East Center. July 24, 2014. http://carnegie-mec.org/2014/07/24 /isis-global-islamic-caliphate-or-islamic-mini-state-in-iraq-pub-56203.

Alireza Doostdar is assistant professor of Islamic studies and the anthropology of religion at the University of Chicago Divinity School.

67. Plastic Religious Art: Playful to Some, Offensive to Others

October 9, 2014
By Spencer Dew

Punk-inspired Argentine artists Marianela Perelli and Pool Paolini attracted international media attention for the show *Barbie the Plastic Religion* that would have featured thirty-three dolls of various characters from religious traditions, primarily Christianity. The collection—made from the iconic Mattel dolls and packaged to look like mass-produced objects in the Barbie line— struck many as cheap provocation. What better tactic for grabbing headlines than to crucify a Ken doll?

The show was set to open October 11, 2014, in Buenos Aires. However, in an apologetic public statement released last week, the artists, who go by the collective title Pool & Marianela, announced that they were removing the dolls from the show, declaring: "We never wanted to hurt the feelings of people of faith." The host gallery canceled the show altogether, citing, even in the absence of the dolls, "threats of destruction" to the gallery space.

Never shying from the controversial, Pool & Marianela have made dolls and paintings of "villains" of history like Charles Manson, Al Capone, and Margaret Thatcher. They have crucified before, too, depicting famed Argentine soccer star Diego Maradona nailed to a cross, his legs severed and standing at its base, rendered in gold.

The pair claims to be shocked at the offense caused by *Plastic Religion* because they never meant the dolls to be read as criticism of religion but rather as engagement, motivated out of "love," with "our religion"—that "our" explicitly a marker of cultural and national identity.

Plastic Religion was an exploration of *Argentine religion* and so included sculptures of Catholic and folk saints. Guided by "respect" for religious diversity, the show was, according to the artists, conceived as a tribute to and manifestation of a distinctly Argentine "melting pot of races and religions living together in harmony." Hindu and Buddhist friends requested the inclusion of figures from their own traditions (Barbie as Kali; Ken as Siddhartha), further highlighting the range of religious identities in Buenos Aires.

The title, *Plastic Religion*, surely generated some of the outrage. "Plastic," as historian of religion David Chidester reminds us, is a term with two valences. On the one hand, "plastic" can signify "the cheap, the tawdry"—that which "is almost immediately disposable." On the other hand, "plastic" also means malleable, fluid, protean—after the Greek god Proteus, who shape-shifted. When we speak of *the plastic,* we are speaking of something with which we can engage in infinite and creative ways.

When Chidester, in *Authentic Fakes,* discusses "plastic religion," he is noting the "transformative capacity for unlimited shape shifting" characteristic of certain religious stories, practices, and beliefs. The veneration of an Argentine folk saint like Gauchito Gil is a textbook example of this "transformative capacity." Narratives surrounding this figure vary: some involve romance, some focus on his criminal activities in defense of the poor, some valorize his military career, but all emphasize his healing of a sick child before his murder by police. Veneration of this figure likewise varies, hinging upon individual expressions of creativity as devotees construct shrines using doll-like figures, red crosses, and pieces of red cloth.

It is Chidester's valence of "ongoing experiment in the making" that Pool & Marianela explore in their sculptures: not throwaway religion but living, creatively vibrant, distinctly Argentine religion. For *Plastic Religion,* Pool & Marianela fashioned a doll of Gauchito Gil by taking the traditionally blond Ken and adding long hair, a mustache, and stubble, along with the bolas of a gaucho and Gil's characteristic red shawl. On the packaging are the words *pídele tu milagro* ("ask him for your miracle").

Many of the other figures intended for the show are of New World origin. Among them is Santo Niño Doctor, a Mexican tradition, popular throughout Argentina, of the Christ child as a medical doctor, complete with stethoscope. Ekeko is another—a pre-Columbian god of prosperity, popular throughout the lower half of the South American continent, garlanded here, in typical fashion, with objects reflecting wealth and abundance.

Also featured is Difunta Correa, here depicted dead in her grave, her child still miraculously feeding from a bare breast; she is a folk saint linked to legends about gauchos discovering such a baby still alive in the arms of a woman who died during the Argentine civil wars. The box for Difunta Correa, in standard Barbie pink, includes a fringe of bottles and roses along the bottom edge of the package's window similar to the accoutrements of veneration seen at any of the hundreds of roadside shrines to this figure.

Locals of San Juan, Argentina, joined the protests over *Plastic Religion,* specifically citing Pool & Marianela's depiction of Difunta Correa. One citizen quoted in several international news stories claimed that their rendition of the saint was "out of place, [because] this is a figure of faith which we care for very much and it is why we patented her image and name years ago."

But part of what Pool & Marianela are saying, quite rightly, is that there is no possibility of patent on popular religious practices. Argentine religion as plastic religion is what the artists are celebrating here. Engagement in stories and images of folk saints such as Gauchito Gil, Santo Niño Doctor, Ekeko, and Difunta Correa are ever changing, personalized. Moreover, material objects—dolls and statues and artwork—are central to the practices of interacting with these figures.

As the artists say, "It is difficult to apologize when our goal was never hurt, but on the contrary, seek to build a message of unity and love of/for religions, framed in the existing social-cultural context." They also speak of *Plastic Religion* as being, instead of canceled, "suspended." Perhaps, if and when the show finds a new home, it can lead not to offense but to appreciation of the dynamic of plasticity in Argentine religious practice.

Resources

Chidester, David. *Authentic Fakes: Religion and American Popular Culture*. Berkeley: University of California Press, 2005.

Roterman, Natalie. "Artists Create Religious Barbie and Ken Dolls Sparking Controversy." *Latin Times*. September 21, 2014. http://www.latintimes.com/artists-create-religious-barbie-and-ken-dolls-sparking-controversy-argentina-263175.

Spencer Dew (PhD, University of Chicago Divinity School) is assistant professor of religious studies and Centenary College Research Professor in the Humanities at Centenary College of Louisiana.

68. #JeSuisCharlie: Blasphemy in Hinduism and Censorship in India

JANUARY 22, 2015
BY WENDY DONIGER

Free speech, under attack in France, is also contested in India, where violence ignited by videos or messages deemed "blasphemous" or "insulting" by orthodox Hindus has long been a reality. In 2014 alone, eighty-five religion-related attacks on the media were reported.

Blasphemy and censorship in India have a complex history because Hinduism in ancient times was primarily orthoprax (and hence often intolerant of violations of social norms), not orthodox; its polytheism included even monotheism among its many doctrines. One god or another was often mocked; there was no concept of divine blasphemy.

To keep the length of today's *Sightings* manageable, let's fast-forward to Britain's colonization of India, which began in 1757. Not only were they British Protestants but they were also Victorian Protestants. They rejected as filthy paganism the sensuous strain of ritual, polytheistic Hinduism, what they regarded as all those kitschy images of gods with all those arms. It reminded them of Catholicism.

But the British respected the more ascetic strain of Indian philosophy, including Indian monism and idealism (so appealing to European philosophers from Schlegel to Hegel) and the Bhagavad Gita (so appealing to the American transcendentalists), and the monotheistic strains of bhakti, on the whole (in their view) a more reasonable sort of religion.

Some Protestants within the British Raj tried to recast Hinduism as a monotheism, with a bible—the Bhagavad Gita—thus also validating the worship of Krishna/Vishnu (the god of the Gita) as a monotheistic god. (The British tended to prefer the company of Muslims to Hindus for a number of reasons, including the simple fact that Islam was a monotheism that revered the Hebrew Bible and the Christian New Testament.)

The many English-speaking Hindus who worked for and with the British came to accept the British evaluation of Hinduism and developed several new forms of so-called Reformed Hinduism, such as the Brahmo Samaj and, later, the Arya Samaj, which valued the philosophical, ascetic aspect of Hinduism and devaluated the worldly, householder aspect.

Such Hindus went about trying to silence the love songs to the gods, to cover up the erotic sculptures, and to kick the temple dancers out of the temples. They were doubly inspired to position the Gita as their bible, both in response to British pressure and in competition with the Muslims, whose monotheism contributed greatly to the Hindus' desire to elevate the monotheistic Gita (as the counterpart to the Muslims' Qur'an) over polytheistic Hinduism.

This sanitized strain of Hinduism, also sometimes called Sanatana Dharma, the Eternal Law, was just one form among many, and a minor strain at that. It thrived primarily among the middle castes, who aspired to raise their social class by aping Victorians, this whole strategy aping the much older Hindu strategy of lower classes aping Brahmins, in a process that the great sociologist M. N. Srinivas called "Sanskritization."

Those at the top and the bottom went on telling their stories and dancing their dances and worshipping their many gods. But the middle castes began to enforce the idea of orthodoxy and to embrace the concept of blasphemy against the gods. Now, for the first time, Hindus of one sort denied the authenticity of other Hindus. Yet the middle castes could not sue the blasphemers, for there was no law against blasphemy in India, not even in British India.

Since British law in India upheld freedom of speech, the authorities needed to employ other means of controlling possibly subversive voices. The laws against libel and sedition became the British Empire's censorship tools in the subcontinent. Prime among these was Indian Penal Code 295(A), which was passed in 1927 at a time of intense conflicts between Hindus (particularly Arya Samaj Hindus) and Muslims.

When the Muslim community demanded a law against insults to religious feelings, the Colonial British Government enacted Section 295(A). The law stated:

> Whoever, with deliberate and malicious intention of outraging the religious feelings of any class of [citizens of India], [by words, either spoken or written, or by signs or by visible representations or otherwise,] insults or attempts to insult the religion or the religious beliefs of that class, shall be punished with imprisonment or either description for a term which may extend to [three years], or with fine, or with both.

Other cases followed, most of them protesting insults against Islam, and some defending Catholics—that is, defending religious minorities against Hindus.

The situation changed dramatically after India's independence from Britain, in 1947, with the rise of a new form of Hindu nationalism, no longer directed against the British but against other religions in India, primarily Islam and then Christianity.

Hindus have long prided themselves on their tolerance, and indeed the worldly, polytheistic, orthoprax strain of Hindus has always been admirably tolerant of the beliefs (if not necessarily the actions) of other religions. But Hindus of the more orthodox strain remain intolerant of any slur cast against their tolerance.

Shortly after Partition, which split the Indian subcontinent into India (with a Hindu majority) and Pakistan (with a Muslim majority), M. S. Golwalker, a member of the nationalist and anti-Muslim Hindu association, the RSS, remarked that since Hindus are, as is well known, the most tolerant people in the world, they deserve to have the land of India to themselves, and therefore the (purportedly less tolerant) Muslims should be disenfranchised.

This movement began to call itself Hindutva, "Hinduness," a term that was invented by the nationalist Vinayak Damodar Savarkar in his 1923 pamphlet *Hindutva: Who Is a Hindu?* Hindutva is both orthoprax and orthodox, and its adherents have inspired violence against both Muslims and Christians.

India still prides itself on having no blasphemy laws (in contrast with Pakistan, which does indeed have them). But 295(A) functions as a blasphemy law, and calls for a nuanced judgment on whether the "outraged religious feelings" of the plaintiffs stem from a lying insult against a group religion or caste, which could lead to violent disorder, making it the equivalent of slander against an individual, or from a reasoned argument or artistic venture intended to uncover the meaning of, or contradictions within, such a group.

In fact, 295(A) has been used more often to incite violence against non-Hindus than to curb it.

The territory of 295(A) is a treacherous no-man's-land in which to maneuver. To prove that one had, or did not have, "deliberate and malicious intention" is a slippery matter. Fear of prosecution under this highly subjective law has silenced a number of writers and publishers in India today.

Resources

Akyol, Mustafa. "Islam's Problem with Blasphemy." *The New York Times.* January 13, 2015. https://www.nytimes.com/2015/01/14/opinion/islams-problem-with-blasphemy.html.

Gold, Daniel. "Organized Hinduisms: From Vedic Truth to Hindu Nation." In

Martin E. Marty and R. Scott Appleby. *The Fundamentalism Project*. Vol. 1, *Fundamentalisms Observed*. Chicago: The University of Chicago Press, 1991.

Golwalkar, M. S. *We or Our Nationhood Defined*. Nagpur: Bharat Publications, 1939.

Hansen, Thomas B. *The Saffron Wave: Democracy and Hindu Nationalism in Modern India*. Oxford: Oxford University Press, 1999.

Islam, Shamsul. *Golwalkar's We or Our Nationhood Defined: A Critique, with the Full Text of the Book*. Pharos Media & Publishing, 2006.

Jaffrelot, Christophe. *The Hindu Nationalist Movement in India*. New York: Columbia University Press, 1998.

Nussbaum, Martha. *The Clash Within: Democracy, Religious Violence, and India's Future*. Cambridge, MA: Belknap, 2009.

———. "Law for Bad Behaviour." *The Indian Express*. February 21, 2014. http://indianexpress.com/article/opinion/columns/law-for-bad-behaviour.

Ren, Chao. "Religion and Nationhood in Late Colonial India." *Constructing the Past* 12, no. 1 (2011): 2–8. https://digitalcommons.iwu.edu/constructing/vol12/iss1/8/.

Savarkar, V. D. *Hindutva: Who Is a Hindu?* New Delhi: Hindi Sahitya Sadan, 2003.

Singh, Sunit. "The Doniger Affair: Freedom of Scholarly Inquiry Takes an Ominous Turn in India." *Sightings*. February 27, 2014.

Srinivas, M. N. *Social Change in Modern India*. Berkeley: University of California Press, 1966.

Wendy Doniger is Mircea Eliade Distinguished Service Professor of the History of Religions at the University of Chicago Divinity School. She also has joint appointments in the Department of South Asian Languages and Civilizations, the Committee on Social Thought, and the College.

69. After the *Charlie Hebdo* Massacre: Islam Must Open Itself to Critique

January 29, 2015
By Jean-Luc Marion

Note: This article was originally published in French in *Le Point*. It was translated by Myriam Renaud.

France is at war; we can no longer doubt that this is the case. But this war has at least three fronts.

The first front is obvious: an act of war occurred in Paris, against a magazine, leaving more than a dozen dead. The government and the nation have started to respond. The government is taking up its principal role—the protection of citizens, handling the security concerns with which it has been entrusted. It is acting as quickly and as well as it can.

As for the nation, we have already witnessed that, far from crumbling and yielding to fear, it is uniting. A republican reflex will bolster this coming together, and extremists will not benefit in the slightest from the crisis.

Finally, the danger posed by Islam is not new—it is familiar to France since the seventeenth century. In fact, the history of France proves that such wars have already been waged and won. The recent history of Europe confirms that democracies eventually vanquish totalitarianism and fascism. Thus, this front will hold. However, when it comes to the other two, nothing is certain.

The second front comes into view as soon as one considers that the attack targeted a political and satirical newspaper that caricatured (I underscore this point) all of the religions, based on the principle that one can laugh about anything "and mock everything else."

If this newspaper was tolerated and even supported by the public, although it was often shocking, it owed this to a fundamental and ancient trait of French society—the freedom to think and to speak—first secured under the Ancien Régime. It rose to the level of principle in the Declaration of the Rights of Man, took effect when all legislation against blasphemy was abolished at the beginning of the nineteenth century, and was reinforced by the law separating Church and State.

In a way, this crime targeted a central tenet of French society: secularism. Here the second front opens out. What is secularism worth today? We must recognize the ambiguity of this concept and its application. Because, if the State is secular, society is not.

More exactly: the State must be secular (it must refrain from showing favoritism for any particular religion, permit them all to exist under the protection of the law, showing a preference neither for religious belief, nor for unbelief), a stance that I hope no one contests.

But society is not secular and cannot be secular, because upon becoming citizens, men and women do not lose their freedom of conscience—their religious freedom—but, on the contrary, exercise it fully. Besides, the neutrality of the State must never be based on neutralization, forced or tacit, of the religious dimensions of the real men and women who make up society.

However, "French-style secularism" has too often tended to understand itself and to comport itself like an army fending off the religions (especially Catholicism), behaving as if it were another religion, substituting itself, in the name of Reason, for the historical religions. Today, this tendency reveals itself in so-called "social" reforms, more or less imposed on people who are more or less in agreement, manipulated, or simply ignored.

This tendency is sometimes imposed on Christians but also Jews and, henceforth, on Muslims as a secularism of prohibition, of punishment, even of repression.

The second front consists of—and is much more difficult to secure than the first front—a reformation of the secular pact in France (and thus in Europe). To defend secularism, an emergency no one debates, we must redefine it, in positive terms, and not as a constraint. Because we can't require all of France's citizens to emasculate themselves religiously.

This is a problem with which we've struggled for the past twenty years. Will we know how to address it? It seems to me doubtful that French politicians, still extremely ideological and rather ignorant on the question of religion, are capable of this today.

There is also the third front, the most difficult of the three. The terrorist attacks have a common, though hazy, cultural and political origin: the world of Islam. To recognize this is not equivalent to a facile rallying to the banner of "culture wars" or lack of integration or discrimination. It merely entails acknowledging that our fellow citizens of Muslim faith (and also acknowledging, one hopes, that this is the case for a majority of the world's Muslims) suffer from a terrible situation.

The situation can be summed up in this way: the religions demonstrate their excellence only by allowing—and even better, by choosing, for themselves, to undergo the ordeal of self-critique—tests of their religious validity. Religions that do not do this either disappear or degrade ideologically.

Islam has not yet opened itself up to a close analysis (including philological analysis to understand how its texts came into being, an assessment of the interpretations of these texts, in-depth research into their actual religious history, et cetera) for historic reasons which themselves would be worthwhile to examine.

In contrast, other religions have done so and are still doing so, including the Catholic tradition, the Protestant traditions, and the Jewish tradition. This is the main reason that certain Muslims have so much difficulty stepping into the secularism that the other religions embrace in France.

This issue must not be set aside due to the emotion of the moment. It is essential not to confuse or stigmatize. But we owe that much to Muslims; we owe it to them to point out this difficulty. And, if possible, to help them confront it. That, more than the State and the elected class, is the help that the other religions, especially Christianity, can contribute.

The fundamental debate which has not set French society ablaze can play itself out in interreligious dialogue. During the attacks on the cartoonists of *Charlie Hebdo*, by some significant and providential irony, representatives of French imams were meeting with Pope Francis in the Vatican. We cannot say or do better.

Resource

Marion, Jean-Luc. "Jean-Luc Marion: 'L'islam doit faire l'épreuve de la critique.'" *Le Point.* January 12, 2015. http://www.lepoint.fr/politique/jean-luc-marion-l -islam-doit-faire-l-epreuve-de-la-critique-12-01-2015-1895795_20.php.

Jean-Luc Marion is the Andrew Thomas Greeley and Grace McNichols Greeley Professor of Catholic Studies and professor of the philosophy of religions and theology at the University of Chicago Divinity School.

70. A Reply to Jean-Luc Marion's "After *Charlie Hebdo*, Islam Must Critique Itself"

FEBRUARY 12, 2015
BY BRUCE LINCOLN AND ANTHONY C. YU

Our University of Chicago colleague Jean-Luc Marion, who is the Andrew Thomas Greeley and Grace McNichols Greeley Professor of Catholic Studies, wrote a passionate response to the horrific attacks in *Charlie Hebdo*'s offices in Paris this past January. The final toll: sixteen dead and twenty-two injured.

Marion's outrage and grief are not only understandable but also shared by countless individuals and communities around the world. We are grateful that in the face of such repugnant atrocities, our colleague throughout his brief essay has emphasized setting aside "the emotion of the moment," not wanting "to confuse or stigmatize," and that "our fellow citizens of Muslim faith . . . suffer from a terrible situation."

Despite deep sympathy for our esteemed colleague and the French people at large, we also feel compelled to address some troubling aspects of Marion's statements concerning religion, because our common profession is defined by its attempted study and understanding.

Announcing clearly from the beginning that "France is at war," Marion's essay proceeds to define the homicides committed by three militants, all of whom were French citizens, as an act of war, followed by a second point that such an act will more closely unite the nation to resist with greater courage and resolve.

Marion's prediction that the homicides would "unite the nation" was largely fulfilled as subsequent events have unfolded, although one must note the young Muslims who refused a moment of silence for the victims. Even so, construing the situation as "war"—something usually understood as armed hostility between nation-states—is dangerous hyperbole or, worse yet, a self-fulfilling act of performative speech that initially misconstrues, then dramatically expands both the problem and conflict.

Such hyperbole is also evident in Marion's assertion that "the danger posed by Islam is not new—it is familiar to France since the seventeenth century. . . . The recent history of Europe confirms democracies eventually vanquish totalitarianism and fascism." We wonder what evidence there is for so characterizing the entire faith of Islam as one endangering France for so long.

The implied equation of Islam with totalitarianism and fascism is even more inflammatory and disturbing. Western civilization, after all, owes an immense debt to Islam and to Arabic communities for helping to preserve and transmit the priceless intellectual legacy of antiquity, without which the modern West would have been immeasurably impoverished. There would have been no Descartes without Plato's and Aristotle's works, which were recovered and translated by medieval Arabic philosophers. The Arabic bequest not only benefited Westerners but also, for example, Chinese and other Asian people, who profited (in mathematics, astronomy, and medical knowledge, to name three forms coming to mind) from contact with Islam.

We do not disagree entirely with Marion's earnest plea for Muslims to engage in "self-critique," but he seems to be unfamiliar with the cogent essays Talal Asad has addressed to this issue, demonstrating that "Islam" (if one must, for the sake of convenience, reduce a complex and diverse tradition to a simple monad) constantly reflects on itself, cultivates internal debate and critique, and identifies problems and shortcomings, which it then struggles to address.

Once this is recognized, Marion's point becomes more problematic, for he is urging "Islam" to engage in the same kind of self-examination and revision that "Christianity" experienced during the Reformation and Enlightenment. What was an internal critique for one tradition thus becomes an imperative that one tradition would impose on another, something the latter experiences as alien to its own history, precepts, and sense of integrity; something it associates, moreover, with European claims of cultural superiority and a history of colonial aggression.

Even if "Islam" were to follow Marion's prescription, we wonder what criteria he would recommend that "they" follow to "test their religious validity." Does a secular state have the final say in defining what is "religious validity," much as the People's Republic of China avers in its constitution that only those who practice "normal religion" will be tolerated by the state? The question of how to make all religions equally acceptable to a secular republic of the French sort is not identical to—nor easily reconciled with—the question of how to create a society fully tolerant of religious difference.

Marion justly urges us to avoid "a facile rallying to the banner of 'culture wars,' or lack of integration, or discrimination." Noble as that counsel may be, one needs to say more about the social and cultural ground for breeding hatred and violence, i.e., the sharply disadvantaged situation of Muslims in France (and not just France) with regard to employment, education, housing, protection under law, and simple dignity.

It is one thing for *Charlie Hebdo* to mock the pope, and quite another to mock Muhammad. To poke fun at the icons revered by the powerful is a courageous act of iconoclasm; to ridicule those of the weak is cheap bullying, as it subjects people who already suffer abuse of multiple sorts to public humiliation, making sport of their (perceived) inability to defend the things they hold sacred.

We understand the need to rally in defense of *liberté*, and we also understand that free speech includes forms of critical speech that may be cruel and offensive, such as iconoclasm, blasphemy, ridicule, and derision. But one also has to realize that when those who enjoy the full benefits of citizenship use their *liberté* to mock others to whom basic rights are abridged or denied, something has gone badly amiss.

The most important front on which France needs to wage a sustained struggle today is precisely the one Marion ignores: the struggle to extend *égalité* and *fraternité* to its Muslim population. Here, progress depends on understanding the criminal events in Paris not as salvos that open a new front or new phase in a long-running war, but as symptoms that follow on—and point to—sustained failures of sociocultural integration, socioeconomic equity, moral sensibility, political accountability, and human understanding.

France may be the flashpoint of the moment, but the issues extend far beyond.

Resources

Asad, Talal. "The Limits of Religious Criticism in the Middle East: Notes on Islamic Public Argument." In *Genealogies of Religion: Discipline and Reasons of Power in Christianity and Islam*. Baltimore: Johns Hopkins University Press, 1993.

Marion, Jean-Luc. "After the *Charlie Hebdo* Massacre, Islam Must Open Itself to Critique." *Sightings*. January 29, 2015.

Bruce Lincoln (PhD, University of Chicago Divinity School) is Caroline E. Haskell Distinguished Service Professor of the History of Religions, Middle Eastern Studies, and Medieval Studies at the University of Chicago Divinity School. He is also associate faculty in the Departments of Anthropology and Classics at the University of Chicago. Anthony C. Yu (PhD, University of Chicago Divinity School) is Carl Darling Buck Distinguished Service Professor Emeritus in the Humanities and professor emeritus of religion and literature at the University of Chicago Divinity School; also in the Departments of Comparative Literature, East Asian Languages and Civilizations, English Language and Literature, and the Committee on Social Thought at the University of Chicago.

71. Another Take on "After *Charlie Hebdo,* Islam Must Critique Itself"

FEBRUARY 19, 2015
BY MATTHEW KAPSTEIN

Despite my agreement with my esteemed colleagues Professors Bruce Lincoln and Anthony Yu in most aspects of their response in last week's *Sightings* to an earlier *Sightings* piece, "After the *Charlie Hebdo* Massacre: Islam Must Open Itself to Critique," by a third distinguished colleague, Professor Jean-Luc Marion, their conclusions strike me as ignoring important dimensions of the issues at hand.

The terrible events of January 7–9 in Paris were not, as they aver, the symptoms of social and economic disadvantage or similar factors. Symptoms of such problems manifest themselves in France, as in many other countries, in increased petty crime, gang activity, drug use, elevated unemployment, occasional car-jackings, arson and riot, and the like.

Among these symptoms, I do not see fit to include targeted, cold-blooded murder, which is what took place in Paris.

These acts of murder, moreover, are part of a pattern whereby certain individuals who regard themselves as acting on behalf of Islam take aim on two particular groups: "blasphemers" and Jews.

As none of my three learned colleagues addressed the wantonly anti-Semitic dimensions of the crimes that were perpetrated, and the manner in which they continue an ongoing series of related assaults on Jews in France—including the kidnapping, torture, and murder of Ilan Halimi by the so-called "Gang des Barbares" (2006), the slaughter of children at a Jewish day school by Mohammed Merah (2012), the carnage unleashed at the Jewish Museum of Brussels by French national Mehdi Nemmouche (2014)—I believe that there is an obligation to set the record about this straight.

If these are "symptoms," they are symptoms not of the deficit of *égalité* and *fraternité* in France, but of the manipulative use of anti-Semitic propaganda in large parts of the contemporary Muslim world, whereby the powers that be have encouraged political objections to Israel to morph into global hatred of Jews.

To achieve this, the tools of classical European anti-Semitism, as exemplified in the calumnies of the czarist forgery, *The Protocols of the Elders of*

Zion, have been trotted out, dusted off, and given new life in the contemporary Arab media. The perpetrators of the acts under discussion here had all been trained by radical organizations in the Middle East in which they were indoctrinated in this poison, and this became one of their key motivations.

It must be stressed that Jews in France face similar circumstances to French Muslims in several respects.

Many, like France's Muslims, hail from North Africa and live in the same working-class suburbs. Jews who are observant (like those gunned down in the Hyper Casher supermarket by Amedy Coulibaly) share with Muslims the sense that France's commitment to public *laïcité*—which prohibits Muslim headscarves and Jewish kippahs in many venues and ensures that halal and kosher meals are unavailable in most school and office cafeterias—presents them with particular obstacles, and sometimes indignities, that other French citizens and residents do not have to face.

French Jews and Muslims have both resented being the objects of derogatory humor and of far-right-wing polemics. And just as some parts of the French Muslim community have been susceptible to the lures of anti-Semitism, so there are French Jews who have embraced Islamophobia. But even the French chapter of the Jewish Defense League, which is not prone to shy away from a fight, has not seen fit to express French Jewish discontent through cold-blooded murder.

The events of January were due to the legitimation and encouragement within some quarters of the Muslim world of the murder of "blasphemers" and Jews. And although the vast majority of French Muslims, as also Muslims elsewhere, by no means condone this, the condemnations have not been nearly loud or prevalent enough to diminish the attraction, for some, of extreme militancy.

This is not to say that the alienation from French society felt by some French Muslims, which is to be explained in large measure by socioeconomic factors, has played no role at all here. It is this, in part, that has inspired French jihadis to reaffirm their Muslim identity by joining militant groups and seeking training in arms and explosives among them.

At the same time, we must recognize that the French social contract has historically been exceptionally generous and *pace* Professors Lincoln and Yu, Muslims in France who are citizens or legal residents—and most by far are—enjoy the benefits of France's systems of public education, health care, unemployment insurance, aid to families with dependent children, et cetera.

It is true that those who live in poorer neighborhoods must deal with poorer facilities, particularly in the area of housing, and with elevated crime and diminished security. The poorer neighborhoods, too, harbor larger proportions of illegal immigrants, who are not eligible to receive all of the benefits others enjoy, a factor that does contribute to the overall impoverishment of some quarters.

Moreover, the French historical commitment to *mixité*, ensuring that neighborhoods are occupied by persons of varied social class, has increasingly given way to American-style economic segregation. None of this has been helped by the poor performance of the French economy in recent years, its inability to generate sufficient jobs and to secure long-term prosperity.

So France faces genuine challenges if it is to maintain its social contract and ensure that its Muslim population universally comes to be included within it. Part of that challenge, unfortunately, now inevitably involves the costly, divisive, and painful task of identifying, surveilling, and inhibiting ideologically motivated killers.

Postscript: In the days since the above was written, Copenhagen has seen a murderous incident apparently copying the Paris attacks, three hundred Jewish graves have been desecrated by a teenage gang in eastern France, and Roland Dumas, a former French foreign minister, has crudely castigated the present prime minister, Manuel Valls, for being "influenced" by his wife, who happens to be Jewish, in respect to Jewish affairs.

As the malediction of anti-Semitism continues to spread, willful ignorance or silence are no longer acceptable options.

Resources

Adida, Claire, David D. Laitin, and Marie-Anne Valford. "Terror in France: Implications for Muslim Integration." *The Washington Post*. January 14, 2015. https://www.washingtonpost.com/news/monkey-cage/wp/2015/01/14 /terror-in-france-implications-for-muslim-integration.

Alcindor, Yamiche, and Elena Berton. "Four Killed at Paris Grocery Store Were All Jewish." *USA Today*. January 11, 2015. https://www.usatoday.com /story/news/world/2015/01/10/details-about-victims-of-terror-attacks-in -france-emerge/21567281.

Associated Press. "Deadly Shooting at Jewish Museum in Brussels." CBS News. May 24, 2014. https://www.cbsnews.com/news/brussels-jewish-museum -scene-of-deadly-shooting.

———. "French President: Anti-Semitism and Islamophobia Are Threats to the Nation." *Haaretz*. February 17, 2015. https://www.haaretz.com/jewish/news /1.642893.

Friedersdorf, Conor. "Europe's Increasingly Targeted Jews Take Stock." *The*

Atlantic. February 17, 2015. https://www.theatlantic.com/international /archive/2015/02/anti-semitism-europe-france-grave-desecration-Zvika -Klein/385547.

Lincoln, Bruce, and Anthony C. Yu. "A Reply to Jean-Luc Marion's 'After *Charlie Hebdo*, Islam Must Critique Itself.'" *Sightings*. February 12, 2015.

Marion, Jean-Luc. "After the *Charlie Hebdo* Massacre, Islam Must Open Itself to Critique." Sightings. January 29, 2015.

Sayare, Scott, and Steven Erlanger. "4 Killed at Jewish School in Southwestern France." *The New York Times*. March 19, 2012. http://www.nytimes.com/2012 /03/20/world/europe/gunman-kills-3-at-a-jewish-school-in-france.html.

Smith, Craig S. "Torture and Death of Jew Deepen Fears in France." *The New York Times*. March 5, 2006. http://www.nytimes.com/2006/03/05/world /europe/torture-and-death-of-jew-deepen-fears-in-france.html.

Wakin, Daniel J. "Anti-Semitic 'Elders of Zion' Gets New Life on Egypt TV." *The New York Times*. October 26, 2002. http://www.nytimes.com/2002/10/26 /world/anti-semitic-elders-of-zion-gets-new-life-on-egypt-tv.html.

Matthew Kapstein is Numata Visiting Professor of Buddhist Studies at the University of Chicago Divinity School and director of Tibetan studies at the École Pratique des Hautes Études, Paris.

72. Rifts in the Mormon Family:
What Just Happened?

NOVEMBER 19, 2015
BY GRANT HARDY

Earlier this month, on November 5, the First Presidency of the Church of Jesus Christ of Latter-day Saints quietly changed a handbook that is available only to church leaders.

The changes stipulated that any Mormons in same-sex marriages were to be considered apostates, which would likely result in their excommunication. In addition, their minor children were to be denied naming blessings, baptism, confirmation, and priesthood ordinations (universal for adolescent males), which would likely result in their alienation from the faith.

When the new policies were leaked, there was an immediate outcry from Latter-day Saints on social media, including those who accept the church's categorization of homosexual behavior as sin, but who nevertheless feel the new rules punished children for their parents' choices.

On November 6, one of the Twelve Apostles gave a hastily arranged interview to explain the changes to the faithful, noting that the new policies followed the precedent of dealing with polygamists, and that the intent was to protect minor children from religious conflict in their homes.

The current controversy stands in contrast with the events in June; after the Supreme Court struck down state bans on same-sex marriage, the First Presidency sent a letter to all local church leaders in the United States reiterating the church's position that while same-sex marriage was now legal, it was still prohibited for Latter-day Saints. Mormon bishops were forbidden to perform such marriages or allow church facilities to be used for same-sex weddings or receptions.

Leaders were instructed to read the letter to all adults and teenagers in Sunday meetings, and because the letter was in line with what most Mormons already believed, it was taken in stride.

However, the recent, non-public change to the leaders' handbook continued to cause turmoil as many pointed out that Mormon children are often raised by parents who are not keeping LDS standards—resulting in religious tension at home—and that most of those affected by the new policies would be children in joint-custody situations.

The First Presidency responded in a statement on November 13 indicating that the rules were only to be applied to families in which the same-sex parents were the primary caregivers, and thus would apply to far fewer children.

The next day, November 14, a rally was held in Salt Lake City at which some 1,500 Latter-day Saints were reported to have resigned their membership, the largest such protest in the history of the LDS Church.

More troubling to top church leaders, however, is that many of those who expressed concerns were active, believing Latter-day Saints, including some of the local leaders charged with implementing the new policies. This is nearly unprecedented in Mormondom.

What changed between June and November?

The new regulations, intended to prevent the normalization of same-sex families in church settings, represent a significant shift in how gay and lesbian Mormons interact with other church members. The regulations also appear to set basic doctrinal principles at odds with one another.

For instance, core tenets of Mormonism include agency, the innocence of children, and the rejection of original sin. Withholding baptism from the children of willing parents is virtually unheard of. And to suggest that some teenagers will do just fine without the gift of the Holy Ghost—which is conferred at confirmation—does not square with standard LDS teachings.

It's true that the LDS Church employed stringent policies to stamp out polygamy in the early twentieth century, but same-sex marriage today is quite different. One practice was illegal and scorned; the other lawful and increasingly accepted. The children of polygamists are often socialized to become polygamists while children of same-sex marriages are overwhelmingly heterosexual.

Given the history of polygamy in early Mormonism, those who cling to the practice claim higher religious authority and are often part of an underground movement. In other words, they are apostates. By contrast, the decision to marry someone of the same sex cannot be supported with quotations from Joseph Smith or Brigham Young.

Apostasy, in Mormon thought, entails a direct challenge to church authority and requires mandatory disciplinary councils, along with murder, incest, and child abuse. Other sins, even serious sins, do not rise to the same level, and disciplinary councils are left to the discretion of local leaders.

Many LGBT Mormons accept the church's high valuation of marriage and children, yet labeling same-sex marriage as apostasy makes a lifetime, legally binding commitment between gays or lesbians a more serious sin than gay promiscuity.

Furthermore, the mandatory disciplinary councils suggest that same-sex marriage is worse than attempted murder, rape, sexual abuse, or spousal abuse, all listed in the handbook as sins for which "formal church discipline *may* be necessary" (emphasis in the original).

It should be noted that although LGBT issues have roiled many American denominations in recent years, the stakes are higher for Latter-day Saints. Salvation in Mormonism occurs at the level of families rather than individuals. The highest degree of heaven is reserved for husband and wife pairs, with a promise of eternal procreation, just as all humankind began as spirit children of a heavenly Father and Mother.

Family members must be sealed to each other through ceremonies in LDS temples. The loss of any family member from the faith breaks this chain, yet it is not at all clear how gays or lesbians would fit into the grand family scheme of heaven.

At this point, there is no theology for how to integrate LGBT siblings or children into the church other than lifelong celibacy. And if Mormons are forced to choose between church and family, many will choose family.

Another area of contention concerns church authority. While there is some flexibility in policy-making, fundamental doctrines are revealed, it is believed, not only in scripture but also to modern prophets and apostles.

However, the distinction between doctrine and policy is not always sharp, and despite an assumption that the highest church leaders are not infallible, there is a sense that it is disloyal to point out any potential mistakes. It has also been troubling to some faithful LDS that changes of such significance seem not to have been well-thought-out beforehand.

So gay and lesbian Mormons, whether married or not, are upset; extended families of LGBT Latter-day Saints are upset; some devout members are upset at policies they perceived as draconian or doctrinally problematic; conservative Mormons are upset with fellow congregants who questioned the wisdom of the changes or the inspiration of leaders; and senior church leaders are undoubtedly upset at how all these decisions were rolled out. That's a lot of unhappiness over a few lines in a handbook.

For Mormons, anxiety over the changing definition of marriage is not simply a matter of conservative prejudice; it is an issue with deep theological consequences which appear to contradict God's plan for eternal families.

Yet many LDS families in the here and now are feeling keen discomfort, and the Mormon community as a whole, which operates more like a worldwide family than most other denominations, has discovered rifts that go beyond the old distinctions between active and inactive members.

Resources

Bailey, Sarah Pulliam. "Mormon Church to Exclude Children of Same-Sex Couples from Getting Blessed and Baptized until They Are 18." *The Washington Post*. November 6, 2015. https://www.washingtonpost.com/news/acts-of-faith/wp/2015/11/05/mormon-church-to-exclude-children-of-same-sex-couples-from-getting-blessed-and-baptized-until-they-are-18.

"Church Leaders Counsel Members after Supreme Court Same-Sex Marriage Decision." The Church of Jesus Christ of Latter-day Saints. July 1, 2015. https://www.lds.org/church/news/church-leaders-counsel-members-after-supreme-court-same-sex-marriage-decision?lang=eng.

Healy, Jack. "Mormon Resignations Put Support for Gays over Fealty to Faith." *The New York Times*. November 15, 2015. https://www.nytimes.com/2015/11/16/us/mormon-resignations-put-support-for-gays-over-fealty-to-faith.html.

Riess, Jana. "Mormon Apostle Stands By New Policy Barring Children of Same-Sex Marriages." Religion News Service. November 7, 2015. http://religionnews.com/2015/11/07/mormon-apostle-stands-by-new-policy-barring-children-of-same-sex-marriages.

Smith, Julie M. "Consequences, Intended or Otherwise, in Light of the Update." *Times and Seasons*. November 13, 2015. http://www.timesandseasons.org/index.php/2015/11/consequences-intended-or-otherwise-in-light-of-the-update.

Welch, Rosalynde. "The Handbook Changes from the Institutional Perspective." *Times and Seasons*. November 6, 2015. https://www.timesandseasons.org/index.php/2015/11/the-handbook-changes-from-the-institutional-perspective.

Grant Hardy is professor of history and religious studies at the University of North Carolina at Asheville.

73. Historic Paris Climate Agreement Reflects Years of Advocacy by Religious People

December 17, 2015
By Sarah E. Fredericks

Last Saturday, world leaders from 196 nations who had gathered in Paris adopted a historic agreement about climate change.

Millions of religious people and their secular partners around the world have worked for years to make this agreement possible.

While religious people care about climate change for a host of reasons, many consider it to be the most significant social justice issue that human civilization has faced.

People are already feeling the effects of climate change. More extreme weather events around the globe disrupt agriculture, damage homes, and kill people. The government of Kiribati, a South Pacific nation, has preemptively bought land in Fiji (from the Church of England) so that its population can emigrate to escape rising seas.

Climate change will have the largest impact on people who lack the resources to respond sufficiently. Additionally, those experiencing the worst of climate change generally contributed least to the problem. Thus, climate change is an issue of justice.

Religious people have worked for decades to convince their fellow believers that climate change is important using sermons, prayers, rituals, and educational materials.

Formal statements have also drawn attention to climate change. Pope Francis's encyclical *Laudato si'* calls upon Catholics and "all people of goodwill" to take action. Similarly, the global Islamic Climate Change Declaration issued in August articulates the religious dimensions of climate change and urged leaders meeting in Paris to "an urgent and radical reappraisal" of existing policies and quick decisive action.

Religious non-governmental organizations (NGOs) focused on poverty, social justice, women's rights, and children increasingly recognize that climate change affects their work and advocate, educate, and fund projects accordingly.

In Paris, members of religious NGOs, and religious people motivated by their consciences but acting in secular leadership roles, have played an active role in the climate discussions. The Global Catholic Climate Movement, the ACT Alliance, Religions for Peace, and Our Voices combined efforts to present a petition for climate justice with 1,833,973 signatures to Christiana Figueres, the top climate official at the UN, who was "visibly moved."

Demonstrations were limited due to heightened French security but ecumenical prayer services at Notre Dame, a "Fast for Climate," and, of course, advocacy work continued. Religious NGOs and their secular partners did incredible work online to educate people about the talks and help them maintain pressure on climate negotiators.

What did the Paris talks achieve?

World leaders agreed to "hold[ing] the increase in the global average temperature to well below 2°C above pre-industrial levels and to pursue efforts to limit the temperature increase to 1.5°C above pre-industrial" temperatures. Compared to earlier international discussions, this statement better recognizes the needs of the most vulnerable for whom even 1.5°C will be catastrophic.

Nations also pledged individual targets for greenhouse gas emissions reductions. Understanding that, if met, current emissions pledges will only halt global temperature rise at approximately 2.7°C, the agreement sets up a framework to have nations review their emissions levels every five years and periodically adopt more stringent emissions targets.

The agreement also provides for financial and technological assistance to developing nations to deal with climate change. The Green Climate Fund, a mechanism set up before the Paris talks, is a prime method of funding to aid those who need it most; Secretary of State John Kerry pledged in Paris to double US contributions.

How did people respond?

Paul Cook, advocacy director of Tearfund, an international Christian group focused on poverty alleviation, responded as religious people with insight into the negotiations did:

> We welcome the agreement brokered at these crucial climate talks. This is a good step forward, but let's not be complacent. This doesn't give us everything we need—nations will need to go further in reducing their emissions over the next few years to ensure the global temperature does not rise by more than 1.5 degrees to avoid the worst impacts of climate change.

Indeed, within hours of the agreement, many NGOs already had updated their websites to reflect the new aims of their advocacy work: to ensure that promises made in Paris are kept and, hopefully, exceeded, as is necessary to ensure justice for the most vulnerable.

Resources

Brown, Stephen. "UN Climate Chief Thanks Pilgrims for 'Every Single Step' to Climate Justice." World Council of Churches. November 30, 2015. https://www.oikoumene.org/en/press-centre/news/un-climate-chief-thanks-pilgrims-for-201cevery-single-step201d-to-climate-justice.

Caramel, Laurence. "Besieged by the Rising Tides of Climate Change, Kiribati Buys Land in Fiji." *The Guardian*. June 30, 2014. https://www.theguardian.com/environment/2014/jul/01/kiribati-climate-change-fiji-vanua-levu.

Chan, Sewell, and Melissa Eddy. "Leaders Move to Convert Paris Climate Pledges into Action." *The New York Times*. December 13, 2015. https://www.nytimes.com/2015/12/14/world/europe/leaders-move-to-convert-paris-climate-pledges-into-action.html.

"Climate Change Statements from World Religions." The Forum on Religion and Ecology at Yale. http://fore.yale.edu/climate-change/statements-from-world-religions.

"Climate Change 2014: Synthesis Report." Intergovernmental Panel on Climate Change, 2014. http://www.ipcc.ch/report/ar5/syr.

"Climate Pledges Will Bring 2.7°C of Warming, Potential for More Action." Climate Action Tracker. December 8, 2015. http://climateactiontracker.org/news/253/Climate-pledges-will-bring-2.7C-of-warming-potential-for-more-action.html.

"Islamic Declaration on Global Climate Change." International Islamic Climate Change Symposium, 2015. http://www.ifees.org.uk/declaration.

Kerry, John. "Remarks on COP21 and Action beyond Paris." US Department of State. December 9, 2015. https://2009-2017.state.gov/secretary/remarks/2015/12/250502.htm.

Kim, Grace Ji-Sun. "Religious Leaders at COP21 Issue Urgent Plea for Care of Creation." *Sojourners*. December 7, 2015. https://sojo.net/articles/religious-leaders-cop21-issue-urgent-plea-care-creation.

"Paris Agreement." United Nations, 2015. http://unfccc.int/files/essential_background/convention/application/pdf/english_paris_agreement.pdf.

Pope Francis. "*Laudato si': On Care for Our Common Home*." Vatican, 2015. http://w2.vatican.va/content/francesco/en/encyclicals/documents/papa-francesco_20150524_enciclica-laudato-si.html.

Voorhaar, Ria. "Civil Society Responds as Final Paris Climate Agreement Released." Climate Action Network. December 12, 2015. http://www.climatenetwork.org /press-release/civil-society-responds-final-paris-climate-agreement-released.

Sarah E. Fredericks is assistant professor of environmental ethics at the University of Chicago Divinity School.

74. Southern Baptists

FEBRUARY 8, 2016
BY MARTIN E. MARTY

Last Monday's *Sightings* surveyed recent online religion stories and found only one about Southern Baptists. This was strange or exceptional or meant some overlooking of items on our part.

A sample of more representative and reliable accounting has since appeared in a Religion News Service story by Jonathan Merritt, "Does Russell Moore Really Represent Southern Baptists?" Most readers may not know or care about one individual in one denomination, and some readers may not care about any individual in any denomination. But there are good reasons to take at least occasional note of some. Russell Moore is one of them.

Many actively religious citizens "do" much of their religionizing in local gatherings: congregations, churches, parishes, synagogues, mosques, et cetera, which are public squares, even if they often get labeled "private." Among denominations, the media pays attention to the Southern Baptist Convention (SBC), since, among other things, there are more Southern Baptists in the United States alone than there are Jews in the whole world. And SBC people do have ways of making news, if, among other reasons, they are often in conflict and they sometimes spin off, against their wishes, sizable new movements of at least quasi-denominational character.

Paradoxes abound among Southern Baptists. From one angle they are traditionally religious, founded and defined. From other angles they are secular, by most definitions, including the devotion of many "public-life" Baptists to worldly and materialist concerns. A sociologist of religion some decades ago wrote that three words could connote these extremes: Texas Baptist Millionaire.

In polity, they are fiercely devoted to local autonomy, yet they are also more mobilizable as groups for common declarations and actions than are adherents in most denominations. Traditionally, they were uneasy about political involvements, but in the most recent half century their level of involvement has increased dramatically, and those who cover politics cannot avoid mention of them.

Back to Russell Moore, who is president of the always on-the-spot Ethics and Religious Liberty Commission of the SBC. He succeeds Richard Land, usually tabbed a founder of the New Christian Right. Moore is perceived as being more moderate, but he knows that the word "moderate" does not always work in the SBC. And Jonathan Merritt, veteran commentator on things Southern Baptist, is not always seen as neutral when addressing his subject.

In the little space remaining, let's notice what Merritt found noteworthy in Moore's scope. Skipping items on political campaigns, here are some: Is Moore "soft" on gay marriage and abortion? Too ready to support "reform that 'establishes a path toward legal status and/or citizenship'"? Right to have denounced "ex-gay therapy" as a "cure" for homosexuality? Right to have written "Let's take down that flag" of the Confederacy from the South Carolina capitol? Should he have signed a letter asking Congress to "reject damaging changes to the U.S. refugee resettlement system"?

Was Moore right when he told Merritt, "One thing you have to remember about Southern Baptists is, if you're 9 percent out in front of them, you're a trailblazer. If you're 10 percent out in front of them, you're dead"?

I've not met Russell Moore, but I've read enough to wish him "happy 9.5 percent in front" status, relief from Baptist wars, and freedom for happier Baptist worship.

Resources

Marty, Martin E. "What Makes 'Religion' News?" *Sightings*. February 1, 2016. https://divinity.uchicago.edu/sightings/what-makes-religion-news.

Merritt, Jonathan. "Does Russell Moore Really Represent Southern Baptists?" Religion News Service. February 3, 2016. http://religionnews.com/2016/02/03 /does-russell-moore-really-represent-southern-baptists.

75. Easter's *Deus ex Machina*

MARCH 24, 2016
BY JEFF JAY

Even in Hollywood, Easter's approach rekindles hope. A hope for profit, that is, since films about Jesus seem to make their debut in late February. *The Passion of the Christ*, for instance, was released in theaters on the 25th in 2004, *Son of God* on the 28th in 2014, and *Risen* on the 19th of this year. As the self-chosen sacrifices of Lent grind on and the light of springtime brightens, Hollywood marketers bank that Christian moviegoers will itch and pine to see Jesus on the big screen.

The relationship between Easter and dramatic narrative runs much deeper. In the Gospel of Mark, which is the earliest extant gospel, the story of the empty tomb in chapter 16, verses 1–8, recalls the *deus ex machina* (meaning "god from the machine") scenes that occur at the end of ancient Greek tragedies (most frequently in plays by Euripides). In these tragedies, a god or demigod swings into view and, while hovering over the stage suspended from a stage-crane, he or she commands mortals to embrace the fate that awaits them. The *deus ex machina* also calms the mortals frightened by the sudden epiphany of his or her unexpected appearance, predicts the future, and issues commands with which the mortals comply, although in some cases, only grudgingly.

This is exactly what happens in the Gospel of Mark 16:1–8. An otherworldly youth dressed in white appears in the tomb to the women who stand in awe of this epiphany (16:5). He calms them with the message of Jesus's resurrection, "It is Jesus you seek, the Nazarene, the crucified one. He was raised. He is not here" (16:6; all translations are by the author). Like a *deus ex machina* the otherworldly youth commands the women, "Go! Tell the disciples" that Jesus will meet them in Galilee (16:7). The women obey the first command, for they flee the tomb, but they fail to comply with the command to tell the disciples. The Gospel of Mark thus ends at 16:8, seemingly coming to a close in failure and distress: "Trembling and distraction seized them, and they told no one anything, for they were afraid" (16:8).

Despite the efforts of later scribes to tame this radical Easter story by appending verses 16:9–20, which describe Jesus's visits to the disciples (likely added in the second century), it is all but certain that the Gospel of Mark originally ended at 16:8.

After all, the *machina* scenes in the Greek tragic dramas function as a signal to spectators that the drama has reached its finale. In some cases, the gods' commands to depart, to go, to sail, or to exit serve as a means to clear the stage and thus unequivocally indicate the conclusion of the play. The *machina* in this regard is analogous to the curtain of our modern stages.

Likewise in the Gospel of Mark. The *deus ex machina*—in this case the heavenly figure—commands the women "Go!" and the women "exited" and "fled from the tomb" (16:8). If one envisions this part of the story as though it were unfolding on a stage, as the affinities with the *machina* scenes of ancient Greek tragedies encourage, then the women's departure at this point serves as a device of closure.

This similarity lends credibility to the claim that the Gospel of Mark ends and has always ended at 16:8. Using the *deus ex machina* as a plot device, Mark brings closure to the story and leaves us with a very definite sense of what he is trying to tell us. In spite of the famous last words, "for they were afraid," Mark's Gospel does not end with the fright of the non-compliant women in flight. They are gone, and there alone remains in the mind's eye or on the "narrative stage" the image of a tomb, empty except for an awe-inspiring otherworldly figure.

The oldest account of Easter, therefore, concludes with the absent Son of God ("He is not here"; 16:6), who is restored to life and soon-to-be present with followers in Galilee. This final vision is truly in keeping with the heavenly consolations that appear throughout the Gospel of Mark. At the end, precisely where the otherworldly youth announces the resurrection, these consolations go hand-in-hand with divine absence, uncertainty, shuddering, and frightful emotion. The analogy to tragedy thus remains fully intact. The drama of Easter is not a make-believe invention of Hollywood marketers; it has deep roots, and even deeper disclosures, in this most ancient of Gospels and its narrative devices.

Resources

Dunn, Francis M. *Tragedy's End: Closure and Innovation in Euripidean Drama.* Oxford: Oxford University Press, 1996.

Jay, Jeff. *The Tragic in Mark: A Literary-Historical Interpretation.* Hermeneutische Untersuchungen zur Theologie 66. Tübingen: Mohr Siebeck, 2014.

Sourvinou-Inwood, Christiane. *Tragedy and Athenian Religion.* Lanham, MD: Lexington Books, 2003.

Tracy, David. "On Tragic Wisdom." In *Wrestling with God and with Evil: Philosophical Reflections*, edited by Hendrik M. Vroom, 13–24. Amsterdam: Rodopi, 2007.

Jeff Jay (PhD, University of Chicago Divinity School) is instructor of New Testament and early Christian literature at the University of Chicago Divinity School.

76. The Last Trump?

SEPTEMBER 8, 2016
BY ROGER GRIFFIN

> In a moment, in the twinkling of an eye, at the last trump: for the trumpet shall sound, and the dead shall be raised incorruptible, and we shall be changed. For this corruptible must put on incorruption, and this mortal must put on immortality.
>
> —1 CORINTHIANS 15:52–53

To English eyes the run-in to the US presidential election sometimes suggests that the Olympic Organizing Committee has been commissioned to run politics. I hope some remarks from a historian from across the pond and three thousand miles outside the Washington bubble will add more light than heat.

Trump and Christianity

Throughout history state power and state violence against the vulnerable have formed an unholy alliance with religion, perverting creeds which (if the sacred texts are read selectively in a compassionate spirit) may even encourage respect for nature and compassion for all human beings. The Aztecs; the ancient Egyptians, Jews, and Romans; the Crusaders and Conquistadors of Christianity; the countries fighting in the First World War, whether Christian or Islamic and whatever alliance they were part of, all believed they had, as Bob Dylan once put it, "God on their side." The horrors of Japanese imperialism were enacted by a regime legitimized by Shinto, a nature religion. Hitler invoked God repeatedly and has convinced at least one scholar he was a true Catholic. The Sinhalese extermination of the Tamil Tigers was justified by Buddhism. Islam has been invoked by all the most brutal tyrants of the Middle East. Religious sectarianism and interfaith wars have probably cost millions of lives throughout history.

So when we learn that James Dobson, founder of the group Focus on the Family, claimed Donald Trump recently accepted "a relationship with Christ," adding, "I know the person who led him to Christ," jaws should not drop. Both George W. Bush and Tony Blair, who almost double-handedly are responsible for the collapse into anarchy of Iraq and the consequent rise of ISIS, both claimed a special relationship with (an allegedly Christian) God. Christian supporters of Trump should perhaps be urged to reread some of the key passages of the New Testament in which Jesus reveals his gospel of compassion for different ethnicities and the socially deprived, and the tolerance of violence directed against oneself. The sword he brought divided Christians from Jews in terms of salvation, not Americans from the rest of the world militarily.

Trump and Fascism

Despite the frequent stigmatizing of Trump by his critics as a "fascist," it would be refreshing if more journalists used political categories with greater nicety. Trump is a populist, or to be exact, a radical right-wing populist. He owes his power to voicing in hardly sophisticated rhetoric widespread prejudices and simplistic diagnoses to complex problems which, if translated into practice, would prove counterproductive, discriminatory, and inhuman in many areas, both domestically and on the international stage. The flamboyant Vladimir Zhirinovsky in pre-Putin Russia was a right-wing populist who said he wanted to charge foreigners in Russia a fee if they could not speak Russian, make vodka dirt cheap, and force all of Europe's homosexuals to live in Holland. Putin is another, far more dangerous form of populist with geopolitical ambitions, while Berlusconi was a more lightweight, comic, less puritanical version; whatever their considerable weaknesses neither can be accused of fascism.

To be fascists they would, like Mussolini and Hitler, have to set about seizing power democratically so as to be able to dismantle or pervert the institutions of liberal democracy entirely. Trump, whatever his faults, has given no sign that he intends the destruction of the US constitutional system and its replacement by a totalitarian "new order" with himself as its charismatic leader for (in his case a short) perpetuity. Nor did other so-called "fascists" such as Margaret Thatcher, Angela Merkel, George W. Bush, or Barack Obama, which similarly disqualifies them from the description. I grant that "Trump Is a Radical Right-Wing Populist" has less of a (populist) ring as a headline than "Trump Is a Fascist," and lends itself to less funny cartoons, but that is what he is. He wants America to be great again, but not to be reborn in a totalitarian new order, let alone force its citizens to be subjected to a coercive state monopoly of power, which for one thing would stop billionaires like him from enjoying the fruits of their ill-gotten gains or running for president.

Trump and Fanaticism

Still, Trump embodies and encourages a process that underlies a considerable percentage of the suffering that has been inflicted by a minority of depraved human beings on fellow human beings down through the centuries: Manichaeanization. The Trumpian world is split into good and bad, black and white (or in his case white and anything non-white, or white without an American accent). Like a grotesque parody of Dante's *Inferno*, Trump's hell has many places reserved for a host of those who are beyond redemption as potential American citizens. Manichaeanization combined with unchecked political or religious power leads to inhumanity, because those "in darkness" are demonized and dehumanized to a point where their suffering and death is regarded as *moral* and compassion for them is hence legitimately suspended.

All anti-state and state terrorists apply a Manichaeanized ideology to reduce the irreducibly complex realities of the world to a simple dualistic narrative. At this point the newborn "visionary" sees him- or herself (curiously) as entrusted with a mission to represent, or even fight for, Good. A close study of the atrocities of Nazism, the massacre of Breivik, or the horrors (not at all "medieval") of ISIS will reveal different groups of human enemies to be demonized and persecuted, but the same dualism, fundamentalism, and fanaticism at work. "Fanatic," from the Latin for a temple (thus a "profanity" is something outside the temple) implies that the Manichaean has a religious sense of fervor about the Truth, and *in extremis* will regard violence and inhumanity committed against alleged enemies of the Truth (or the culture/nation that is its guardian) as a sacred duty. But because Trump is operating in a rationally constructed, liberal constitution, there are countervailing powers that would restrain him from undertaking the most extreme actions. Once his hysteria and incompetence revealed themselves as a bad basis for a successful US presidency he would in any case soon be removed democratically and peacefully, like Thatcher or Berlusconi, without being shot like Mussolini, committing suicide like Hitler, or being lynched like Saddam Hussein.

A Bottom Line

So what are genuine American humanists—Christian, Muslim, or secular—to do as the great political Superbowl approaches? Perhaps they should bear in mind that the crises of the present world system demand forms of non-fanatical activism which refuse to demonize or dehumanize anyone, even Mr. Trump. He is not the first simple-minded demagogue to appear on the political stage of a major nation. Nor will he be the last. Trump is no more (politically) immortal than his predecessors, and it is for those who can live with the complexity and tragedies of the world without being seduced by simplistic diagnoses and solutions to make sure they outlive him.

Resources

Anthony, Michael. "Exclusive Interview with Dr. James Dobson—Did Donald Trump Recently Accept Christ?" Godfactor.com. June 24, 2016. https://god factor.com/exclusive-interview-with-dr-james-dobson-did-donald-trump -recently-accept-christ.

Kagan, Robert. "This Is How Fascism Comes to America." *The Washington Post*. May 18, 2016. https://www.washingtonpost.com/opinions/this-is-how-fas cism-comes-to-america/2016/05/17/c4e32c58-1c47-11e6-8c7b-6931e66333e7 _story.html.

Matthews, Dylan. "I asked 5 fascism experts whether Donald Trump Is a Fascist. Here's What They Said." *Vox*. May 19, 2016. http://www.vox.com/policy-and -politics/2015/12/10/9886152/donald-trump-fascism.

Shekhovtsov, Anton. "Vladimir Zhirinovsky and the LDPR." *Foreign Policy Journal*. November 7, 2011. https://www.foreignpolicyjournal.com/2011/11/07 /vladimir-zhirinovsky-and-the-ldpr.

Roger Griffin is professor in modern history at Oxford Brookes University. He is widely acknowledged to be one of the world's foremost experts on the socio-historical and ideological dynamics of fascism, as well as the relationship of various forms of political or religious fanaticism, and in particular contemporary terrorism, to modernity.

77. Children on Christian or Secular Swings?

OCTOBER 24, 2016
BY MARTIN E. MARTY

Trinity Lutheran Church of Columbia v. Pauley is a grabbing lawsuit name for those of us who do sightings of religion in American public life. It features in a story in *The Kansas City Star*. The suit has to do with whether children playing on swings and merry-go-rounds on the playground of a Christian day school in Columbia, Missouri, are engaging in religion-related activities, which are protected by law but in this case could present a problem for the American tradition(s) of church-state relations. The lookers-on who watch for tough cases on the US Supreme Court's docket predict that this parochial issue, and the Court's decision about it, will have an enduring influence on how government relates to religion.

These little swingers take their place on the regular merry-go-round of Court agendas. One year they, their schools, their practices, and their counterparts nationally are the subjects of decisions which appear to be "religious" and, on the next go-round, appear to be "secular." Picture yourself as a judge who must deal with issues of this sort, as detailed in Rick Montgomery's story in the *Star*. I myself am a product of parish-related (a term I like better than "parochial") education of the Lutheran brand; our own parish, St. Luke Lutheran in Chicago, supports an academy; and I can testify to the quality of education in many such schools as well as to the pervasive influence of faith in the teaching and formation of children. So, what's the problem?

Sightings has dealt with these issues as early as April 17, 2001, when we cited Walter Berns. He was a conservative constitutional scholar who regularly pointed out that a republic like ours—whose Constitution says, in its First Amendment, that "Congress shall make no law respecting an establishment of religion, or prohibiting the free exercise thereof"—must locate religious institutions as legally subordinate to the state. If not, we'd live in a theocracy, however benign it may seem to be. Berns knew that saying things like that did not settle the matter. The Founders, he noted, "solved" the religion problem by *not* solving the religious problem, which is why we still have to debate it each year.

The Columbia, Missouri, case involves a Lutheran parish's day school, whose stewards want state-supported funds to pay for a minor but safety-enhancing resurfacing of the school's playground. The American Civil Liberties Union argues, and lower courts have agreed, that subsidizing the upkeep of such a playground violates the canons of "separation of church and state," because everything that happens on the school's premises is "religious" or religion-related. The Alliance Defending Freedom disagrees and says that play and playground at schools like Trinity Lutheran are not a religious activity and site, even by extension. They are simply recess-related.

As I read Montgomery's article, I find reasons to agree with the ACLU on one aspect of the case, which will be adjudicated in the months ahead, and, a few lines later, with the ADF, whose reasons are also somehow compelling. And, like many other citizens, I have sympathy for the Court and lower courts when they have to deal with these never-solved and never totally solvable religious issues. I hope that *Sightings* readers will read the story and follow the case. Some will regard the issue as "solved," and the Court to be ideologically "religious" *or* "secular" once more. They may regard this columnist as ideologically muddled or wishy-washy. But I remember and note how the best Christian (and, I suppose, other parochial) schools take "holistic" approaches, whereby the faith is to be developed and realized all over the place and all of the time. But, then again, one can be aware of such and also celebrate the fact that the institutions of a republic are free of state influence and control, that the institutions of religion are not dependent on state support, including the financial support of people who do not share a particular faith. We can celebrate that we live in a republic that deals with the addressable but not solvable issues of life. Can't we?

Resources

Marty, Martin E. "State over Church." *Sightings*. April 17, 2001. https://divinity.uchicago.edu/sightings/state-over-church-martin-e-marty.

Montgomery, Rick. "Columbia Church Finds Itself at Center of U.S. Supreme Court Squabble." *The Kansas City Star*. October 19, 2016. http://www.kansas city.com/news/politics-government/article109276117.html.

78. How Waiting 108 Years Makes the Good Life

OCTOBER 27, 2016
BY HOLLY SWYERS

For years, people have been asking me what I will do if the Chicago Cubs ever win the World Series. I don't actually know. The closest I've come to what that moment might be like was when the Cubs won the National League Division Series against the Cardinals in 2015. I was as surprised as anyone when I burst into tears on the spot, overwhelmed by emotion. It was the biggest game at which I had been in the ballpark, caught up not only in my own excitement but in the energy of the crowd, participating in a roar of joy in which I could not distinguish my own voice. Émile Durkheim would call this "collective effervescence," and he would point out that those present had entered a sacred time/space, from which we would return the next morning to our profane lives and realize the everyday bodiliness of them in contrast to the spiritual experience of that moment at the end of the game.

As an anthropologist, I am accustomed to writing about sports this way. Durkheim's *Elementary Forms* and sports go together like a 6-4-3 double play. Recently, though, a special issue of *HAU: Journal of Ethnographic Theory* led me to revisit the life of a Cubs fan. The special issue deals with happiness, and Joel Robbins's afterword reflects on the dichotomy in the issue between articles on ephemeral moments of joy and those assessing the long-term happiness of a "good life." Robbins asks "if in fact the contributors do routinely conflate two different things under the term 'happiness.'" He rejects this idea to posit that "we can find a core element shared by these two kinds of happiness, and that this core has crucially to do with the way both kinds of happiness involve values." I propose to illustrate this piece of his argument via the long-suffering of Cubs fans.

To connect values to joy, Robbins points out that "effervescence attends not only the revelation of a value, but also the performative realization of it." In other words, my sudden tears were both about how much I cared about the Cubs winning the game and about everyone around me realizing through our actions that we all cared, that we were sharing something larger than ourselves. The shared thing seems trivial: a sports team. But the sports team is a social lubricant, a thing relative strangers can talk about to form connections, a source of excuses for friends to gather. The Cubs are the representation of our connections to one another, "realized . . . in the performance of a concrete activity." The games make concrete the often-inchoate links we share with others.

The ability of sports to facilitate social ties illustrates well how Robbins connects moments of joy to a life well lived. Drawing on Erving Goffman and Randall Collins, Robbins observes that social interactions have a ritualistic quality. When they go smoothly, participants experience satisfaction, "at least some effervescence . . . [and] some quantum of the kind of happiness that we have tied to the disclosure and realization of values." Imagine a new coworker in an office who proposes a visit to the bar on the corner to watch the game after work. If her colleagues accept, she experiences the pleasure of being part of the group, of working in an environment with others who share her enjoyments. This feeling persists even if the Cubs lose, possibly amplified over postgame pints. Robbins argues, "We might take a life well lived to be one that produces a steady flow of effervescence by virtue of moving regularly through a wide range of successful interactions across the life-course."

The Cubs fan gets that frisson of effervescence when among fellow fans, watching the games season after season, occasionally swept away by a stunning win when the place explodes with full-on collective effervescence, all of which contributes to a general sense of satisfaction with life. For someone else, the same experience might be had through another passion or commitment. What Robbins's argument highlights is the idea that a life well lived relies on others, on evincing at least respect for what we value: a little indulgence for the elderly man retelling the story of buying his first car, or the kid explaining snails in excruciating detail, or if I am so lucky, the woman bursting into tears at the end of the World Series.

Resources

Durkheim, Émile. *Elementary Forms of the Religious Life*. Translated by Karen Fields. New York: Free Press, 1995.

Robbins, Joel. "On Happiness, Values, and Time: The Long and Short of It." *HAU: Journal of Ethnographic Theory* 5, no. 3 (2015): 215–33.

Holly Swyers (PhD, University of Chicago, Department of Anthropology) is an associate professor of anthropology at Lake Forest College.

79. An Event to Celebrate

November 10, 2016
By Peter J. Paris

September 24, 2016, marked one of the most significant moments in America's history when its first African American president, Barack Obama, opened the National Museum of African American History and Culture on the nation's mall in Washington, DC. Though that magnificent structure shares a space with memorials to both Abraham Lincoln and Martin Luther King, Jr., its uniqueness lies in its purpose of providing a permanent context for all future generations of Americans to engage in conversation about the nation's dreadful past that prevented African peoples from participating in and contributing to the nation's civic and cultural life. Their accomplishments were amazing nonetheless, and the museum makes them visible through thousands of artifacts and accompanying narratives. Thus, for the first time in our history, schoolchildren and citizens of every race and nationality will be able to see all dimensions of that experience and be challenged in numerous ways to celebrate its enduring legacy.

This museum strives to present all phases of the African American experience including the ubiquitous presence of religion in the personal, associational, and aesthetic lives of its people. Accordingly, the stories and artifacts of prominent individuals, churches, mosques, civil rights organizations, women's clubs, schools, businesses, and fraternal and youth associations receive careful attention in this great assemblage of historical and cultural data. Most important, the religion of African Americans is presented as integrally related to their continuing struggle for freedom and justice.

Recognition of African American contributions to the nation's history and culture began in 1925, when Carter G. Woodson and the organization he founded, the Association for the Study of Negro Life and History, called for an annual celebration during a week in February, because the month contains the birthdays of two iconic leaders, Abraham Lincoln and Frederick Douglass. For the first half century the week was celebrated largely by blacks alone. But, prompted by the nascent rise of black studies programs from the 1960s onward, the weeklong event was extended during the 1976 Bicentennial to the entire month and thereafter called Black History Month, which is declared each year by a presidential proclamation.

Since racism has been called America's original sin, the thought and action of African Americans have been both corrective and redemptive forces aimed at healing the nation of its devastating disease. The most vivid example of that mission is seen in the many and varied acts of resistance rendered by African Americans from the time of enslavement up to the present day, as evidenced most graphically in the Black Lives Matter movement.

Locating the museum on the mall certainly gives African American history significant status, but that does not mean it is fully integrated into the nation's history. That remains an unfinished task. Thus, contrary to those who think that America has two histories, one white and the other black, the truth is that it has one history in which a sizable number of people were enslaved, oppressed, and excluded from citizenship for centuries. Yet those excluded ones and their allies have struggled over the centuries to achieve full inclusion, believing that their claim to citizenship is as valid as that of any European.

By documenting those strivings and giving them national visibility, this museum moves that struggle a step forward toward its ultimate goal of equal citizenship. Most important, perhaps, it represents a fitting finale to the administration of our first black president.

Peter J. Paris is the Elmer G. Homrighausen Professor Emeritus of Christian Social Ethics at Princeton Theological Seminary. He received his PhD in ethics and society from the University of Chicago Divinity School in 1975 and was named Alumnus of the Year in 1995.

80. In Defense of the Liberal in the Study of Religion

December 22, 2016
By Jeffrey Stackert

In the aftermath of the US presidential election and the political divisions it highlighted, I noticed that Nicholas Kristof's May 7, 2016, *New York Times* column, "A Confession of Liberal Intolerance," began trending online. In this piece, Kristof argues that American universities, especially in their humanities and social science departments, are problematically dominated by liberal faculty and ideas. Himself an avowed liberal, Kristof suggests that the American academy should actively work to include within it conservative thought and, in particular, evangelical Christian perspectives:

> The stakes involve not just fairness to conservatives or evangelical Christians, not just whether progressives will be true to their own values, not just the benefits that come from diversity (and diversity of thought is arguably among the most important kinds), but also the quality of education itself. When perspectives are unrepresented in discussions, when some kinds of thinkers aren't at the table, classrooms become echo chambers rather than sounding boards—and we all lose.

Kristof goes on to cite statistics reflecting the low proportion of Republicans represented in American university faculties as well as social scientific data and anecdotal evidence of bias against Republicans and evangelical Christians in university contexts. (Kristof subsequently defended his view against his critics in his May 28, 2016, column, "The Liberal Blind Spot." On December 10, 2016, he updated—and largely restated—his argument in light of the Trump election; see "The Dangers of Echo Chambers on Campus.")

Though Kristof's special concern is not the academic study of religion, consideration of it might yield fruitful insights regarding his claims and proposed remedies. In his diagnosis of liberal bias, Kristof focuses on non-sectarian higher education—primarily public universities and private, non-religious universities. I will thus focus my attention there, even as I acknowledge that there are a significant number of confessional colleges and universities that this focus ignores and that, if considered, might reorient the discussion, at least in part.

As the quote above exemplifies, Kristof frames his consideration of diversity in the academy in terms of *perspectives* and *kinds of thinkers*. In both cases, his interest is *content*—what is thought and whether it is identifiably liberal or conservative. The good that Kristof seeks is a diversity of *perspectives*.

What Kristof omits is any consideration of *method* or, even more important, *methodology*. In the study of religion, this distinction between claim and methodology is a vital one, especially as it relates to the value of diversity. As a critical biblical scholar, my methods and methodology are shaped by the Enlightenment principles of empiricism and rational thought. I thus reject claims that appeal to authority—human or divine—rather than empirical evidence and reason. Such perspectives are not valuable to my work because they are founded in a fundamentally different set of principles for inquiry and argumentation. Kristof's torchbearers of conservatism, evangelical Christians, have oftentimes championed religious authority rather than empirical evidence to support their claims. In such cases, critical scholars reject their perspectives.

Curiously, Kristof acknowledges precisely this issue but rejects its cogency. He notes that, in a Facebook discussion he initiated on this topic, one respondent wrote, "Much of the 'conservative' worldview consists of ideas that are known empirically to be false." Kristof characterizes this response as "scornful" and the conversation overall as one that "illuminated primarily liberal arrogance."

Yet insistence upon a shared set of methods and methodology (which are themselves constantly being challenged and refined), such as in critical biblical studies or the academic study of religion more broadly, hardly limits a diversity of *perspectives*. It instead makes discussion possible, clarifying a baseline for valid argumentation while leaving ample room for marshaling and evaluating different evidence, a process that inevitably leads to conflicting claims. These features of scholarly discourse also underscore that, notwithstanding Kristof's assertion, the academy does not value an unqualified diversity; indeed, it never has.

Finally, I would note that insistence upon critical methods and methodology—or what we might term more generally, with Michel Foucault, "the critical attitude"—does not *necessarily* exclude those who hold conservative or specifically evangelical Christian views. All comers, whatever their political or religious persuasion, may engage productively on such terms *and should be welcome to do so*. At the same time, some may choose not to engage, preferring, for example, creed over critical inquiry. The academy need not exhibit hostility toward such individuals, but neither must it include their *perspectives* in its discourse.

Resources

Foucault, Michel. "What Is Critique?" In *The Politics of Truth*, edited by Sylvère Lotringer, 41–82. Translated by Lysa Hochroth and Catherine Porter. Los Angeles: Semiotext(e), 2007.

Kristof, Nicholas. "A Confession of Liberal Intolerance." *The New York Times*. May 7, 2016. http://www.nytimes.com/2016/05/08/opinion/sunday/a-con fession-of-liberal-intolerance.html.

———. "The Dangers of Echo Chambers on Campus." *The New York Times*. December 10, 2016. http://www.nytimes.com/2016/12/10/opinion/sunday/the -dangers-of-echo-chambers-on-campus.html.

———. "The Liberal Blind Spot." *The New York Times*. May 28, 2016. http://www .nytimes.com/2016/05/29/opinion/sunday/the-liberal-blind-spot.html.

Stephens, Randall J., and Karl W. Giberson. *The Anointed: Evangelical Truth in a Secular Age*. Cambridge, MA: Belknap, 2011.

Jeffrey Stackert is associate professor of Hebrew Bible at the University of Chicago Divinity School.

81. Many Sightings of Hope

JANUARY 2, 2017
BY MARTIN E. MARTY

For more than a year I engaged in the visual and oral analog to "fasting." Fasters discipline themselves not to eat. I chose not to comment on the election campaigns. A digital word-search will find no mention in fifty Monday *Sightings* of any presidential candidate or party. The choice was an implicit protest against or retreat from the grossness, waste, distortion, and distraction in what elections have become. Now the bad year of 2016 is past, and it is time to join everyone else in the sighting-and-commentary professions and to re-emerge actively.

What struck me all year was the sense and sight of extreme despair on many fronts, accompanied by some new notices of the meaning and potential of hope. The headline of a column by fellow Chicagoan Neil Steinberg was "The Necessity of Hope." The column began with a quotation from Michelle Obama: "Now we're feeling what not having hope feels like." It ended: "Hopelessness is not an option. Hope is a tool, a hammer. Never let it go. You're going to need it."

This paralleled the long holiday essay in *The Economist* on "the agony of hope," which focused on President Obama, who had written at book length on "hope," and who kept embodying and exemplifying it against all odds, as the story recalled. The article traces the president's career and evidences of his outlook through his bad recent year, in which he had no choice but to act and speak. Conclusion: he had to do the best he could. "Sometimes it was all he could do. The possibilities seem shrunken. After its collision with history, so might hope itself."

The third came from Vatican City, by Philip Pullella for Reuters. The headline was unsurprising: "Pope's Christmas Message Offers Hope in World Hit by Terrorism, War." The report inspires readers to retrace steps to the roots of their religious traditions or any nurturing bases. At the end of this column I cite two extended Muslim discussions of hope, articles which might surprise any Americans who are fed on Islamophobia and hatred. Continuing in the Abrahamic line, we include Jonathan Sacks's bold treatment which argues, with a bit of a wink and a good bit of credibility, that Judaism "invented" hope.

Christians find immeasurable resources of hope in their scriptures and witness. For me and mine, Jürgen Moltmann's *The Theology of Hope* (1967), a shaping but not isolated influence, is typical. Believers can go to their friendly neighborhood pastor or counselor or bibliophile for many more suggestions. We can't meander through the rich library offerings, being already at the point of overstaying our welcome in this turn-of-the-year essay.

It's time for a parting shot, recalling a base from which I've sometimes drawn comfort and counsel. Back in the 1970s, on a panel at a university in California, Buckminster Fuller, historian Daniel Boorstin (my PhD adviser, a great teacher, later the Librarian of Congress), and I wrestled with an assigned topic. It was the latest version of an enduring theme, "the decline of the West." Fuller was a utopian, so he did not let talk of decline enter his mind. Boorstin and I used historians' eyes and outlooks, which combine realism and hope. At intermission, however, our program hosts chided us for not being "declinist" enough to make the promised point of it all. Boorstin winked at the two of us as the host left our recess chamber: "Don't worry. I'll take care of this." When we got back on stage he reported that we had been scolded for not being pessimistic enough. He then announced that we had concluded, "We do not know enough about the future to be *absolutely* pessimistic."

Starting from there, one can begin to find impulses to revisit hope, which awaits responsible people who are ready to appraise realities, revise their thinking, and act. One day late, then, let *Sightings* join hopers with a warm "Happy New Year."

Resources

Laila, Tanim. "The Phenomenology of Hope." In *Hope: Global Interdisciplinary Perspective*, edited by Whitney Bauman. Oxford: Inter-Disciplinary Press, 2008.

Moltmann, Jürgen. *The Theology of Hope: On the Ground and the Implications of a Christian Eschatology.* Translated by James W. Leitch. Minneapolis: Fortress Press, 1993.

Osmani, Noor Mohammad. "Phenomenology of Hope and Despair: A Qur'anic Perspective." In *Hope: Global Interdisciplinary Perspective*, edited by Whitney Bauman. Oxford: Inter-Disciplinary Press, 2008.

Pullella, Philip. "Pope's Christmas Message Offers Hope in World Hit by Terrorism, War." Reuters. December 25, 2016. http://www.reuters.com/article /us-christmas-season-pope-idUSKBN14E09I.

"A Reflection on Barack Obama's Presidency." *The Economist*. December

24, 2016. http://www.economist.com/news/christmas-specials/21712062
-barack-obamas-presidency-lurched-between-idealism-and-acrimony
-some-his.

Sacks, Jonathan. "Future Tense—How the Jews Invented Hope." *The Jewish Chronicle*. April 1, 2008. http://www.rabbisacks.org/future-tense-how-the-jews-invented-hope-published-in-the-jewish-chronicle.

Steinberg, Neil. "The Necessity of Hope." *Chicago Sun-Times*. December 21, 2016.

82. Dylann Roof, the Radicalization of the Alt-Right, and Ritualized Racial Violence

January 12, 2017
By Joel A. Brown

Dylann S. Roof, the self-professed white supremacist known infamously as the "Charleston church shooter," was convicted last month of killing nine black churchgoers at (Mother) Emanuel African Methodist Episcopal Church in Charleston, South Carolina, on the evening of June 17, 2015. This week, Roof was sentenced to death.

While there is an argument to be made for the religious valence of the Charleston church massacre (which hasn't been made to my knowledge), I'm simply going to posit for the moment that the massacre carried out by Roof at Mother Emanuel was a performance of *ritualized racial violence*, consistent with what recent scholarship has identified as the "religion of lynching" in American history. The religion of lynching does not simply sanction violence against black bodies; rather, through ritualized performance, it creates blackness as part of the profane world. Radicalized white supremacist ideology breeds ritualized racial violence. Thus, rather than focus on the religious dimension of Roof's massacre here, I want to investigate its ideological roots.

Dylann Roof is the face of the radicalized "alt-right."

This is admittedly a provocative and controversial statement, principally because the primary spokesmen (they're all men) for the movement have publicly disavowed Roof and condemned his violence. However, when one looks past the trendy haircuts and tweedy outfits of this self-described "intellectual movement," one finds a racist ideology strikingly coherent with Roof's.

The clearest evidence of this connection is Roof's own acknowledgment in his manifesto that one of the websites associated with the alt-right, that of the Council of Conservative Citizens, was responsible for his "racial awakening." It is also revealing that the same alt-right spokesmen who denounced Roof's massacre—Richard Spencer, a founder of the movement, and Jared Taylor, who is widely regarded as its leading "intellectual"—both admitted Roof had "legitimate concerns" and expressed "legitimate grievances" in his manifesto. Spencer, in fact, stated that he wished the alt-right could write Roof off as a "madman" but simply couldn't, because "what he published [in his manifesto] was no insane screed, the kind of thing in which madness is palpable. . . . His writing indicates that he was capable of critical thought and had seriously pondered the implications of race on American society."

And when one scratches below the surface of the alt-right, moving past its members' style to the substance of their thought, one discovers that Roof shares their basic racial ideology. For instance, Roof's thoughts on race (as expressed especially in his manifesto, but also in his prison journal) correspond almost point-for-point with the racial theory outlined by Taylor. In a speech given at an alt-right press conference a few months ago, Taylor argued that the alt-right exists largely to refute the false virtues promoted by liberal "identity politics," namely egalitarianism and multiculturalism (Roof, too, made this argument, referring to a "melting pot" fallacy). Taylor continued by insisting that "race is real . . . not a social construct," and that the reality of race must be recognized as the chief distinguishing mark between groups (Roof wrote about the need for raising "complete racial awareness"). Science is on the side of the alt-right, according to Taylor. He posited that a "century's worth of studies" confirm differing average IQ levels between the races, with "whites" second in the rankings only behind "Asians." (Roof featured the IQ argument in the section of his manifesto dedicated to "blacks," and confided later on that he has "great respect for the East Asian races.") Taylor (like Roof) then moved immediately to indicate that a race's average IQ correlates directly with its "capacity for moral reasoning." On this point, Taylor (like Roof) underscored that the white race is far more "ethically inclined" than "blacks." Taylor admits this is a "harsh doctrine," but "whites" must be compelled to talk about it because the fate of white culture depends on it.

Culture is of paramount value for the alt-right, and the preservation and protection of white culture are at the center of its racial ideology. Such is also the crux of Roof's manifesto. Only Roof perceives that white culture will be perpetually threatened and ultimately corrupted by close proximity to "blacks." At least in theory, Taylor and other alt-right apologists imagine that the goals of white nationalism (i.e., the separation of the races) can be achieved without violence, although they admit it is at times necessary to cause "momentary chaos." Roof departs from them on this point, believing that the achievement of racial separation and cultural purity will necessarily be bloody. In feeling the need to "do something," Roof radicalized, and nine black lives were extinguished because of it.

The alt-right wants to convince us that its adherents are not Dylann Roof. They want us to believe they represent a brand of white supremacy we haven't encountered before in American history—intelligent, civil, clean-cut, not like the hillbilly racists of ages past—and therefore deserve a seat at the table of mainstream American social and political life. But the truth is it's a disguise, an age-old game of deception which plays upon our assumptions that racism is the provenance of poor, uneducated white folks. Nicole Hemmer, a historian who has covered the alt-right for some time, is right when she writes, "Attitudes like white supremacy are about power, and they dress up in whatever way they need to in order to protect that power. Only when that truth is fully understood can [we] set aside [our] awe at dapper Klansmen and hip racists—and begin to offer clear-eyed accounts of the dangerous ideology still in our midst."

Again, this is nothing new. Since their initial organization in the nineteenth century, white supremacist groups have turned the same trick, playing on notions of cultural respectability and assuming the guise of intellectualism to give the impression of a novel, more sophisticated incarnation of white supremacy. But, as Kelly J. Baker has recently argued, "the alt-right only appears novel if we ignore the continuum of 'intellectual' white supremacy from which it emerged: scientific racism in the 19th and early 20th centuries, the national Ku Klux Klan of the 1920s, and the Citizens Councils of the 1950s and '60s." The makeover is one of style, not substance. It's a trick. And yet this timeworn scheme has proven effective time and again.

We should not be fooled by the alt-right, but recognize it for the farce it is. Its ideology is not only racist, antiquated, and "politically incorrect"—it is these things—but also dangerous when it becomes radicalized. Ritualized racial violence is the bedfellow of radicalized white supremacy. That's not speculation; it's the story of American history.

Resources

"The Alt-Right Press Conference." YouTube. September 9, 2016. https://www .youtube.com/watch?v=aJWLjRK2SRo.

Baker, Kelly J. "White-Collar Supremacy." *The New York Times.* November 25, 2016. https://www.nytimes.com/2016/11/25/opinion/white-collar-supremacy .html.

Bokhari, Allum, and Milo Yiannopoulous. "An Establishment Conservative's Guide to the Alt-Right." Breitbart. March 29, 2016. http://www.breitbart.com /tech/2016/03/29/an-establishment-conservatives-guide-to-the-alt-right.

"The Dylann Roof Trial: The Evidence." *The New York Times.* December 9, 2016. http://www.nytimes.com/interactive/2016/12/09/us/dylann-roof-evidence .html.

Hemmer, Nicole. "Tweedy racists and 'ironic' anti-Semites: the alt-right fits a historical pattern." Vox. December 2, 2016. http://www.vox.com/the-big -idea/2016/12/2/13814728/alt-right-spencer-irony-racism-punks-skinheads.

Mathews, Donald G. "Lynching Is Part of the Religion of Our People: Faith in the Christian South." In *Religion in the American South: Protestants and Others in History and Culture*, edited by Beth Barton Schweiger and Donald G. Mathews, 53–94. Chapel Hill: University of North Carolina Press, 2004.

Robles, Frances, Jason Horowitz, and Sheila Dewan. "Dylann Roof, Suspect in Charleston Shooting, Flew the Flags of White Power." *The New York Times*. June 18, 2015. http://www.nytimes.com/2015/06/19/us/on-facebook-dylann-roof -charleston-suspect-wears-symbols-of-white-supremacy.html.

Roof, Dylann. "Prison Journal." Administrative Office of the US Courts. http:// www.uscourts.gov/courts/scd/cases/2-15-472/exhibits/GX500.pdf.

Spencer, Richard B. "Dylann Roof and Political Violence." Radix Journal. June 23, 2015.

Wood, Amy Louise. *Lynching and Spectacle: Witnessing Racial Violence in America, 1890–1940*. Chapel Hill: University of North Carolina Press, 2009.

Joel A. Brown is a PhD student in religions in America at the University of Chicago Divinity School.

83. Myths Debunked: Why Did White Evangelical Christians Vote for Trump?

JANUARY 19, 2017
BY MYRIAM RENAUD

Why did a record 81 percent of white evangelicals vote for Donald Trump in the recent presidential election? A common explanation in the media is that these voters wanted to safeguard the empty seat on the Supreme Court with the hope of overturning *Roe v. Wade*. Though widely accepted, there are at least two problems with this explanation.

First, while abortion rights have been a consistent preoccupation (for conservatives and progressives alike), white evangelical support for Republican presidential candidates has been inconsistent. Pew Research data shows that 78 percent of white evangelicals voted for George W. Bush in 2004, 74 percent for John McCain in 2008, and 78 percent for Mitt Romney in 2012. Ballots cast for Trump hit a new high.

Second, despite the claims of pundits who speak on their behalf—pastors and other religious leaders—the abortion issue was not a primary concern for white evangelicals in this election. When, in November 2016, a LifeWay Research poll asked white evangelicals what one issue they considered most important when voting, only 10 percent said "Supreme Court nominees," and a mere 4 percent said "abortion." In contrast, 20 percent of pastors said "Supreme Court nominees," and 10 percent said "abortion."

WHITE EVANGELICALS		WHITE EVANGELICAL PASTORS	
26%	Improving the economy	27%	Personal character of the candidate
22%	National Security	20%	**Supreme Court nominees**
15%	Personal character of the candidate	12%	Religious freedom
10%	**Supreme Court nominees**	10%	**Abortion**
7%	Religious freedom	6%	Improving the economy
5%	Immigration	5%	National security

WHITE EVANGELICALS		WHITE EVANGELICAL PASTORS	
4%	**Abortion**	2%	Immigration
11%	None of these	13%	None of these

In total, nearly half of white evangelicals considered the economy or national security most important when choosing between presidential candidates. Even when the Pew Research Center asked them which issues—not limited to a single one—were "very important" to them in deciding how to cast their votes, terrorism (89 percent) and the economy (87 percent) ranked higher than Supreme Court appointments (70 percent) and abortion (52 percent).

Terrorism	89%
Economy	87%
Immigration	78%
Foreign Policy	78%
Gun policy	77%
Supreme Court appointments	70%
Health care	70%
Social Security	70%
Trade policy	62%
Education	59%
Abortion	52%
Treatment of racial/ethnic minorities	51%
Environment	34%
Treatment of LGBT community	29%

For many white evangelical voters, then, worries about the Supreme Court and *Roe v. Wade* were not primary factors. Simply put, the amped-up obsession with the Supreme Court and *Roe v. Wade* in the media points to an opinion gap between the people in the pews and their clergy.

Why this disconnect? Reporters may not be aware that some white evangelical pastors hold different views than the lay people whom they supposedly represent. Also, religious leaders may themselves not be aware that their views differ from those of their congregants. Regardless of the reasons, when Franklin Graham, president of the Billy Graham Evangelistic Association, told NBC that "This election is about the Supreme Court and the justices that the next president will nominate," he was not speaking for all white evangelicals. Neither was Richard Land, president of Southern Evangelical

Seminary, who, NBC reported, "believes evangelicals were motivated to vote in unprecedented numbers because of Hillary Clinton's record on abortion."

Contra Graham and Land, the unprecedented numbers of white evangelicals who voted for Trump were principally motivated by worries about the economy. This may seem odd. Scratch the surface of the US economy and all appears to be well. According to Bureau of Labor Statistics data released in late 2016, the number of private sector jobs has grown for eighty consecutive months, 178,000 people were added to payrolls in November, and the unemployment rate dropped to 4.6 percent. Wage growth, though slower, was still running ahead of inflation, and consumers were expressing the highest levels of confidence in nearly a decade.

Still more confounding, based on data alone, is the fact that white Trump supporters—white evangelicals among them—are somewhat better off than other Americans, including other whites. According to Nate Silver the median household income for Trump's non-Hispanic, white supporters was about $72,000, or $10,000 higher than that of all non-Hispanic whites.

Nonetheless, many white evangelicals are, or see themselves as, left behind financially.

To understand why this is the case requires a closer look at the median household income since the Great Recession of 2007–2008. Six years into the economic recovery, the US Census Bureau reported that incomes in the middle range—when adjusted for inflation—were still 1.6 percent below the previous 2007 peak of $57,423 per household. Also problematic, these incomes remained 2.4 percent lower than the high reached during the late 1990s. Most of the registered income gains have bypassed middle-income workers, like the average white evangelical Trump voter, and gone to those at the top of the income ladder. Seen in the broad context of the past few decades, the average wage earner has failed to get ahead. Though more people are back at work, *The New York Times*'s Binyamin Appelbaum wrote, "many of them are still struggling to maintain their standard of living."

Patricia Cohen, also writing for *The New York Times*, echoed these grim assessments. Despite recent good news about the economy, she said, "tens of millions of Americans understandably feel that the recovery has passed them by." Many without skills are stuck with low-paying jobs plagued by irregular and unreliable schedules and by little or no security or benefits. Others, laid off from the well-compensated manufacturing jobs that left the US for other countries, have had to accept lower-wage positions, if they found work at all.

Eric Hoffer, in his classic book *The True Believer*, described what he called the "new poor." He found that the intensity of the discontent found among the new poor is not necessarily tied to economic hardship. Indeed, individuals born into misery do not usually revolt against the status quo—their lot is bearable because it is familiar and predictable. Discontent, the emotion Trump tapped into so adeptly, is more likely to afflict people who have experienced prosperity. When their comfortable life is diminished in some way, the result is intolerable. According to Hoffer, it is usually "those whose poverty is relatively recent, the 'new poor,' who throb with the ferment of frustration. The memory of better things is as fire in their veins."

Actual financial struggles, along with the memory of better things, may explain why more white evangelicals voted for the Republican candidate than in previous elections. It may also explain why worries about the economy took precedence over distaste for Trump as a person. Surveys showed that many white evangelicals objected to Trump's sexism, racism, anti-Muslim-ism, anti-immigrant-ism, and other ugly "isms." Barna Group found that 49 percent of white evangelicals felt that Trump lacked a strong moral character. Only 15 percent saw him as "authentically Christian."

Still, Trump successfully tapped into their economic anxiety—justified or not—with his slogan "Make American Great Again." Hillary Clinton, with her insistence that America was already great, probably appeared horribly out of touch. Trump, in contrast, agreed with the new poor that the nation's economy was in trouble. He promised seemingly quick fixes like eliminating trade agreements that appeared to favor foreign companies over American ones, forcing US-based companies to keep jobs stateside instead of shipping them overseas, and reducing competition for jobs with a tough stance toward illegal immigrants. In his first press conference as president-elect last week, Trump pledged to be "the greatest jobs producer that God ever created."

Why bother to try to understand the motivations of white evangelical voters? Because, according to Pew surveys, they make up 26 percent of the American electorate, giving them significant political clout. (That percentage has held since 2008.) Of course, white evangelicals do not constitute a single voting bloc. They cover the spectrum of political affiliations. But the fact that more than four out of five placed their trust in Trump deserves attention.

Trump paid attention to the power of this group and assembled an evangelical advisory council to assist his campaign. Going forward, future campaigns would do well to do the same. Most importantly, though, rather than relying on the opinions of pastors and religious leaders, or on economic reports that fail to take the larger picture into account, those who wish to succeed in understanding and responding to the concerns of white evangelicals ought to reach out to them directly.

Resources

Appelbaum, Binyamin. "Fed Raises Key Interest Rate, Citing Strengthening Economy." *The New York Times*. December 14, 2016. http://www.nytimes.com/2016/12/14/business/economy/fed-interest-rates-janet-yellen.html.

Casselman, Ben. "Inequality Is Killing the American Dream." FiveThirtyEight. December 8, 2016. http://fivethirtyeight.com/features/inequality-is-killing-the-american-dream.

Cohen, Patricia. "President Obama Is Handing a Strong Economy to His Successor." *The New York Times*. December 2, 2016. http://www.nytimes.com/2016/12/02/business/economy/jobs-report.html.

Edsall, Thomas B. "Trump Voters Are Feeling It." *The New York Times*. December 8, 2016. http://www.nytimes.com/2016/12/08/opinion/trump-voters-are-feeling-it.html.

Glueck, Katie. "Trump's Religious Dealmaking Pays Dividends." *Politico*. December 7, 2016. http://www.politico.com/story/2016/12/trump-religious-dealmaking-dividends-232277.

Hoffer, Eric. *The True Believer: Thoughts on the Nature of Mass Movements*. New York: Harper Perennial Modern Classics, 2010.

Johnson, Alex. "What's behind Evangelical Support for Donald Trump? Less Than You Think." NBC News. October 16, 2016. http://www.nbcnews.com/politics/2016-election/what-s-behind-evangelical-support-donald-trump-less-you-think-n666146.

Khazan, Olga. "Why Christians Overwhelmingly Backed Trump." *The Atlantic*. November 9, 2016. http://www.theatlantic.com/health/archive/2016/11/why-women-and-christians-backed-trump/507176.

Kuruvilla, Carol. "After Trump's Win, White Evangelical Christians Face a Reckoning." *The Huffington Post*. November 9, 2016. http://www.huffingtonpost.com/entry/evangelicals-election_us_5820d931e4b0e80b02cbc86e.

Porter, Eduardo. "America's Inequality Problem: Real Income Gains Are Brief and Hard to Find." *The New York Times*. September 13, 2016. https://www.nytimes.com/2016/09/14/business/economy/americas-inequality-problem-real-income-gains-are-brief-and-hard-to-find.html.

Silver, Nate. "The Mythology of Trump's 'Working Class' Support." FiveThirtyEight. May 3, 2016. http://fivethirtyeight.com/features/the-mythology-of-trumps-working-class-support.

Smith, Gregory A., and Jessica Martínez. "How the Faithful Voted: A Preliminary 2016 Analysis." Pew Research Center. November 9, 2016. http://www.pewresearch.org/fact-tank/2016/11/09/how-the-faithful-voted-a-preliminary-2016-analysis.

Wojcik, Natalie, Mack Hogan, and Mike Juang. "Transcript of President-Elect Trump's News Conference." CNBC. January 11, 2017. http://www.cnbc .com/2017/01/11/transcript-of-president-elect-donald-j-trumps-news-con ference.html.

Zylstra, Sarah Eekhoff, and Jeremy Weber. "Top 10 Stats Explaining the Evangelical Vote for Trump or Clinton." *Christianity Today*. November 4, 2016. http:// www.christianitytoday.com/gleanings/2016/november/top-10-stats-explain ing-evangelical-vote-trump-clinton-2016.html.

Myriam Renaud is a PhD candidate in theology at the University of Chicago Divinity School. A former editor of Sightings, *Renaud is also a previous Martin Marty Center junior fellow and two-time recipient of the Langdon Gilkey Scholarship.*

84. Rock, Paper, Scissors

FEBRUARY 9, 2017
BY SARAH HAMMERSCHLAG

With each passing day since the inauguration of Donald Trump the news cycle gets more punishing. Power is consolidated within the executive branch. The three-headed monster of authoritarianism, fear mongering, and intimidation takes another step on its march to trample checks and balances. Attempting to counter this force with reasoned argument has come to feel a bit like wielding scissors against an opponent who plays only with a closed fist in a relentless game of Rochambeau (rock, paper, scissors).

For a scholar the situation can seem disheartening to say the least.

Some of us—even those who do not like crowds—have thus taken to demonstrating. "You know it's bad when even the librarians are marching," read one of the signs I saw at the Women's March on January 21 in Washington, DC. As many have reported, the march itself *felt* extraordinary: not only the experience of seeing and hearing hundreds of thousands reaffirm a commitment to civil rights, women's rights, gay rights, immigrant rights, but also the sheer civility of it all, the wave upon wave of people making room for one another, a crowd whose desire was neither to get somewhere, nor to buy something; not to sell something or even to see something.

In a context of neoliberal capitalism where everything is measured in profit, this might seem pointless to some or like mere consolation to others. David Brooks in his January 24 column in *The New York Times* wrote, "These marches can never be an effective opposition to Donald Trump" because protestors "have a social experience with a lot of people and fool themselves into thinking they are members of a coherent and demanding community." Furthermore, he continued, in what might seem a strange juxtaposition if not a contradiction, "Identity politics is too small for this movement."

What Brooks sees as a twofold weakness in this conjunction, I want to insist is exactly the strength of these demonstrations and even their most potent force, the fragile but pervasive and prevailing paper to Trump's rock. This is not only because the march itself has given rise to a network of participation and a series of precise and delimited strategies ranging from the organization of canvassing efforts in swing states to phone campaigns directed at members of Congress to plans for more marches and more rallies, each of which brings its own flurry of media attention at a time when such attention seems to be the most sought-after currency in our world (as Farhad Manjoo recently argued in *The New York Times*). Rather, it is because the community created in these moments, ephemeral as it is, is one made up of people whose identities do not always overlap. Their differences and grievances might, in a different context, even be set against one another, but now highlight a shared sense of injustice. It may be that the community created in these moments is neither "coherent" nor "demanding," certainly not in the way that we perceive a tribe or a church to be coherent in its criteria for belonging and historical consistency, but neither is this new community restrictive or exclusionary. If our current political battle is about "securing our borders," these protests reveal the potency of decentered networks in *overcoming* borders.

At the more recent protests against the immigration ban at airports around the country, Jews, Muslims, and Catholics have gathered together, both because they themselves were once refugees and because they fear for those who are or will be. Rabbis from Jewish congregations have followed representatives of Palestinian rights organizations in the speaking lineup. These communities show up because they or their families have suffered, because their identities are marked by that fact. Such a politics of identity is exactly what Brooks and political philosopher Mark Lilla think the left should overcome, even as Trump's policies are targeted not only at identity politics but also at the very identity and practices of anyone who isn't a white Christian male.

It is ironic that a new form of identity politics may be emerging as a consequence of the very policies bent on suppressing it. As our family histories of immigration and persecution are re-invoked by this new wave of bigotry, we recognize that our political identities are anything but abstract. Particularity is also the key to perspective. To see the plight of others doesn't require overcoming difference, but it does require thinking analogically. While Brooks claims that identity politics is splintering, a shared sense of threat to the very institutions that once protected us in our abstract freedoms and particular histories is surely a strong enough common cause. I read the other day that the strength of this new grassroots movement cannot be measured by its size, because it is now so easy to mobilize people into action. Isn't that precisely the point?

None of this is to say that there is no room for reasoned argument, only that its potency now is not in direct confrontation with the blunt force of Trump and Steve Bannon. Trump is not going to change his policies because three thousand scholars signed a petition against him, but neither can he silence our paper machines. Spreading the word—or dissemination, as some of us like to call it—has perhaps never been more important. It ensures we'll keep showing up in droves.

Resources

Brooks, David. "After the Women's March." *The New York Times.* January 24, 2017. https://www.nytimes.com/2017/01/24/opinion/after-the-womens-march .html.

Lilla, Mark. "The End of Identity Liberalism." *The New York Times.* November 18, 2016. https://www.nytimes.com/2016/11/20/opinion/sunday/the-end-of -identity-liberalism.html.

Manjoo, Farhad. "The Alt-Majority: How Social Networks Empowered Mass Protests." *The New York Times.* January 30, 2017. https://www.nytimes .com/2017/01/30/technology/donald-trump-social-networks-protests.html.

Sarah Hammerschlag (PhD, University of Chicago Divinity School) is director of the MA program and associate professor of religion, literature, and visual culture; philosophy of religions; and history of Judaism at the University of Chicago Divinity School.

85. Sacred Sites Violated

FEBRUARY 13, 2017
BY MARTIN E. MARTY

What if the Sioux Nation decided to build a pipeline through Arlington Cemetery? This question from Faith Spotted Eagle—who lacks a PhD in comparative religion and who would never be employed to teach the phenomenology of burial ritual—got at the heart of at least one of the three main issues in the prolonged debate over the Dakota Access Pipeline project. Opposition to wealthy oil companies and their potential profits if and after the pipeline is completed would have been sufficient to attract the thousands who came to support Sioux protestors at Standing Rock. Meanwhile, environmentalists, who care and worry about what such a pipeline under the plains and river might do, have raised appropriate questions. But "grandmother"—a technical title among the Sioux for women like Spotted Eagle—really got at the heart of what animates the protesters and their sympathizers.

Why the comparison to a sacred place like Arlington Cemetery? Or the Tomb of the Unknown Soldier, or key monuments at Gettysburg? What makes this Sioux site sacred, inviolable in the eyes of those for whom this place in North Dakota has drawn so much national attention? The environmental concerns alone would have been ominous enough to agitate the Native Americans on the scene. But the Cannonball River, which flows nearby, and the complex of tributaries connected to the Missouri River, are not merely sources of water. No, Spotted Eagle has said, water is "the best medicine," the sustainer of life from a mother's womb until its issue, years later, breathes no longer. Water is necessary for the sweat lodge, so important in Sioux worship, and it serves as a purifier and calmer in sacred ceremonies. And much more.

Spotted Eagle spoke to interviewers about women gathered on the river's bank to sing stories: "One hundred years from now, somebody's going to go down along the Cannonball River and they're going to hear those stories." What motivates her and her fellow worshippers, above all, is concern that the pipeline will profane the burial sites over and around and through which it will flow. All of the governmental action is thus, in the eyes of the Native Americans, a profanation.

Sightings spends so many lines on this one out of many contested revered sites in the "flyover country" of the Great Plains—my homeland—in the interest of giving attention to the rites of some of the peoples who have been plundered, exploited, silenced, and murdered for more than 500 years by us newcomers, who now make the rules, establish the rituals, and bring the edicts and the guns to enforce them. Weekly, if not daily, we hear and read of the ins and outs, the ups and downs, of this most recent conflict. We observe how readily disdained the protesters are. But we are moved by the fact that leaders and sympathizers of many religious bodies, including Jews and Muslims, Catholics at the highest level, mainline Protestants, and some evangelicals, have publicly sided with the Sioux.

Many of them know that there are other sides (and undersides) to conflicts like this one. They know how complex are the valid economic issues on the opposing sides of such ventures. Even some close-to-the-scene Native Americans are concerned about the potential economic loss, should the Native Americans win. (They won't.) Sympathetic religious leaders are urging that the spiritual concerns and the human rights of the protesters be respected in the face of often-brutal economic and political forces and realities. And the Standing Rock Sioux, by their witness, are teaching the nation that "the sacred" takes many forms and deserves to be handled with care, and with awe, even in our profane days and ways.

Resources

Brekke, Gregg. "PC(USA) Offers Support for Standing Rock Sioux Protest in North Dakota." Presbyterian Mission Agency. August 26, 2016. http://www.presbyterianmission.org/story/pcusa-offers-support-standing-rock-sioux-protest-north-dakota.

"Churches Uniting in Christ Support Standing Rock Pipeline Protests." Churches Uniting in Christ. October 21, 2016. http://www.churchesunitinginchrist.org/news/164-churches-uniting-in-christ-support-standing-rock-pipeline-protests.

"ELCA Presiding Bishop Issues Statement Addressing Dakota Access Pipeline." Evangelical Lutheran Church in America. September 9, 2016. http://elca.org/News-and-Events/7857.

Erasmus. "Standing Rock Is a New Turn in Christian Ties with Native Americans." *The Economist*. November 27, 2016. http://www.economist.com/blogs/erasmus/2016/11/church-and-dakota-pipeline-protests.

Hodges, Sam, and Doreen Gosmire. "Pipeline Protest Supporters Cheer Re-Rout

Ruling." United Methodist Church. December 5, 2016. http://www.umc.org /news-and-media/supporters-of-pipeline-protest-cheer-re-route-ruling.

Macpherson, James, and Blake Nicholson. "Tribe Files Legal Challenge to Stall Dakota Access Pipeline." ABC News. February 9, 2017. http://abcnews.go.com /US/wireStory/company-set-finish-work-dakota-access-oil-pipe-line-45366233.

Ravitz, Jessica. "The Sacred Land at the Center of the Dakota Pipeline Dispute." CNN. November 1, 2016. http://www.cnn.com/2016/11/01/us/standing -rock-sioux-sacred-land-dakota-pipeline.

Schuck, Michael J. "Catholic Tradition Meets Native American Spirituality at Dakota Pipeline Protest." *America*. December 8, 2016. http://www .americamagazine.org/politics-society/2016/12/08/catholic-tradition -meets-native-american-spirituality-dakota-pipeline.

White, Jon. "Episcopal Church Formally Asserts Its Support of Pipeline Protestors." Episcopal Café. October 24, 2016. https://www.episcopalcafe.com /episcopal-church-formally-asserts-its-support-of-pipeline-protestors.

Winsor, Morgan, and James Hill. "Cheyenne River Sioux Tribe Files 1st Legal Challenge over Dakota Access Pipeline Easement." ABC News. February 9, 2017. http://abcnews.go.com/US/cheyenne-river-sioux-tribe-files-1st-legal -challenge/story?id=45373370.

86. The Church Militant

February 27, 2017
By Martin E. Marty

Headlines in the *Detroit Free Press*, which reached us recently via *USA Today*, and the *Chicago Sun-Times*, from the second-to-last day of last year, were wake-up alarms alerting readers to yet another extremist group of the sort that prospers in these years. One local paper tabbed it as "Right-Wing Group Builds Empire near Motor City," which was an accurate but provincial-sounding notice for a national phenomenon. In all those stories the phrase "Church Militant" was prominent, as it was in another December 30 story, this one by Samuel G. Freedman in *The New York Times*, which goes into details we cannot provide here. Indeed, we might have dozed past the words "Church Militant" altogether had Freedman not moved the concept from the fourth to the twenty-first century: "'Church Militant' Theology Is Put to New, and Politicized, Use."

Until modern-day right-wing religio-political activists seized the term, twisted its historic meaning, and made it their banner, the now-misused "Church Militant" was conveniently shelved in the collection of "old, unhappy, far-off things" like the Crusades, Inquisition, and Thirty Years' War. In 1992 Pope John Paul II and company replaced it with the more appropriate term "Pilgrims on Earth." One of the useful side effects of the current religio-political battles is that they may force commentators, and the rest of us, to trace our way back to vestiges of the olden ways, and understand them. Then, the "Church Militant" referred to spiritual warfare, which was far more serious and soul-destroying than the mere Thirty-Years' War. Some of us grew up with hymnals featuring "Christian Warfare" sections: "Rise! To Arms!"—rendered pacific by line two, "With Prayer Employ You"; "Fight the Good Fight with All Thy Might"; and "Stand Up, Stand Up for Jesus," which children sang while sitting down in Sunday School.

No longer? In these latter days—as they may well be—of our free republic, the formal term "Church Militant," which balanced the promise of the "Church Triumphant" in heaven, is now the name for an organization, a ".com" host of websites, a cluster of organizations far from the Motor City, to which publics have to pay attention because it is the announced slogan, animator, and battle cry of some people in high positions. The founder and leader, TV personality and organizer Michael Voris, promotes extremely extreme Catholic worldviews which (he complains) are no longer held or honored by most Catholics. He perceives a "breaking down into forces that believe in God and those that don't. . . . Largely, [Voris] would say this is a war of religion versus nonreligion." Religion, according to his definition, does not include Islam, "Rabbinic Judaism," and presumably Protestantism, not to mention the views of the vast majority of Catholic leaders and Catholics in general.

Freedman quotes White House chief strategist Stephen K. Bannon, who in a speech at the Vatican in 2014 "called on the 'church militant' to fight a global war against . . . 'Islamic fascism' and international financial elites," et cetera. Freedman condenses the "Church Militant" agenda to stances against—surprise, surprise!—"globalism, immigration, social-welfare programs and abortion," and for "an existential war against radical Islam."

The Church Triumphant was historically promised to outlast the enemies of the Church Militant. Whoever reads and hears of these present-day contentions may well wonder if the words or their promise can outlast the militancies in our present chaos. Still, many "pilgrims on the earth" do continue their pilgrimage, freely.

Resources

Allen, Robert. "How a Right-Wing Ferndale Fringe Group Is Building a Multimedia Empire." *Detroit Free Press*. February 19, 2017. http://www.freep.com /story/news/local/michigan/oakland/2017/02/18/church-militant-growing -influence/97735914.

Freedman, Samuel G. "'Church Militant' Theology Is Put to New, and Politicized, Use." *The New York Times*. December 30, 2016. https://www.nytimes .com/2016/12/30/us/church-militant-theology-is-put-to-new-and-politicized -use.html.

87. The Time Has Passed

MARCH 2, 2017
BY EMILY D. CREWS

On February 16, 2017, *Sightings* published an article entitled "Why Milo Scares Students, and Faculty Even More," by University of Chicago professor Rachel Fulton Brown. In the piece Fulton Brown theorizes about the discomfort that Milo Yiannopoulos, the then-rising star of the far right's pyrotechnics show, inspires in many students and faculty at American universities. Her argument relies on an assertion that Yiannopoulos "speaks about the importance of Christianity for the values of Western civilization" in a context in which "these issues, most especially the civilizational roots of culture and virtue in religious faith, are . . . purposely avoided." The twenty-first-century American university, she states, "does not allow students to keep an open mind" because "their minds are already open—and being filled with what they are given in place of religion: multiculturalism; race, class, gender; the purportedly secular ideals of socialism and Marxism." Yiannopoulos, by contrast, returns us to a conversation about "people's deepest convictions," and the backlash against his presence at institutions of higher education is "evidence of a deep crisis in religious thinking."

In the days since its release, the article has inspired a storm of controversy. On social media, in classrooms, and throughout the University of Chicago people have reacted either with disbelief, disgust, and outrage, or with support and enthusiasm. Within twenty-four hours the piece was featured in a post on Breitbart, the far-right online news outlet that prior to February 21 employed Yiannopoulos, and to which Fulton Brown herself has previously contributed. It has since been quoted and discussed elsewhere.

Members of the University of Chicago community have advocated for a variety of responses to Fulton Brown's article, at least one of which is to offer no response at all. "Don't add fuel to the fire," these voices say. Others go so far as to argue that the piece should be removed from the *Sightings* website altogether. I understand the logic of these approaches, and I am persuaded by them in certain instances. They are supported by a number of my colleagues and mentors, who have spoken about them with wisdom and eloquence and whose training in theology or medieval European Christianity makes them

234

far more qualified critics of Fulton Brown than I am. Even so, I disagree that removal and silence are the best courses of action in this particular case. I believe that these would act in contravention to the fundamental goals of the academy as I understand them, and would prevent what is, in fact, an opportunity for scholars of religion to provide much-needed critical commentary on issues of public concern. Fulton Brown's piece, not in spite of but *because of* its problematic nature, offers us this opportunity.

The time for saying, "Let's not dignify this with a response," has passed. That method has been painfully unsuccessful. The reality facing us now is that the things we have thought would disappear if we looked the other way have not only remained but put down roots. They've set up camp. They've been elected president. And so it seems to me that Fulton Brown's piece, as objectionable as many find it, provides scholars of religion with an ideal opportunity to do something we have, by and large, failed to do in recent years, and particularly in the months since the election of Donald Trump: step into the fray. While political scientists, pollsters, and countless other kinds of pundits have commented on Trump's campaign and victory, the vitriol spewed by members of his new administration, and the agenda of the "alt-right," scholars of religion have been largely silent. We have neglected to make use of our skills and our unique ability to offer to interested members of the public valuable and necessary insight into pressing issues of our time, from the ban on Muslim immigrants entering the United States to the role of evangelical Christianity in twenty-first-century American culture.

Fulton Brown's major critique of American higher education is that it "lacks any clearly articulated and tested faith." She is wrong. Our faith is in the fundamental commitment to the rights of any person, regardless of perspective, to enter into principled, disciplined debate and advance an argument supported by credible evidence. From this commitment comes the duty to object to work in which our peers do not uphold this standard. Fulton Brown's position within the University alone—one that Breitbart has been all too happy to use as a means of authorizing Yiannopoulos's agenda— demands that we address the claims she has made and work to counter them where we see such acts as appropriate, not only for ourselves as scholars but also for the many members of the public who read and take very seriously the essays published via the University's online media, including *Sightings* and the *Religion & Culture Forum*.

In that spirit, let me highlight a few points on which one might critique Fulton Brown's article. First is her nostalgia for the medieval European university, which stems from the fact that it welcomed theological reflection. What the medieval university did *not* welcome was the presence of women or Jews or homosexuals or countless other classes of people who make today's universities the thriving places they are, and whose willingness to counter patriarchal hegemony has made it possible for a woman to hold the position of professor—and for a certain provocateur who identifies as queer to be treated as a full human being, despite his unwillingness to do the same for others.

I disagree, too, with her assertion that religion is the "wellspring" of culture. In this she has, I would argue, misunderstood the relationship between these two deeply contested categories. Religion is not the wellspring of culture; it is the structures, biases, prerogatives, and asymmetries of culture projected into and justified by a realm beyond the human. It is culture naturalized as supernatural.

Most problematic of all, to me, is Fulton Brown's claim that universities do not allow students and faculty openly to address religion. This suggests that, despite her own affiliation with the University of Chicago Divinity School, she has never set foot in Swift Hall, where, for better or worse, religion in its many forms is constantly discussed, debated, and defined by people of diverse faith commitments, including Christians who practice the theology they teach (and preach) as well as the atheists and humanists of whom Fulton Brown seems so afraid.

In encouraging engagement with Fulton Brown's piece I do not mean to say that we should tolerate the kind of hateful speech that has been so thoroughly and effectively utilized by the Trump administration and many of its supporters, including Yiannopoulos. Nor should we fall prey to the trap in which we play patty-cake with fascists in order to show our support for the First Amendment or to hush murmurs of intolerance. But it is time for academics to take their conversations out of elite circles and into the public square. In the era of "alternative facts," we are uniquely qualified to undertake the painstaking labor of historicizing, contextualizing, and falsifying. This process is not sexy, it's not flashy, and it's certainly not efficient. It is, nonetheless, the response to which I feel we're obliged by our membership in this profession. And it is a response we lose the opportunity to offer if we remove this article from the *Sightings* website or continue to look away from the issues staring us in the face.

Resource

Fulton Brown, Rachel. "Why Milo Scares Students, and Faculty Even More."
Sightings. February 16, 2017. https://divinity.uchicago.edu/sightings/why
-milo-scares-students-and-faculty-even-more.

*Emily D. Crews is a PhD candidate in history of religions at the University of
Chicago Divinity School. A 2015–16 Martin Marty Center junior fellow, she is a
former editor of the* Religion & Culture *Forum and currently serves as interim
director of the undergraduate program in religious studies.*

88. Alien Citizens

MARCH 6, 2017
BY MARTIN E. MARTY

NOT BREAKING NEWS! Overdosed on "Breaking News," which in the case of religion usually means news of clerical sex scandals, parochial embezzlements, or stories of some evangelicals acting unevangelically, *Sightings* sometimes likes to train its sights on religious stories that do not "break," but focus on what serves the citizenry in largely unobserved ways. This week we observe a long-longtime favorite of ours, the Bruderhof. Recently we sighted the "Benedict Option," which sets out to serve the faithful by retreating *from* the world. The Bruderhof, by contrast, would serve the faithful and others by gathering (and publishing) in order to advance *into* the world in distinctive ways.

The Bruderhof is probably not a household word, so let it explain itself: "an international community of people seeking to follow Jesus together . . . committed to a way of radical discipleship in the spirit of the Sermon on the Mount" and in the tradition of the first Christian community (Acts 1 and 2). There are tiny settlements in the US and in four other countries. Census-takers, pollsters, pundits, and statisticians would not notice them, but *Sightings* readers can find out more via their website. They publish our favorite religious quarterly, *Plough*, whose winter issue is what prompts this notice.

The quoted passage mentions Jesus and Christianity, a fact which might alienate citizens who are not Christian or have been schooled to be "spiritual but not religious." However, we believe that one can learn more and act more citizenly when Jews are Jews, Muslims are Muslims, et cetera, than when they are muffled or wishy-washy. When we are articulate speakers/writers and good listeners, we can often share citizenship better and, one hopes, understand and cooperate with "others."

The current journal cover is red-stamped "ALIEN CITIZENS," and the lead editorial is called "Our Alien Citizenship." We get the point. The editors draw on a 1989 book by William Willimon and Stanley Hauerwas titled *Resident Aliens*. Willimon himself appears in these pages, with an article in which he quotes theologian Karl Barth as being anti-Hitler, as well as Bruderhof founder Eberhard Arnold, who would perhaps have agreed with Hauerwas when the latter famously said, "The church doesn't have a social policy; the church *is* God's social policy."

Willimon seems to enjoy, more than perhaps he should, the irritation of and criticism by a dozen reviewers who dismissed his books with Hauerwas as "politically irrelevant, sectarian escapism from the great issues of the day." At times I share such irritation and criticism, but I can't say that I've not been warned by the authors who—from many angles of vision—*do* go out of their way to alienate citizens who they wish were "resident aliens."

By the way, Bruderhofers can scarcely go even a few paragraphs without pointing to exemplars like Lutheran Dietrich Bonhoeffer, Catholic Dorothy Day, and an ecumenical cast of characters as influences. The major address by Arnold included in the current issue, first delivered in August 1934, is "Becoming Flesh and Blood: The Church and Its Dangerous Politics." Aha! See! This supposedly non-political approach has its own form of politics. Its approach to issues having to do with the environment, the use of resources, the regard for all humans as having equal rights, is distinctive but also very much a part of the political mix today. We'll keep reading the Bruderhof journal and related materials, to be challenged when we disagree and cheered when, as so often happens, we are jarred into agreement with these residents-with-a-difference.

Resources

Arnold, Eberhard. "Becoming Flesh and Blood." *Plough Quarterly*. Winter 2017. http://www.plough.com/en/topics/justice/politics/becoming-flesh-and -blood.

Coon, John. "5 Beliefs That Set the Bruderhof Apart from Other Christians." Newsmax. May 7, 2015. http://www.newsmax.com/FastFeatures/bruderhof -christians-beliefs-set/2015/05/07/id/643320.

Dreher, Rod. "Ben Op Meets Bruderhof." *The American Conservative*. December 13, 2016. http://www.theamericanconservative.com/dreher/benedict-option -bruderhof.

Mommsen, Peter. "Our Alien Citizenship." *Plough Quarterly*. Winter 2017. http:// www.plough.com/en/topics/justice/politics/our-alien-citizenship.

Weizel, Richard. "Of Family, Spirituality and Power." *The New York Times*. December 8, 1996. http://www.nytimes.com/1996/12/08/nyregion/of-family -spirituality-and-power.html.

Willimon, William H. "Alien Citizens." *Plough Quarterly*. Winter 2017. http:// www.plough.com/en/topics/justice/politics/alien-citizens.

Zimmerman, Christopher. "The Bruderhof, Another View." *The New York Times*. December 15, 1996. http://www.nytimes.com/1996/12/15/nyregion/l-the -bruderhof-another-view-698415.html.

89. Look for the Jews

March 9, 2017
By Erika Tritle

Various news outlets have addressed the fact that the US president's published statement on International Holocaust Remembrance Day intentionally omits specific reference either to Jews or to anti-Semitism. It does honor "the victims, survivors, heroes of the Holocaust" and acknowledge the unfathomable "depravity and horror inflicted on innocent people by Nazi terror." As reported by CNN, the White House defends its statement by insisting that "we are an incredibly inclusive group and we took into account all those who suffered." Social media conversations and public comments about this statement reveal debate over whether it is important to mention Jews and their history, or whether it is sufficient to imply Jews as constituents of a more universal notion of humanity. Given that the Nazis killed many people who were not Jews, perhaps we could let the Holocaust stand for general human suffering brought about by a generic concept of evil.

Many implied Jews populate the public statements and tweets of the current presidential administration and its preceding campaign. If the Holocaust Remembrance Day statement implies Jews but does not name them explicitly, so does the six-pointed star next to an opponent's face and atop a pile of cash. Equally so does suggesting a conspiracy among certain leaders in the world of business and finance, all of whom are well known to be Jewish. The second and third examples draw upon a history of anti-Semitic tropes without ever using the words "Jew" or "Jewish." This strategy contrasts with Nazi propaganda, which often included the word "Jude" over an image to be crystal clear.

The omission of Jews from the Holocaust Remembrance Day statement is even more insidious than the imagery of the above examples because it is more easily explained away by those who would, in fact, denounce overt expressions of anti-Semitism. At worst, the statement ignores or minimizes the fact that the Nazis' final solution explicitly aimed to exterminate flesh-and-blood Jews from the earth and to expunge their memory from the human story. At best, the statement incorporates Jews and their particular history and identity into a universal notion of humanity.

Yet while universalist ideals may sound attractive and may appeal to our best inclinations to unity, too often they serve to advance the perspectives, assumptions, and interests of one group of human beings over those of other groups. In the history of Christianity, for example, one method used by the earliest followers of Christ to define themselves involved contrasting their universal faith, in which "there is no longer Jew or Greek, there is no longer slave or free, there is no longer male and female; for all of you are one in Christ Jesus" (Galatians 3:28), with what they described as the Jews' slavish adherence to the restrictive prescriptions of the Law (e.g., Galatians 4:21–31). That utmost marker of Jewish particularity, circumcision, became for many Christian authors a symbol of that Jewishness which was nullified or transcended by the death and resurrection of Christ. The apostle Paul wanted to spiritualize it (Romans 2:29), while the second-century Justin Martyr argued that circumcision had been commanded to mark the Jewish people for deserved suffering. True Israel, Justin taught, belonged to Christians, leaving Jews who did not accept the universal faith of Jesus mired in obsolescence.

Given that we do not have the space to recount a complete and nuanced history of Christian self-definition against Judaism or of the ways in which such rhetoric has informed actions and policies against flesh-and-blood Jews, let us turn to an insight from linguistic theory regarding the way the human brain and human cultures tend to assign normative weight to certain members of a group. Statements that appear to promote "inclusive," universalist notions of humanity without acknowledging important human differences often advance the interests of one group as prototype while subtly undermining the equal membership of other groups. With respect to the category "bird," for instance, one could assume that American robins or songbirds in general represent all birds, thereby pushing other groups like owls, penguins, and flamingos to the margins. Scholars of race, gender, anti-Semitism, postcolonial theory, et cetera, have called attention to how such strategies have similarly caused certain subgroups to attain prototypical status within the category "human being."

Statements such as the one produced by the White House for Holocaust Remembrance Day that omit Jews—that subgroup of human beings which was the explicit target of the Holocaust and which has so often been singled out for discrimination and aggression precisely because of its particularity—fail to worry many people of goodwill because the language sounds inclusive and universal. Nevertheless, avowedly anti-Semitic organizations have applauded this statement that omits Jews just as they have voiced their approval of campaign images drawn from anti-Semitic tropes. For some proponents of anti-Semitic policies, it has not been a question of centrality to the category "human being," but a question of membership itself. Whether they are insinuated to evoke a history of fearful stereotypes or whether they are omitted in favor of claims to universality, we should be wary of implied Jews.

Resources

Boyarin, Daniel. *Border Lines: The Partition of Judaeo-Christianity*. Philadelphia: University of Pennsylvania Press, 2006.

"Defining the Enemy." United States Holocaust Memorial Museum. https://www.ushmm.org/wlc/en/article.php?ModuleId=10007819.

Jackson, Henry C. "ADL Head Rips Trump Team over Holocaust Statement That Doesn't Mention Jews." *Politico*. January 27, 2017. http://www.politico.com/blogs/donald-trump-administration/2017/01/anti-defamation-league-trump-holocaust-statement-234285.

Justin Martyr. *Dialogue with Trypho*. Edited by Michael Susser. Translated by Thomas B. Falls. Rev. ed. Washington, DC: Catholic University of America Press, 2002.

"Lauder Criticizes ADL Reaction to Trump Statement on Holocaust Remembrance Day." World Jewish Congress. January 28, 2017. http://www.worldjewishcongress.org/en/news/lauder-criticizes-adls-negative-reaction-to-trump-statement-on-holocaust-remembrance-day-1-6-2017.

Milbank, Dana. "Anti-Semitism Is No Longer an Undertone of Trump's Campaign. It's the Melody." *The Washington Post*. November 7, 2016. https://www.washingtonpost.com/opinions/anti-semitism-is-no-longer-an-undertone-of-trumps-campaign-its-the-melody/2016/11/07/b1ad6e22-a50a-11e6-8042-f4d111c862d1_story.html.

Nirenberg, David. *Anti-Judaism: The Western Tradition*. New York: W. W. Norton & Company, 2014.

"Statement by the President on International Holocaust Remembrance Day." White House Press Office. January 21, 2017. https://www.whitehouse.gov/the-press-office/2017/01/27/statement-president-international-holocaust-remembrance-day.

Tapper, Jake. "WH: No Mention of Jews on Holocaust Remembrance Day Because Others Were Killed Too." CNN. February 2, 2017. http://www.cnn.com/2017/01/28/politics/white-house-holocaust-memorial-day/index.html.

Erika Tritle received a PhD in history of Christianity from the University of Chicago Divinity School. She currently teaches courses in religion, history, and philosophy at South Dakota State University.

90. Being Hip-Hop, Being Job, and Being

MAY 4, 2017
BY JULIAN "J.KWEST" DESHAZIER

The opening of De La Soul's "Intro" (from the *Stakes Is High* album) is an expertly mixed chorus of four voices saying these six words . . .

When I first heard "Criminal Minded"

. . . which refer to Boogie Down Productions' 1987 album of that name, one of the most acclaimed albums in hip-hop history. De La Soul's sentiment is clear and can easily be translated to, "When I first heard *that album that changed my life*," be it from BDP or Black Thought or Bob Dylan—the moment the listener hears an album that is both talking *to* and *for* them, bearing witness to a reality and helping to create a better reality. BDP and its lead rapper KRS-One became entertainers, journalists, and prophets to a South Bronx, NY, context full of poverty, drugs, and pop music—whether disco or rock—that was served to them but not made by them. As invisible as the politics of the day made them, hip-hop represented the soundtrack of resistance.

The notion of creating music as a way of creating or articulating reality has its roots in other genres. James Cone reminds us that blues music was created in the midst of the black struggle for being in another era, King David of Israel becomes a brilliant psalmist (that's "songwriter") in the midst of deep pain, and Samuel Livingston traces humankind's first songs to the African concept of *neferu* (cultural manifestations of functional beauty). In other words, music has always had a purpose before it had an industry, and its economy was purely social, made up of those who would listen, identify, and be identified by those artists.

When I first heard "Criminal Minded"
When I first heard 2Pac's "All Eyez on Me"
When I first heard Common's "One Day It'll All Make Sense"
. . . It changed my world
. . . Because I heard myself, for the first time

243

Rap is scary to some because it is loud, which is entirely the point. It is a response with deep intention toward the systemic silencing by privileged whites, the wealthy, and the ignorant men who hold the center at this particular moment in time. It is the first bell that rings after the death around us young black Chicagoans has silenced us.

It is the cathartic response of Job after being stunned over and over, pathologically pummeled to the brink of nonbeing, and his first words—"Let the day perish on which I was born. . . . Let that day be darkness!"—which begin to reaffirm and reconstruct his being. His words are harsh and explicit and feel grossly emotional; in our context they would seem anti-intellectual when in fact they are *super*-rational, transcending intellect.

In 1988 and today, N.W.A's "F— tha Police" is shocking and controversial—"uncalled for" by most tastes—until you hear the songwriters recall their inspiration, being pulled over in Los Angeles, handcuffed, and forced to lie on the ground for being one thing: black. Was N.W.A having a Job moment, or was Job having one of the first hip-hop moments? Either way, both texts comprise wisdom, both utterances remain necessary.

If you want to understand the violence epidemic in Chicago, listen to the "drill" music of the shooters. You will hear the struggle for being that too often describes and destroys. If you want to understand the beautiful complexity of our youth, listen to Chance the Rapper's "No Problem," where he talks about "scoopin' all the blessings out my lap" and by the end of the same verse brusquely reminds us that his "shooters come for free." His message is clear: he's keeping his, by any means necessary.

What he's really saying—perhaps in every verse Chance has ever written—is that his being matters. His album *Coloring Book*, along with BDP's *Criminal Minded*, expresses the "courage to be" without probably ever hearing (and certainly never caring about) the name Paul Tillich. These are theological projects as much as they are musical ones, and hip-hop has a way of reminding us that the separation of the head and heart is mostly an academic and superficial one. Job should have written an album; maybe Notorious B.I.G. was reading the famous text when he settled on a name for his first album, *Ready to Die*.

Growing up on the South Side of Chicago in rap's "Golden Era," I had no need for church; I had already found an adequate object of worship in the music that blared through my cassette player—music from Christians and Muslims and Five-Percenters and Black Hebrew Israelites—music that was loud and confident and confrontational, *explicit* in every sense of the word. For all I had seen and endured, it needed to be.

We—that is, most young, black boys—take our cues from rappers, perhaps to a fault, but at least they show better journalistic integrity in accurately describing reality than most news outlets. This trust in *entertainer as journalist* evolves rappers into a greater role: the poets who shape culture, the poetry whose purpose is to create a new reality. You hear rappers who don't understand this and use their microphone to spread a dangerous gospel of misogynist and capitalist urges—no different from some pulpits. But you also hear the proclamation and affirmation of the #BlackLivesMatter movement, its anger and its spirit engorged as a people fight to be made visible. In the rhythm and lineage you see Africa. It is *neferu*. It is the catharsis of Job. And for those hearing it for the first time . . .

> *When I first heard "Criminal Minded"*
> *When I first read Job*
> *When I saw myself*

. . . it is like coming alive again. It is that Resurrection that many classically trained theologians spend too many words describing. It is a hip-hop moment.

Julian "J.Kwest" DeShazier (MDiv, University of Chicago Divinity School) is pastor of University Church in Chicago, and a rapper.

91. The Meaning of Religious Exemptions

May 11, 2017
By Franklin I. Gamwell

Governmental recognition of religious liberty is a pressing issue in our current politics. The 1993 Religious Freedom Restoration Act states that a generally applicable federal statute may not substantially burden "a person's exercise of religion" unless the law "furthers a compelling governmental interest" and "is the least restrictive means of furthering that compelling governmental interest." In *Hobby Lobby v. Burwell* (2014), the US Supreme Court exempted some "closely held corporations" from a provision of the Affordable Care Act (ACA) because their owners object to certain forms of contraception. In *Zubik v. Burwell*, which the Court returned last year to lower courts with instructions to seek compromise, some religiously affiliated institutions claim an exemption because, for them, a particular governmental directive authorized by the ACA means complicity with insurance coverage for contraception, which they oppose. Religious exemptions will likely be a prominent issue the future Court, now again at full strength, is called to decide.

Some critics have challenged the Court's refusal to ask whether religious exercise has been "substantially burdened." But that focus is misplaced. As Justices Scalia and O'Connor have said, judges should not determine what is "central" to a given religious belief. Instead, I argue, the relevant question asks *what kind* of religious activities qualify for exemption.

Approach to an answer requires that "religious" in "religious freedom" has a broad meaning: any conviction about the ultimate basis for evaluating all human activity should be, for political purposes, called religious. Thereby, any comprehensive belief, whether conventionally religious or secularistic, is constitutionally protected. Moreover, such First Amendment protection is essential to our democracy because each adult citizen must be free to advocate any political evaluation she or he finds convincing. If "we the people" are sovereign, each person should be sovereign over her or his belief about the ultimate basis of evaluation. It also follows that popular sovereignty is impossible when differing religious beliefs are assumed immune to public discussion and debate because they are somehow suprarational and thus "solely a matter of faith." Our democracy implies government through full and free discussion and debate inclusive of differing comprehensive beliefs.

Whether or not free exercise exemptions should be sanctioned constitutionally or only by statute is controversial. But religious freedom cannot mean granting such exemptions whenever the compelling interest test is inapplicable and some law is contrary to some citizen's comprehensive belief. Any dissent from a generally applicable law might then be grounds for a claim to exemption. Moreover, something is amiss if such dissent could be used as the basis for religious free exercise. The claim to exemption does not disagree with a given law's general applicability. Opposition to a democratically decided statute denies its rightful enactment, but seeking exemption does not contest the law itself.

To be sure, certain religious adherents might assert that a particular law or aspect thereof directly denies one of their religious beliefs—for instance, an ACA requirement that certain employers provide health insurance inclusive of legal contraception. In that case, however, the claim against the state asserts its violation of religious disestablishment, because the law is said to teach something about the ultimate basis of evaluation. A given law is said to target a certain religious belief or kind of religious belief, and the claim for exemption is irrelevant. Moreover, the real issue is not whether some religious adherents *assert* this; in fact, any law can be said to deny a religious belief. The proper question is whether a particular law does in fact explicitly say something about comprehensive evaluation. And the proper test is then whether the law restricts a full and free political discourse by teaching something about how citizens should evaluate political decisions. The ACA teaches no such restriction; each member of "we the people" is entirely free to evaluate and oppose the law, and a claim against its general applicability has no merit.

Hence, free exercise claims make sense only if the candidate activities are limited in a way independent of political dissent. What's distinctive to religious practices is the kind of cultivation they require. As comprehensive, religious belief must evoke in adherents an innermost commitment and must develop competence in applying ultimate evaluative terms to diverse situations of human life—and many religious communities include activities of symbolic expression and associated teaching designed for this cultivation. Because they assume the given comprehensive belief, these activities are rightly prescribed only for adherents of it. Politically, then, such practices facilitate participation in the public discourse, where the comprehensive evaluation is advocated.

Here, then, is a proposal: only cultivating activities in preparation for (among other things) public discourse can be candidates for free exercise exemptions. Claims for an exemption are improper unless the activity in question is prescribed only for adherents of a given comprehensive belief. In contrast, dissent from a generally applicable law has no claim to exemption because failure to prevail in the full and free discourse is not grounds for release from the law's requirements. Free exercise exemptions are meant to enhance how the public determines generally applicable laws, not as compensation when the public finds one's political view wanting.

Given a relevant constitutional provision or statute specifying religious exemptions, use of peyote in worship ceremonies or the drinking of wine in certain eucharistic celebrations or a certain personal appearance in the military or in prison are, to cite some examples, possibly exempt from generally applicable laws prohibiting such activities—*if* in each case the activity is prescribed only for those who cultivate the comprehensive belief they already confess. Perhaps this mediation is mostly found in conventionally religious communities, but so-called "religious" liberty should also provide exemption for the cultivation of secularistic beliefs.

What is *not* a candidate for exemption, however, is activity that opposes a generally applicable law itself; no person can be exempted from democratically determined laws she or he takes to be wrong. And because activities prescribed only for adherents should be distinguished from political advocacy by claimants themselves, there is no harm in allowing them to determine when the former have been sufficiently burdened. Given this account, neither *Hobby Lobby v. Burwell* nor *Zubik v. Burwell* includes a claim fit for a free exercise exemption.

Franklin I. Gamwell (PhD, University of Chicago Divinity School) is Shailer Mathews Distinguished Service Professor Emeritus at the University of Chicago Divinity School, where he taught religious ethics, theology, and philosophy of religions for many years.

92. Taking the Unitarian Universalist Diversity Crisis Seriously

MAY 15, 2017
BY MARTIN E. MARTY

How did the Unitarian Universalist Association (UUA), a merger of two most liberal church bodies, escape notice in this column for two decades or so? Since it made big news (given its small size), it has received national attention for the past month, a notice that prompted some research on our part. The conventional research instrument Google provides access to many features of UUA life and history. For example, look up "Unitarian Universalist jokes," and you will find it to be as capable as are far larger bodies of being the butt of jokes, some the subject of mini-feuds with, e.g., humorist Garrison Keillor, who finds them funny. Let's take them seriously.

At issue recently was the furor over racial policies and practices in this most liberal denomination, sparked by the resignation of its president, the Rev. Peter Morales, in the face of a ruckus over the appointment of what critics see as too many privileged (i.e., white) candidates and leaders. Let it be noted that the UUA's language and stated intentions are all on the side of changing the image of a denomination that has a very small percentage of minority or marginalized leaders. Morales's stepping down was followed by two more resignations at the highest level. To no one's surprise, a variety of caucuses and rights-and-interest groups quickly organized and spoke up. Finger-pointing and soul-searching among members made headlines wherever the UUA has local congregational representation.

The public relations embarrassment has served notice not only to liberal denominations but, at this moment, to them especially. There is no place to hide for a group whose language may be "correct," its public pronouncements *up front*, but whose pews and letterheads *down home* continue to embarrass many Unitarians and Universalists. The same is true for the majority of largely white Protestant bodies. What is most obvious is that there are no quick fixes, no matter how much argument, energy, posturing, and reforming is in evidence.

The church bodies with which I am most at home have spent the most recent half-century repenting, revising, and revisiting formerly underserved publics. Their proclamations, preachments, and voting patterns reveal impressive evidences of efforts to bring about change. But what we have learned during these decades is that, even in religious bodies where one seldom hears defenses of racial segregation or snubbing, it is very difficult to see the development of truly interracial—and, truth be told, interclass—congregations. Let it be noted that not all resistance to integrative change is based on hatred, prejudice, or snubbing on the part of the privileged against the marginalized. Reluctance to change can sometimes be read as a tribute to the enduring power of existing religious communities to contribute positively—in the form of art, creativity, pastoral care, et cetera—to those who make them up.

On these terms, one asks: must all African American or Hispanic or Asian or white, Euro-American cohering congregations abandon their cultural trademarks, even as they feed the soul and motivate generosity? And *can* they, if they try? At their best, many are learning to invest in what they inherited, and to combine that with learning from "the other." Listen to them: they will confess, spiritually and artistically, that their lives and worship are improved. We can hope that the liberal Unitarian Universalist body, as it patches itself up, can find ways to serve the less privileged and, sometimes, less liberal communities of believers. Let the Unitarian Universalist jokes survive, but we may notice, along the way, that "the joke's on us" if we don't learn.

Resources

Banks, Adelle M. "Unitarian Universalist President Resigns amid Diversity Controversy." Religion News Service. March 31, 2017. http://religionnews .com/2017/03/31/unitarian-universalist-president-resigns-amid-diversity -controversy.

Hogan, Susan. "Turmoil over Diversity Strikes Unitarian Universalist Association." *The Washington Post*. April 3, 2017. https://www.washingtonpost.com /news/morning-mix/wp/2017/04/03/turmoil-over-diversity-strikes-unitarian -universalist-association.

Landrum, Cynthia. "Garrison Keillor Is No 'Companion' for Unitarian Universalists." Personal blog. December 17, 2009. http://revcyn.blogspot.com/2009/12 /garrison-keillor-is-no-companion-for.html.

Walton, Christopher L. "Updates to Presidential Resignation and Controversy over Hiring Practices." UU World. April 1, 2017. http://www.uuworld.org /articles/developments-2017-04-01.

———. "Further Updates to UUA Resignations and Controversy over Hiring Practices." UU World. April 8, 2017. http://www.uuworld.org/articles /developments-2017-04-07.

93. The Hidden Roots of Betsy DeVos's Educational Policies

MAY 25, 2017
BY WILLEMIEN OTTEN

Secretary of Education Betsy DeVos favors the injection of a conservatively religious, most likely also corporate, evangelical influence into American educational politics. But the question of what exactly that means digs deeper than just the mere presence of religion in American education through the promotion of vouchers and expansion of charter schools. By sidetracking funds from public education, a shadow system of privately run schools is created that undermines the flourishing of a once-viable national public school system. For a long time that public system served this country well as a social and religious equalizer, allowing immigrants from different backgrounds to assimilate as American citizens.

"Assimilation" may be the key term here, and the concept most resisted by DeVos. For what it stands for in her eyes is not a neutral education but a normative (read: liberal) set of values that clash with the religious beliefs of parents. To her, the latter's voices outweigh any government responsibility.

This religious principle, lying at the heart of DeVos's educational advocacy, is to a large extent the product of a long nineteenth-century Dutch political and religious debate. As in the Netherlands, it could lead to a demand that religious education be subsidized through public funds, which would be a novelty in the American educational system. Growing up in the Christian Reformed Church in western Michigan and attending Calvin College, Betsy DeVos was heavily influenced by Abraham Kuyper (1837–1920), an early Dutch advocate of "Schools with the Bible."

When first introduced in the Netherlands in 1917, Christian, so-called "special" schools—they are not called "private" because they are publicly funded and hence seen as part of the public institutional landscape—were a novelty as well, the result of a long political battle instigated by Kuyper. Kuyper was a Reformed, neo-Calvinist minister and politician who broke away from the Dutch Reformed Church in 1869; founded the nation's first political party, the Anti-Revolutionary Party (ARP), in 1879; created the Free University in Amsterdam in 1880; and became prime minister in 1901. In 1980 his party merged with other confessional parties to form the Christian Democratic Party, while his church reconciled, or rather merged, with the Dutch Reformed Church in 2004 to form the Protestant Church in the Netherlands. Hence his most tangible legacy may well be the network of publicly funded special (i.e., Christian) schools. It is so successful that, with less than half of the Dutch population currently claiming to be religiously affiliated, about 70 percent of Dutch children still attend Christian schools.

How did this system come about, and why does it persist? Throughout the nineteenth century, as the Netherlands recovered from the impact of the French Revolution and tried to build a nation that was "one and indivisible," the church played an important role in channeling the people's religious and nationalist sentiments. But the Protestant church was considered too distant and formal, while the restoration of the Catholic hierarchy in 1853 fueled the nation's dormant anti-Catholicism. The emerging religious and political debates masked a deep underlying tension about the role of the Dutch nation, whose Eighty Years' War of Independence (1568–1648) was seen as closely tied to the Reformation, and whose freedom and identity were considered inherently Protestant. Guillaume Groen van Prinsterer, an important nineteenth-century politician who steadfastly opposed the liberal Johan Rudolph Thorbecke, author of the 1848 Dutch constitution, wrote in support of an early secessionist movement from the Dutch Reformed Church, some of whose adherents left in the mid-1840s for Michigan; there they later formed the Christian Reformed Church, in which Betsy DeVos would grow up. Groen's early warning against the semi-established Protestant church was that such tensions might spill over into the political arena. Driven by his "anti-revolutionary" and "Christian-historical" agenda, he advocated for Protestant schools with government funding, and when denied, insisted on neutral schools that offered no religious education and also made no reference to national history.

The fortune of Groen's failed legislative agenda changed when Kuyper, energized by another denial of government funding for Christian education at public schools, founded the ARP. He uprooted the political landscape by prioritizing the charismatic bond between leader and constituents. Still, it was not until the First World War, in which the Netherlands was neutral, that the ARP and other confessional parties succeeded in what became known as the Pacification of 1917. This Pacification, further aided by the threat of a socialist revolution, consisted in a unique tradeoff by which the left (social-democrats and liberals) gained universal suffrage—first only for men, soon after also for women—and the right (confessional parties) achieved their goal of founding Christian schools with government funding.

Instrumental in winning this drawn-out battle were two central Kuyperian concepts. First, the notion of common grace, the neo-Calvinist version of natural law, by which God has ordered creation for all to work in and enjoy. This is a moral exhortation for Christians to be active in the public realm. The second is sphere sovereignty, the notion that life is an organism consisting of different spheres, in which different constituencies each play their own part without government interference. Kuyper gave an address on sphere sovereignty at the opening of the Free University in 1880. But only in 1917 did he succeed in gaining the government's endorsement for a systemic educational change. A new educational system was put in place, anchored in article twenty-three of the Dutch constitution, which grants freedom of education, meaning that in the educational sphere different constituencies can each found their own schools at the government's expense.

While I am no longer in favor of the Dutch system due to its lack of credible representation, the fact that it is publicly funded has allowed for full accountability as well as facilitating useful government pushback against religious extremes. Special schools can no longer discriminate against teachers based on gender or sexual identity. Also, a recent committee has designed a national canon setting standards for historical education. It highlights universal suffrage but does not mention special schools. Nevertheless, with an appeal to their board, special schools can still refuse to admit Muslim students wearing headscarves, and failing inner-city schools are too often public schools. While it is clearly time for an update of the Dutch system, I would strongly counsel Secretary DeVos and the US to refrain from going down the long and winding Kuyperian road.

Resources

Bratt, James D. "Sphere Sovereignty among Abraham Kuyper's Other Political Theories." In *The Kuyper Center Review.* Vol. 1, *Politics, Religion, and Sphere Sovereignty*, edited by Gordon Graham, 34–49. Grand Rapids: Eerdmans, 2010.

The Dutch canon (in English) can be found at http://www.entoen.nu/en.

Kruse, Kevin M. *One Nation under God. How Corporate America Invented Christian America*. New York: Basic Books, 2015.

Monsma, Stephen V., and J. Christopher Soper. *The Challenge of Pluralism: Church and State in Five Democracies.* Lanham, MD: Rowman & Littlefield, 2009.

Rooy, Piet de. *A Tiny Spot on the Earth: The Political Culture of the Netherlands in the Nineteenth and Twentieth Century.* Amsterdam: Amsterdam University Press, 2015.

Vermeulen, Ben. "Een schets en evaluatie van de kritiek op de overheidsfinan-cieting van het bijzonder onderwijs." In *Geloven in het publieke domein: verkenningen van een dubbele transformative* edited by W. H. B. J. van de Donk et al. Amsterdam: Amsterdam University Press, 2006.

Willemien Otten is professor of theology and the history of Christianity at the University of Chicago Divinity School; she also teaches in the College and is associated faculty in the Department of History. A Dutch native, Otten recently served on a Task Force for Sustainable Humanities instituted by the Dutch minister of education to strengthen the position of the humanities in Dutch universities.

94. Rev. Dr. William Barber and the Sound of Transcendence

JUNE 15, 2017
BY BRAXTON D. SHELLEY

In his address to the 2016 Democratic National Convention, the Rev. Dr. William J. Barber II, then president of the North Carolina Conference of the NAACP and leader of the Moral Mondays Movement, proclaimed, "like our forefathers and foremothers, we are called to be the moral defibrillators of our time." Likening the pursuit of justice to the regulation of an irregular heartbeat, Barber's words offer a valuable window into the politics of prophetic preaching.

While Barber's leadership of the Moral Mondays Movement has brought him to national prominence and granted him entry into many venues, including the stage of the DNC, Barber contends that he is "not a politician, [but] a pastor." In his words,

> The job of a pastor is to touch people where they are hurting and to do what is possible to bind up their wounds. You can only do this sort of work locally—among people whose names you know and who, likewise, know you. But you cannot do it honestly without at some point becoming a prophet. Something inside the human spirit cries out against the injustice of inequality when you know people who have to choose between food and medicine in a country where CEOs make more in an hour than their lowest-paid employees make in a month.

While Barber identifies himself as a pastor, his preaching embodies a kind of political strategy. This strategy does not consist in "political realism," which he argues tends to silence dissent, but instead *faith*, the kind that makes "it possible for a moral voice to cry aloud and spare not." This kind of belief, he writes, is "not blind faith," but "conviction that [takes] the long view. Even when they could not see now how justice would prevail, generations of dissenters knew that it would. Even when they felt alone in the moment, they knew they were part of a 'great cloud of witnesses' in the long movement toward justice."

I argue that Barber's analysis reveals aspects of the public theology he seeks to construct. Further, I am intrigued by his suggestion that faith can serve as a kind of strategy and fuel for protest, for it points to a more central problematic. Namely, while Barber's discourses and actions focus on fusion, joining diverse groups of people in pursuit of common objectives, he recruits aesthetic and ritual resources that are oddly specific. What meanings obtain from the usage of characteristically black religion in the public sphere? What does this case teach about the political value of the black sacred?

As he straddles the line between speech and sermon, Barber's orations use musical affect to motivate the pursuit of justice. When Barber "tunes up," performing the characteristic shift from speech into song near the end of his discourses, he facilitates a communal experience of transcendence. At precisely the moment that he makes this sonic shift toward heightened musicality, he also makes a textual shift toward history, pointing to the victories of those who fought for abolition, suffrage, and civil rights as proof that "the arc of the moral universe bends toward justice." For just a few moments at the end of these messages, then, Barber's deliberate anachronism fashions transcendence as a resource for resistance. As his listeners feel their place on the universe's moral arc, they acquire a renewed commitment to bend it even the more. Thus, an ecstatic practice that previous writers have derided as evidence of black Christians' fundamentally "otherworldly" disposition becomes fuel for political protest.

Barber's homiletic recalls theologian James H. Cone's observation that, by taking audiences "from the present to the past and then thrust[ing them] back into their contemporary history with divine power to transform the sociopolitical context," liberative practices like this mode of address help communities "transcend the limitations of their immediate history and encounter the divine power, thereby creating a moment of ecstasy and joy wherein they recognize that the pain of oppression is not the last word about black life." I want to argue that this black sacred rhetoric gives transcendence a characteristic sound.

By shifting toward heightened musicality and toward content that reaches across temporal borders, Barber subsumes the specific message of an individual sermon within an experience of divine presence, insisting that God is interested in the plight of the oppressed while offering anticipatory proof that justice will have the last word. His "tuning up" is therefore more than a performance strategy; rather, it is a theological assertion that God is present and that God can be expected to act.

Resources

Barber, William J., with Jonathan Wilson-Hartgrove. *The Third Reconstruction: Moral Mondays, Fusion Politics, and the Rise of a New Justice Movement.* Boston: Beacon Press, 2016.

Cone, James H. *God of the Oppressed.* New York: Seabury Press, 1975.

Braxton D. Shelley graduated with an MDiv from the University of Chicago Divinity School and a PhD in the history and theory of music from the University of Chicago's Department of Music. He has recently joined the faculty of the Department of Music at Harvard University.

95. Euthanasia, Dignity, and "Spirituality Lite"

July 10, 2017
By Martin E. Marty

Those (of us) who value the ethical but are not ethicists have good reason to pay attention to those philosophers, theologians, and, yes, ethicists, whose vocation it is to deal with values, whether these have to do with ordinary problems and dilemmas or with extraordinary ones, such as matters of life and death. These are not, and cannot be, right all the time or in agreement with each other much of the time, but they gain credibility in the eyes and minds of ordinary and extraordinary people when they follow their vocation and subject themselves and each other to criticism.

Few problems or issues are more troubling than those code-named "euthanasia." When *The New York Times* (May 25) placed a story about euthanasia on page one and followed through on more pages, there were many reasons for the public to take special note. The story "At His Own Wake: Celebrating Life and the Gift of Death" by Catherine Porter was attention-getting enough, for it followed the career-toward-death of a particularly engrossing candidate for euthanasia, John Shields, a former Roman Catholic priest who, in the language of the church, "left the faith." Among those who read the story of the end of his trail was Gilbert Meilaender of Valparaiso and Notre Dame universities. From their fields in Indiana, this professor has figuratively walked with people in "the valley of the shadow of death" and reflected on its realms.

He did not think much of the *Times* piece and said so in an important response in *Commonweal* (June 30). Assuming that fewer people read that Roman Catholic magazine than read the *Times*, we'll commend both articles to all but concentrate on the little-magazine response. For the title of his article on Porter's account of Shields's end, Meilaender came up with "Pathos, Bathos, and Euthanasia": "Clearly intended to elicit pathos . . . the account is, by my lights, drowning in bathos." He does not admire the euthanized John Shields nor those who chose "to orchestrate and choreograph the homemade rituals, drawn from countless different (and incompatible) cultural and religious traditions."

Meilaender scores Porter and the *Times* for seeking sympathy for Mr. Shields, but sees the article as a "puff piece aimed at evoking support for one side of a complicated moral argument." Not humble, Shields became a "spiritual cosmologist," who announced, "I come forth at this precise moment to contribute my unique gifts to the great unfolding." Not quite Hegelian, thinks Meilaender, who may be sympathetic to Shields but not to his way of coping with always-terminal amyloidosis, as he profited from Canada's newly legalized "medical assistance in dying."

The whole scheme of the Canadian law, the self-advertising of Shields, and the awe-full account by Porter and the colleagues whom she quotes is based on a concept of "self-determination," which Meilaender effectively critiques. For this critic the virtue of compassion, which motivates support for euthanasia, "has a shape and has limits": "The imperative that governs this virtue is not 'minimize suffering,' but 'maximize care.'" The self-invented rituals patched together by Shields and executed after his death led Porter to create traditions which are not likely long to survive; this sort of "spirituality lite" cannot "sustain us in the face of death."

Meilaender ends with a particular and particularized Christian affirmation and response, arguing that "in the face of a culture intent on teaching that to experience decline and loss of capacities is to lose dignity, we need to insist that each of us, whatever our capacities, is equidistant from eternity, and that no one for whom Christ was content to die can lack human dignity." Christianity is not the only anti-bathos faith, but it is representative of values unlikely to be surrendered by those in any community or tradition who celebrate dignity more than advertised self-affirmation. One suspects.

Resources

Meilaender, Gilbert. "Pathos, Bathos, and Euthanasia." *Commonweal*. June 30, 2017. https://www.commonwealmagazine.org/pathos-bathos-and-euthanasia.

Porter, Catherine. "At His Own Wake, Celebrating Life and the Gift of Death." *The New York Times*. May 25, 2017. https://www.nytimes.com/2017/05/25/world/canada/euthanasia-bill-john-shields-death.html.

96. Love Your Enemies: Moral Absurdity or Genius?

July 13, 2017
By Audrey D. Thompson

The Autumn 1942 issue of *Christianity and Society* published an article by Reinhold Niebuhr that began, "In times of social and political conflict there are always Christians who obscure the very genius of the New Testament conception of love by their particular interpretation of one form of the love commandment, namely, 'Love your enemies.'" Fresh on Niebuhr's mind, of course, would have been conflicts at home and abroad centering on the race problem during World War II. Responding to Christian idealists at that time who had used the love commandment to speak out against participating in the war, Niebuhr determined that the applicability of the biblical mandate in such a case would either demand "a psychological and moral absurdity of us" or enjoin an ingenious attitude of spirit, all depending on how the word "love" is interpreted.

Fast-forward to 2017 and Niebuhr's query is still relevant. When a blog recently admonished victims of bigotry who would sacrifice to save the lives of their oppressors to "Let Them F—ing Die" (the title), it was hard not to see this as a sign of the times and, like Niebuhr, ask whether the Christian response to love your enemies is absurd or genius.

The blogger identifies himself as "Son of Baldwin," and fresh on his mind was the June 14 shooting at a congressional baseball practice, particularly the role of black first responders in defusing the situation and saving the life of GOP Representative Steve Scalise. The blog post focuses on the irony that Scalise, who is reported to have self-identified as "David Duke without the baggage" and voted against LGBTQ rights, would be saved by a black lesbian. Son of Baldwin sees a pattern where, under the guise of "loving their enemies," the oppressed hold themselves to a moral standard that serves to enable the very system that oppresses them. To illustrate the point, he compares the Scalise story to an episode of the 1970s and '80s sitcom *The Jeffersons*, in which George Jefferson uses CPR to save the life of a Ku Klux Klan leader. When the latter learns that it was Jefferson who saved his life, he tells his son, "You should have let me die." Son of Baldwin, basing his argument on the premise that life imitates art, implores blacks and queers to learn from George's experience, and, rather than take the moral high road, "turn your compassion inward" and let bigots die.

Son of Baldwin admits: "What I am suggesting will rile us because it operates contrary to our centuries of brainwashing, rejects the religious instruction our oppressors gave us, negates the mounds of propaganda that imagines our oppressors as deserving of our humanity in the face of their lack of such. What I propose will certainly have most white/cisgender/heterosexuals who practice bigotry . . . up in their outrageous feelings because they have become accustomed to our worship, rely on our fealty, and receive sustenance from our sacrifice. . . . Our indifference to their well-being is the *only* [sic] thing that terrifies them."

By recasting racial tensions in America as "a battle between the moral and the immoral" and positing that religious instruction has emphasized morality to give the oppressors "a distinct strategical advantage" over the oppressed, Son of Baldwin's argument compels Christians once again to re-examine whether it is foolish to demand love for your enemies in situations of social and political upheaval. Niebuhr certainly thought so, especially if love is interpreted to mean "emotional attachment," and if the love commandment is misconstrued to deny the possibility of naturally hating those who oppress you or stand in opposition to your cause.

Yet, unlike Son of Baldwin, who dismisses the religious mandate to love your enemies as moral absurdity, Niebuhr thought it possible (and necessary) to address the absurdity by recovering the genius of the New Testament conception of love as *agape*. He critiques the tendency to conceive of love as *eros*, which is ego-driven and thus limited in its ability to extinguish the hatred that invariably exists between those who oppose each other, making the demand to love your enemy not only morally absurd but psychologically impossible. The only way forward, then, is to avoid conflict altogether, as Christian idealists advocated in the 1940s, or to show indifference to the lives of your enemies, as Son of Baldwin now proposes.

Agape, on the other hand, understands love as moving the individual beyond the ego to something transcendent—in the New Testament it is the kingdom of God; for the sons of Baldwin, it could be the Beloved Community or simply a more perfect union. Herein lies the genius Niebuhr saw: "We are not told to love our enemies because . . . they will love us in return" but because the good of our enemies is always bound to that transcendent ideal of which we are also a part.

If Son of Baldwin had carried his analysis of that episode of *The Jeffersons* to its end, he too might see the wisdom in George's sacrificial act. While the

Klan leader remained unrepentant, his son thanks Jefferson for saving his father's life, rips up the Klan fliers, and walks out of the room. The other men present walk out as well, symbolically turning their backs on bigotry and trashing the idea of white supremacy.

Perhaps only time will tell whether loving your enemies is absurd or genius. Son of Baldwin may be right to see George's refusal to let a Klan leader die as absurd; but, considering the number of lives potentially transformed by George saving the life of one bigot, Niebuhr may also be right to see the irony of desiring the good of your enemies as genius.

Resources

Niebuhr, Reinhold. "Love Your Enemies." *Christianity and Society*. Autumn 1942. Reprinted in *Love and Justice: Selections from the Shorter Writings of Reinhold Niebuhr*, edited by D. B. Robertson, 218–221. Louisville: Westminster John Knox, 1957.

Son of Baldwin. "Let Them F—ing Die." Medium. June 16, 2017. https://medium.com/@SonofBaldwin/let-them-fucking-die-c316eee34212.

"Sorry, Wrong Meeting." *The Jeffersons*. Season 7, episode 14. First broadcast on CBS on February 15, 1981.

Audrey D. Thompson graduated with a PhD in homiletics from Princeton Theological Seminary. She teaches in the English Department at Pennsylvania State University Erie-The Behrend College.

97. Closings

July 31, 2017
By Martin E. Marty

Tradition compels us to close shop at *Sightings* for August, but we hope and intend to be back to greet September, ff., with you. However, we keep thinking of one special fact in the human condition and situation: sooner or later, every thing on earth will close and will not reopen. One does not need scriptural reminders of this; we just do our sighting and have evidence. Having read much about "decline" in religion—hereabouts, not always globally—evidences abound. What prompts this choice of topic this week was the combination of two headlines in *The New York Times* last Thursday. One was "An Ode to Shopping Malls" by Steven Kurutz, and the other was "Country Stores Look for Someone to Hand the Keys To" by Julie Turkewitz. The first story is about a film series which chronicles how malls, "pleasure palaces of days past," are reaching their end as "a way of life"; the second, about the slow disappearance of small-town hubs.

Both seem to deal with secular, not religious, subjects. But churches (et cetera) and cultures or societies are so intertwined that their stories overlap and get fused. The religious world is very much a subject or victim of change in its many forms and locations. The internet surveys this, not only in suburban-mall or rural cultures but in cities too. Thus, close to home, in my case, one fairly recent story is being lived out: "[Chicago] Archdiocese May Close Nearly 100 Churches in Next 15 Years." Another offered a more ambivalent judgment: "Thousands of Churches Closing Every Year, but There Is a Silver Lining." The latter, by Lisa Cannon Green of LifeWay Research, saw a cheery upside: "America is launching new Protestant churches faster than it loses old ones, attracting many people who previously didn't attend anywhere." LifeWay found that "More than 4,000 new churches opened their doors in 2014," for example, "outpacing the 3,700 that closed, according to estimates from the Nashville-based research organization based on input from 34 denominational statisticians."

What is more, said Ed Stetzer, then executive director of LifeWay, recently planted churches do better at attracting the unchurched than do existing churches. He observed: "In winning new converts to Christ, church plants are light-years ahead of the average church because of their focus on reaching the unchurched." We'll let readers pursue that topic with LifeWay, since we are for this moment (or month) interested instead in noting how churches and other religious institutions suffer or prosper depending upon their location, environment, and so much else.

Here is where the *New York Times* stories are revelatory. A few decades ago, almost no public institutions had better prospects than suburban malls. Kurutz notes that 1986 was the peak year for malls in America. Hollywood featured mall culture in films. Families organized weekend life with them as the attraction. Kids hung out at them. Now? Don't invest in malls, and, if you don't want to feel haunted, don't stroll in these dead or dying palaces of commerce. As for rural and small-town life, let's say that 1886 might well have been the peak for new enterprises which were created by and catered to country folk. No more.

Thousands of lay and clerical religious leaders and other spiritually hungry and ambitious citizens will engage their environments and find fresh ways to deal with them. But one plus factor in the change is this: heirs of the self-contented ruralists from back when town-and-country stores and schools and churches prospered don't boast any more about their prosperity. They just serve as they can. And the boomers who once mega-prospered in suburban-mall cultures are now succeeded by more modest, but newly hard-working believers and builders, who experience "ups" and "downs" as they try to make personal, philosophical, and theological sense of their surroundings and possible destinies.

Resources

"Archdiocese May Close Nearly 100 Churches in Next 15 Years." Curbed. February 9, 2016. https://chicago.curbed.com/2016/2/9/10953596/archdiocese -closing-100-churches.

Green, Lisa Cannon. "Study: Thousands of Churches Closing Every Year, but There Is a Silver Lining." CharismaNews. December 9, 2015. http://www.char ismanews.com/us/53715-study-thousands-of-churches-closing-every-year -but-there-is-a-silver-lining.

Kurutz, Steven. "An Ode to Shopping Malls." *The New York Times*. July 26, 2017. https://www.nytimes.com/2017/07/26/fashion/an-ode-to-shopping-malls .html.

Turkewitz, Julie. "Country Stores Look for Someone to Hand the Keys To." Published online as "Who Wants to Run That Mom-and-Pop Market? Almost No One." *The New York Times*. July 26, 2017. https://www.nytimes.com/2017/07 /26/us/colorado-markets.html.

98. Visiting a Fellow Human at the Benedictine Monastery

September 7, 2017
By Alan Levinovitz

Nearly fifteen years ago I watched a line of young men file out of a Buddhist temple near the sacred Chinese mountain of Putuo. Then, as now, I had a naive belief in the power of spiritual exercises, if not the spirits to which they are often dedicated. Memorization, meditation, asceticism, devotion, submission—these are the tools with which we sculpt virtue out of the self's raw material, and there in front of me were masters of the craft, clad in saffron robes, their shaved heads surely full of hard-won wisdom, their hearts pure (or at least purer than mine).

So it came as a shock to me and the other assembled tourists when one of the men withdrew a phone from his robe and launched into angry conversation. It was everything I thought he wouldn't need: instant gratification, distance from the moment, emotional expression. And so I reacted as anyone does when their beliefs are challenged, and filed the incident away as an exception, my reflexive judgment as evidence of personal spiritual shortcomings.

I had occasion to reflect on that memory on a recent visit to a Benedictine monastery. The visit was part of research for a piece I wrote about *The Benedict Option*, a bestseller by the conservative author Rod Dreher. His book horrified me—it was what I called "spiritual pornography"—and I wanted to redeem the real Benedict Option by swapping its supposed exegete for a genuine practitioner.

The elderly priest sat me down in his office. "How can I help you?" he asked.

How could he help me? I didn't know, exactly. With a conversation that humbled me, that showed to this nonbeliever the power of a faith diligently practiced to make you wise. Thomas Merton's *Seeds of Contemplation* performed in the flesh.

We spoke for over an hour. At first it was normal introductory small talk: his health, his past as a young Navy recruit, his longstanding desire eventually to become a monk. Then the topic turned to politics. He complained that a nearby Benedictine military school was being forced by the government to teach the acceptability of homosexuality or give up ROTC affiliation.

"So they gave it up," he told me sadly. "They pay for their own uniforms now. See, it's what Dreher talks about in his book. Homosexuality, transsexualism, everyone has to agree with that stuff."

We never once spoke about God, wisdom, virtue, or anything like that. It was a perfectly ordinary conversation with a kindly older man, whose faith and political orientation differed from mine, like many such conversations that I've had. He did not have a unique perspective on those issues. His countenance did not radiate otherworldly wisdom. Decades of spiritual exercises left no discernible mark.

At first I was disappointed. I had hoped that somehow this monk would show me a path through the bleak political landscape of our country and, more importantly, embody a transcendent way of being that crosscut my own petty, worldly concerns. I had hoped he would teach me the true Benedict Option.

It was only later, on the drive home, that I fully realized what he had taught me and how the conversation really had succeeded in humbling me. Spiritual exercises do not dissolve concerns about politics or health. They do not make you a more valuable human being, as I had once thought. In fact, he had told me as much. When I asked him directly about the effects of monasticism, all he said was that it suited him. For others, a different path was best.

In that answer—the only explicit reference to religious practice—he was embodying a virtue that I did not possess: humility about the possibility that a specific set of practices can make you better than others. "A more valuable human being"—what a thought to think! And of course, there was the deeper mistake built into my own judgment of cell phones and emotional expression and being worried about your health. Do sages never anger? Do they have no prescriptions to fill, no families to call?

I had made a mistake—with him, with the Buddhist monks in China, with my whole outlook on what it is to cultivate wisdom. I know this now; my faith is shaken. But I do not want it restored. I want to keep it unsteady, so that in the future, I do not seek out those who have found a better path, but instead remind myself that we are all wanderers on a map with infinite paths, the relative virtues of which are difficult to judge, especially—to borrow from a faith not my own—for sinners in need of grace.

Resource

Levinovitz, Alan. "The Awful Pleasures of Spiritual Pornography." *Los Angeles Review of Books*. May 29, 2017. https://lareviewofbooks.org/article/the-awful -pleasures-of-spiritual-pornography.

Alan Levinovitz (PhD, the University of Chicago Divinity School) is assistant professor of religion at James Madison University.

99. Historical Justice in an Era of #MeToo: Legacies of John Howard Yoder

DECEMBER 7, 2017
BY RACHEL WALTNER GOOSSEN

The surge of reporting about sexual harassment in politics, media, and entertainment is both liberating and harrowing for those who identify as "me too" victims and survivors. Spotlights that *had* focused on abusive priests, professors, theologians, and religious institutions' cover-ups—the stuff of the John Howard Yoder saga—are now shining brightly. And they're reaching into more corners, as new voices challenge male prerogative, power, and humiliating behaviors in corporate life, journalism, and other workaday settings.

All this focus on sexual harassment and assault is jolting. It's also illuminating.

In the midst of this, Stanley Hauerwas's recent explanation of his efforts more than two decades ago to urge restoration of Yoder's reputation is strangely discordant. Hauerwas's handwringing is confessional: "I was too anxious to have John resume his place as one of the crucial theologians of our time. I thought I knew what was going on, but . . . in truth, I probably did not want to know what was going on."

Some of Yoder's colleagues, including a few Mennonites, were sufficiently disturbed in the early 1990s by reports of his sexual aggressions that they ceased referencing his writings. Yet even now Hauerwas commends these works as canonical in Christian nonviolence and ethics, advising that we not let what Yoder "taught us" and "how we think theologically to be lost."

Such misplaced focus—on Yoder's intellect and renown—is precisely the kind of dynamic that contributed to making this abuse so horrific. After grooming, targeting, and sexually exploiting an estimated one hundred or more women, Yoder was largely unrepentant. His flagrancy was amplified by his theologizing about it, perpetrating sexual violence while preaching nonviolence.

The most significant tragedy is that Yoder harmed scores of women, as people of all genders and ages have suffered under similar figures. Institutionally enshrined power let these figures get away with it. Even as Yoder's church sought to bring him to accountability, no denominational representative was appointed consistently to support victims, though substantial time and energy were focused on Yoder.

As a result, fewer women became Mennonite theologians or pursued ministerial positions. Hauerwas's focus on salvaging Yoder's theology is blind to the theological possibilities never brought to fruition by aspiring women who were driven away from seminary or other church leadership paths. Victim-blaming, coupled with deference to Yoder's privilege and power, contributed to the silencing of those already marginalized in a faith tradition dominated by male leaders.

After the publication in 2015 of my article "'Defanging the Beast,'" which described Mennonite and Catholic institutional failures to stop Yoder's theological "experiment," a friend wrote to me about her traumatic experiences as a young adult volunteer in a Catholic diocese: "Many people may feel these are 'dead' stories as those involved can no longer be brought to justice; however, I believe in historical justice as well as criminal justice." She added: "I am literally shaking inside as I type this."

What might "historical justice" mean for survivors of sexual abuse?

In the past two years, among the outpouring of letters and notes I received in response to my article, fewer than a half-dozen were congruent with Hauerwas's concerns. Many people who wrote were survivors of sexual abuse, or their loved ones. For nearly all of these writers, the Yoder chronicle was disconcertingly familiar because of sexual abuse perpetrated by *other* credentialed clergy and academic mentors: Anglican, Evangelical Covenant, Mennonite, Catholic, in the 1980s, '90s, and into the twenty-first century. Details varied: some victims were seminarians who had trusted a gifted professor, others were children targeted by pedophiles in church settings.

Of course, these letters aren't about Yoder. But they are all the more relevant for their #MeToo sensibility. The writers correctly identified Yoder's legacy of abuse as symptomatic of a much larger problem in churches, the academy, and beyond. One correspondent, whose childhood friends were groomed and harmed by a pastor, decried church bodies' lack of transparency: "Information simply isn't known, has been lost, covered up, and so on. What I wanted to know is: how did this happen? Detailed knowledge of the evil processes, the 'how,' will help us see its red flags in the future. Blaming the bad individual, and then moving on as if all other hands are clean and it will surely never happen again, is totally unhelpful."

Twenty years after Yoder's death, resistance and healing *are* part of his tragic legacy. An elderly letter-writer, acknowledging his own theological conservatism, recounted sexual abuse experienced by his young-adult daughters in a tight-knit Old Order Mennonite community, adding, "There are much more important issues than JHY and what drove him. The larger issue has to be with power and accountability, in particular with ordained male leaders."

We *can* practice historical justice. Creating awareness and safety for all in faith-based institutions, and chipping away at patriarchal structures, are everyone's responsibility. Meanwhile, the musings of Hauerwas "trying to make sense" of his colleague's theological scheming, when laid side-by-side with this collection of victims' and families' remembrances and resolve, seem largely irrelevant.

Resources

Chilton, Amy L. "My Rise, Their Fall: A Theologian's Burden in Response to the Reality of Sexual Abuse." Baptist News Global. October 27, 2017. https://baptist news.com/article/rise-fall-theologians-burden-response-reality-sexual-abuse.

Farley, Lin. "I Coined the Term 'Sexual Harassment.' Corporations Stole It." *The New York Times*. October 18, 2017. https://www.nytimes.com/2017/10/18 /opinion/sexual-harassment-corporations-steal.html.

Garcia, Sandra E. "The Woman Who Created #MeToo Long Before Hashtags." *The New York Times*. October 20, 2017. https://www.nytimes.com/2017/10/20 /us/me-too-movement-tarana-burke.html.

Goossen, Rachel Waltner. "'Defanging the Beast': Mennonite Responses to John Howard Yoder's Sexual Abuse." *Mennonite Quarterly Review* 89 (January 2015): 7–80.

———. "Documenting Sexual Abuse: Archival Collections and the Complex Legacy of Theologian John Howard Yoder." *The Mennonite Historian* 42 (March 2016): 2–9.

———. "Mennonite Bodies, Sexual Ethics: Women Challenge John Howard Yoder." *Journal of Mennonite Studies* 34 (2016): 243–55.

Hauerwas, Stanley. "In Defence of 'Our Respectable Culture': Trying to Make Sense of John Howard Yoder's Sexual Abuse." ABC Religion & Ethics. October 18, 2017. http://www.abc.net.au/religion/articles/2017/10/18/4751367.htm.

Hunter-Bowman, Janna L. "The Opportunity Stanley Hauerwas Missed." *The Christian Century*. October 27, 2017. https://www.christiancentury.org /blog-post/guest-post/opportunity-stanley-hauerwas-missed.

O'Hara, Maureen, and Aftab Omer. "Virtue and the Organizational Shadow: Exploring False Innocence and the Paradoxes of Power." In *Humanity's Dark Side: Evil, Destructive Experience, and Psychotherapy*, edited by Arthur C. Bohart et al. Washington, DC: American Psychological Association, 2013.

Scarsella, Hilary. "Not Making Sense: Why Stanley Hauerwas's Response to Yoder's Sexual Abuse Misses the Mark." ABC Religion & Ethics. November 30, 2017. http://www.abc.net.au/religion/articles/2017/11/30/4774014.htm.

Spotlight. Directed by Tom McCarthy. Open Road Films, 2015.

Rachel Waltner Goossen, a professor in the Department of History at Washburn University, is a peace historian specializing in American social history and Mennonite studies.

100. Jerusalem

December 14, 2017
By Paul Mendes-Flohr

With the outset of autumn as determined by the Jewish liturgical calendar, a daily prayer is recited beseeching God to bless the Holy Land with rain: "Turn to us, God, who are surrounded by troubles like water. / For the Jewish people's sake, do not hold back water. / You are Adonai, our God / Who causes the wind to blow and the rain to fall." The prayers were answered this year in early December as the first rains began to fall, eliciting joyous prayers of thanksgiving.

But on the following day, hopes that the "troubles that surround" the land will recede, leaving in their wake the blessings of peace, were severely damped by President Trump's grandiloquent announcement that the United States recognizes Jerusalem as the political capital of the State of Israel. That Jerusalem is the spiritual center of Judaism and the Jewish people few would deny; that it is the political capital of the State of Israel has been questioned since its founding in 1948. Israel's claim to political sovereignty over Jerusalem is contested because it is also a spiritual home for Christians and Muslims worldwide, not to mention that Christian and Muslim Arabs have been denizens of the Holy Land for generations and more.

The seemingly intractable political dispute is compounded by the transmogrification of supersessionist religious claims to supersessionist political claims. The imbrication of religious and political supersessionism has cast the Israeli-Palestinian conflict into an uncompromising zero-sum game of either them or us. The mobilization of realpolitik to secure religious claims to Jerusalem could not but debase the sacrality of the city; indeed, it has desecrated this city holy to Jews, Muslims, and Christians alike with idolatrous overtones of religious chauvinism.

To soften what is widely perceived to be President Trump's fatal blow to the prospects of a peaceful resolution to the Israeli-Palestinian conflict, some political pundits speculate that his endorsement of Israel's political claim to Jerusalem is but a smoke screen to allow Israelis and Palestinians to enter clandestine negotiations without the interference of public opinion. But even if it were true that there is an overarching strategy behind Trump's declaration, it is exceedingly improbable that at this juncture political negotiations would yield a semblance of rapprochement, and not only because the US has irreparably lost its credibility as a neutral mediator. The ultimate impediment to a political solution to the conflict is the abysmal lack of mutual trust.

It is only by laying a firm foundation of mutual trust—trust that the other is not out to "get one," to outmaneuver one on the playing field of politics, not to speak of the battlefield—that a mutual political accommodation can be achieved. Such trust cannot be attained by negotiations, or even polite debate and convivial conversation. It requires the jettisoning of adversarial attitudes and posturing, and marshaling a determined will to honor the existential reality of the other, to listen attentively and empathetically to the spiritual and emotional voice of the other, the voice that is often muffled by words. The existential bonds forged by mutual trust transcend questions of who is right or whom God favors. These bonds of trust have the heuristic effect of highlighting the horizon of a political solution securing the dignity of the peoples and religious communities who are destined to share the Holy Land.

Resource

"Heads of Local Churches Send Letter to President Donald Trump Regarding Status of Jerusalem." Latin Patriarchate of Jerusalem. December 6, 2017. https://www.lpj.org/heads-local-churches-send-letter-to-president-donald -trump-regarding-status-of-jerusalem.

Paul Mendes-Flohr is Dorothy Grant Maclear Professor of Modern Jewish History and Thought at the University of Chicago Divinity School. He is also associate faculty in the Department of History at the University of Chicago, and professor emeritus of Jewish thought at the Hebrew University of Jerusalem.

Index of Contributors

Index of Subjects